Merchants, Farmers, and River Gods

Merchants, Farmers, and River Gods

An Essay on Eighteenth-Century American Politics

ROBERT ZEMSKY

Gambit
INCORPORATED
Boston
1971

Permissions

Excerpts from *Earliest Diary of John Adams* and *Diary and Autobiography of John Adams*, Volumes I, II and supplement. L. H. Butterfield, editor, reprinted by permission of the Belknap Press of Harvard University Press, Copyright © 1961, 1966, by the President and Fellows of Harvard College. Excerpts from *The House of Hancock*, by W. T. Baxter; *The Barrington-Bernard Correspondence,* edited by Edward Channing and Archibald Cary Coolidge; and *History of the Colony and Province of Massachusetts Bay,* by Thomas Hutchinson. Lawrence Shaw Mayo, editor, reprinted by permission of Harvard University Press.

Excerpts from *Colonial Merchants in the American Revolution,* by Arthur Meier Schlesinger, Copyright © 1917, reprinted by permission of Columbia University Press.

Excerpt from *The Francis Bernard Papers* reprinted by permission of the Harvard College Library.

Excerpt from *The Maritime History of Massachusetts,* by Samuel E. Morison, reprinted by permission of Houghton Mifflin Company.

Excerpts reproduced from *The Loudoun Papers* (LO 2262, LO 2929), by permission of The Huntington Library, San Marino, California.

Excerpts from *The Adams Papers* reprinted by permission of the Massachusetts Historical Society.

Excerpt from *King George III and the Politicians,* by Richard Pares, Copyright © 1963, reprinted by permission of the Clarendon Press.

Excerpt from *Who Governs?* by Robert A. Dahl reprinted by permission of Yale University Press.

Excerpt from pages 101-102 of *Political Life: Why People Get Involved in Politics,* by Robert E. Lane, reprinted by permission of the Free Press of Glenco, Incorporated, Copyright © 1959.

Parts of this study were previously published in the *William and Mary Quarterly,* 34th ser., Volume XXVI (1969) 502-520.

Library of Congress Catalog Card Number: 70-116559

Printed in the United States of America

FIRST PRINTING

for

Ann

Contents

Preface

I suspect that we are about to revise again our view of the American Revolution, about to argue that the conflict, having radicalized large segments of the population, brought truly revolutionary mobs into the street and resulted in new definitions of public and private morality. Because traditionally we have portrayed the colonial period of American history as a prelude to that revolution, I presume that we will also come to view eighteenth-century America as an essentially unstable society whose values were in conflict and whose members were burdened by self-doubt, anxiety, and alienation.

Perhaps such post hoc reasoning is inevitable, given the centrality of the Revolution to our understanding of the American experience. But we do pay a price for looking at the eighteenth century through such a prism. Most obvious is the implicit assumption that every event relentlessly led to the bloody confrontation at Lexington and Concord, to the Declaration of Independence, to the chaos under the Articles of Confederation, and eventually to the emergence of a new federal government. Yet the Revolution was not so much inevitable as unexpected. There was no revolutionary vanguard, no period of gestation, no dire warnings of impending conflict. At most there was only a vague feeling that the colonies would require new status and increased autonomy once their population and wealth rivaled that of the mother country. But that day was yet to come, or at least so thought most colonials on the eve of the Revolution.

A second, more pervasive danger in looking at the eighteenth century from the vantage point of the Revolution is that this tends to limit the questions one asks. Were there social classes and were they in conflict? Was prerevolutionary America democratic? Were political and social values sufficiently disjunctive to create the necessary malaise which must precede a genuinely radical upheaval? My quarrel with this, presently the dominant historical approach to prerevolutionary America, is not that the past is being explained in other than its own terms, but that we have forgotten that we cannot put on the shoes of dead men; we can neither think like colonial Americans, nor act like them, nor judge their society by its own standards. But we can—and implicitly, at least, this is what most of us do—employ modern perspectives to inform the images we draw from those artifacts eighteenth-century Americans chose to leave us. While we cannot know what colonial America was like, we can ask, "How different was America in the eighteenth century?"—"How unlike today was it?"

Such at least is the perspective underlying this study of the people and politics of eighteenth-century Massachusetts. In working out my own answer to the question, "How different was that society from our own?" I have drawn on two remarkably rich traditions of scholarship which as yet remain essentially hostile to each other. The first is the historian's longstanding fascination with colonial New England, which has led us to learn more about how New Englanders thought, what they wore, where and why they worshipped, and how they organized their communities than we know about societies far more accessible to the modern researcher. The second tradition results from the development of a highly theoretical—as well as statistical—approach to political behavior. Some historians have responded to this reshaping of what was once a sister discipline by simply ignoring it, denying that statistical models can enrich the historical imagination, and claiming that to be theoretical is to explain the past in other than its own terms. My study is intended as an explicit denial of this point of view.

Still, a word of caution, as well as of definition, is in order. What unites the sciences—natural as well as social—is a common endeavor to build theories for organizing our perceptions of the world about us. Theory, in this sense, defines the data, establishes categories for analysis, and finally organizes our conclusions along preconceived and well-defined continua. Good theories are those which best explain the data at hand. New theories develop whenever new information is discovered or the results of our analysis suggest we should recast our notion of what we are about. Some theories are obviously stronger than others, can be relied upon with more certainty, because there is less expectation that they will prove unsatisfactory. In general, the strength of any theory also reflects the kinds of data available for analysis. The natural sciences put more faith in their theories largely because data drawn from the physical world are more susceptible to systematic analysis. But in both endeavors theory plays the same role: it defines—or, more precisely, creates—rules for reaching conclusions.

Hence theories developed to explore the behavior of modern man can prove inappropriate to the historical task, not because they use modern categories to classify past behavior, but rather because they call for the analysis of certain kinds of data the past has chosen not to provide the historian. What those of us interested in developing a theory of behavior (as opposed to a theory of history) must do, then, is investigate when and under what conditions we can use data from the past to broaden as well as to verify theoretical insights derived from the close and systematic observation of living men.

What this study builds upon, then, is an informed kind of present-mindedness, one that sets the remains of a past society in a theoretical framework for depicting political relationships. Several reasons dictated my choice of provincial Massachusetts for such an enterprise. New Englanders not only took their politics seriously, but they did so in such a way as to leave a remarkably rich record of their experiences. Then, too, eighteenth-century Massachusetts was an especially varied conglomerate of American types: merchant princes and yeoman farmers, men with cosmopolitan aspirations, and parochials who never left their villages or cared about what happened in the outside world. Boston, and to a lesser extent Salem, Ipswich, and Newbury, were already urban centers, while in the west the Connecticut Valley remained under the suzerainty of a handful of land barons who ruled a domain of industrious farmers absorbed in the task of clearing a wilderness and extending the tentacles of settlement. Massachusetts was also a royal colony with a governor appointed by the king, a Council which doubled as an executive cabinet and upper house of the provincial General Court, and a popularly elected Assembly that in fact, as well as theory, gave effective voice to the aspirations of the province's rural majority. Finally, the quarter-century (1730–1755) covered by this study was one of basic political stability. The contest between governor and Assembly over the royal prerogative had largely abated. While disputes flared, the constitutional compromise forged in the 1720s— which granted a measured independence to both parties—remained intact. Even political disputes, though capable of arousing passions, never seemed to threaten basic alignments or attitudes.

The first question I asked of that time and place was simply, "What did government in the eighteenth century do?" Here I was interested in the "what" in Harold Lasswell's definition of politics as deciding "Who gets what, when, how." What precisely did politicians compete for when they sought personal power? How big was the budget? How large was the army? How extensive was the civil service?

I next sought to learn something of the texture of the political fabric: how complex and intricate was its weave? Here the provincial General Court supplied the data. How rigid were its rules and customs? Did young men grow old waiting their turn to exercise power?

Drawing again on data supplied by the General Court, I next asked, "Who were Massachusetts' leaders?" How extensive was their power? What distinguished them from the people they governed? In contests with the colony's royal governor, how did this leadership group fare? Indeed, did the colonial chief executive preside over his colony or could he in fact govern it?

Finally I sought to measure the impact non-officeholders had on public policy. Did Massachusetts' social and economic notables, her merchant princes and river gods, exercise an influence out of proportion to their numbers? Was the colonial leader accountable to those who placed him in office? Can we explain the political rhetoric of which New Englanders were so inordinately fond?

In short, this book is about the business of politics: how men voted; what they sought from their government; and why a few came to exercise special power and influence.

R.M.Z.

March 1970

Acknowledgments

While some scholars work in splendid isolation, my endeavors become almost public enterprises. Hence my debt to others looms large, and while individually they bear no responsibility for my errors, collectively they played a significant role in shaping and improving this study. Among the librarians and custodians of manuscript collections who assisted me, I owe a special debt to Mr. and Mrs. Leo Flaherty of the Massachusetts Archives. Murray G. Murphey, Anthony N. B. Garvan, John Shover, Michael Zuckerman, Melvyn A. Hammarberg, and Gerald Ginsburg each read and substantially contributed to the manuscript's final draft. Lovell Thompson, Mark Saxton, Catherine Dexter, and Eugenia Plunkett of Gambit superintended the study's final metamorphosis. I also benefited from the financial generosity of the Woodrow Wilson Foundation and the University of Pennsylvania.

Originally this study was a dissertation under the direction of Edmund S. Morgan. To the extent that I have succeeded in expressing my ideas clearly and succinctly, he is responsible. Richard Jensen read the entire manuscript more times than even I care to admit and constantly improved my own interpretation of political events and personalities. Not least, this study reflects the understanding and patience of my wife, who assisted with much of the research, compiled most of the statistical data, and edited several versions of each chapter. To Ann, who said it could be done and then lovingly made sure it was, this book is dedicated.

Abbreviations

A&R   *The Acts and Resolves, Public and Private, of the Province of the Massachusetts Bay,* 19 vols. (Boston: the Commonwealth of Massachusetts, 1869–1922).

HP–BL   Hancock Papers, Baker Library, Harvard University, Cambridge, Mass.

JA–Diary Lyman H. Butterfield et al., *Diary and Autobiography of John Adams,* 4 vols. plus supplement (Cambridge, Mass.: Harvard University Press, 1961, 1965).

MHJ   *The Journals of the House of Representatives of Massachusetts,* 39 vols. (Boston: The Massachusetts Historical Society, 1919–   ).

SHG   Clifford K. Shipton, *Sibley's Harvard Graduates,* 15 vols. (Boston: The Massachusetts Historical Society, 1873–   ).

TH3–BL   Thomas Hancock Letter Book (TH3), Baker Library, Harvard University, Cambridge, Mass.

TH4–BL   Thomas Hancock Letter Book (TH–4), Baker Library, Harvard University, Cambridge, Mass.

In quotations from eighteenth-century documents, capitalization, spelling, and punctuation have been modernized.

Merchants, Farmers, and River Gods

Prologue: The Business of Government

O URS IS AN AGE IN WHICH GOVERNMENT ITSELF IS THE
principal business of the nation—an age in which the
public servicing, regulation, and defense of society requires more than sixteen million government employees, or about
one out of every five members of the American labor force.[1]
The magnitude of this enterprise has come to dominate the
political consciousness. Unable to remain free from government,
twentieth-century Americans have instead sought to have a
voice in deciding how these enormous resources are distributed
and toward what goals public regulation channels private energies and endeavors. Americans have also come to describe the
modern political order largely in terms suggested by this desire
to guide the governmental impulse: in terms of competing interest groups, of an electorate divided over how to spend the
resources of government, of public agencies that have become
intricate, highly institutionalized bureaucracies. But it is in their
definition of—indeed, interest in—political democracy that this
awareness of the totality of the public enterprise has had its

---

[1] U.S. Bureau of the Census, *Statistical Abstract of the United States; 1969*
(Washington, D.C.: Government Printing Office, 1969), pp. 211, 215.

greatest impact. Democracy has come to mean a citizenry which is in at least imperfect control of its own destiny, deciding, above all else, who exercises the awesome powers vested in public institutions.

Such interests and preoccupations played limited roles in eighteenth-century politics, largely because of the constricted nature of the government itself. All told, Massachusetts' provincial government annually spent less than £25,000 (roughly equivalent to $.80 per capita), employed six full-time public officials, had a part-time civil service of less than a thousand positions and equally restricted police and military establishments. Jonathan Belcher, then the province's chief executive, indirectly testified to the constricted nature of his government when he told his brother-in-law Richard Partridge that the 1740 Assembly had "supplied the treasury according to the king's instructions, drawn in all the money they are obliged to do to this time, ordered the forts on the frontiers to be repaired [and] a ship bought for the defense of the coasts. [The members] have done all the king has required respecting the expeditions, raised the wages of Castle William, and added 20 men. I am much pleased with the influence I have had on this Assembly for promoting his majesty's honor and service and the welfare of the province." [2] By any standard, these were limited accomplishments. That a governor could take such pride in them simply reflected how little most provincials expected of their government.

In eighteenth-century Massachusetts the business of government was confined to the military defense of the province, the umpiring of disputes between citizens, the supervision of unincorporated areas of settlement, and the maintenance of the prov-

[2] Belcher to Partridge, 5 July 1740, *Collections of the Massachusetts Historical Society,* 6th ser. 7 (1894): 313–14.

ince's governmental establishment. Hence only three issues regularly invited legislative activity: revenues, appropriations, and the currency. Of these three issues, the need to maintain a viable medium of exchange proved the most nettlesome. In part the problem was attributable to England's insistence that all gold and silver flow to the mother country, thus leaving her imperial outposts woefully short of hard money. But most provincials who worried about their struggling economy knew that the real villain was their own appetite for English goods. Massachusetts in the eighteenth century lived beyond her means, annually importing more than she exported. As a result, accounts owed to British merchants constantly drained Massachusetts of what little specie was in circulation.[3]

One perennial solution to this lack of a medium of exchange was for the colony to print her own currency. According to paper-money advocates, an expanding money supply coupled with large-scale deficit financing was what the province's ailing economy required. Massachusetts would prosper, internal commerce would expand, and the resultant affluence would mean ever greater tax revenues with which the government, at some future date, could retire its outstanding bills. All this an expanding paper currency would accomplish by simply returning the province to a natural state of affairs in which the price of money depended on the province's total produce.[4]

Appropriations, by contrast, were much less complicated. Military costs and government salaries accounted for nearly 70 percent of the total budget, while miscellaneous items, such as the maintenance of government buildings, military pensions,

[3] Charles M. Andrews, *The Colonial Period of American History,* 4 vols. (New Haven: Yale University Press, 1934–1938), 4:323–25, 351–52; see also [William Douglass], *A Discourse Concerning Currencies* (Boston, 1740).
[4] See, for example, [Hugh Vance], *An Inquiry into the Nature and Uses of Money* (Boston, 1740).

and an occasional allotment to a troubled community, completed the list of regular appropriations. In theory, the revenues needed to pay for these limited services were to be raised through a general head and property tax which set the terms for valuing property, defined how taxes were to be paid, and set the discount rate at which the government accepted its own notes. But such a system required, first, a citizenry with enough cash to meet its tax bills and, second, a collection agency capable of commanding what was due the provincial government—two conditions colonial Massachusetts seldom satisfied. Hence the provincial government was forced to rely on a variety of expedients. Sometimes the General Court borrowed, always in the hope that next year would be better. At one time or another, lotteries, special taxes on luxuries, and expanded customs duties were tried. Ultimately, however, Massachusetts had to choose between two not very pleasant alternatives: she could simply print enough new money to meet current expenses and thus further inflate her paper currency; or she could do without money altogether and hope that her creditors would remain sympathetic to her plight.[5]

Finally, the province faced the problems already created by a depreciating currency. The most troublesome of these issues forced the General Court to deal with the chaos surrounding the payment of private debts. Everyone agreed that creditors needed some protection against debtors who attempted to satisfy their accounts with depreciated notes. The question was always how much and in what form.[6]

Beyond these attempts to resolve the province's deepening

[5] *The Acts and Resolves, Public and Private, of the Province of the Massachusetts Bay,* 19 vols. (Boston: The Commonwealth of Massachusetts, 1869–1922), 2:1011–12, 1077–78, 3:195–99, 270–80, 408–11, 539–44, 548–49, 575–76, 732, 790–92 (hereafter cited as *A&R*); *The Journals of the House of Representatives of Massachusetts,* 39 vols. (Boston: The Massachusetts Historical Society, 1919–), 29:157ff., 30:47–48 (hereafter cited as *MHJ*).

[6] *MHJ,* 19:66, 108, 174–77.

financial dilemmas, however, the General Court saw little reason to employ its legislative mandate. Consequently, in a heavily agricultural province worried about its lack of domestic industry and the general well-being of its citizenry, there were no farm subsidies, price controls, significant aid to industries, or legislative schemes either to reform or to regulate the social order.

This reluctance to tinker with the basic organization of society had an equally pervasive influence on the General Court's approach to its nonlegislative responsibilities. In the eighteenth century, the provincial legislature was, as its name suggested, a Great and General Court. Besides writing the province's laws, levying taxes, and granting appropriations, the General Court shared in the administering of these statutes and was frequently responsible for providing the limited goods and services it had authorized. No less important, the legislature was simultaneously a court of law, capable of resolving conflicts among individuals and between the citizen and his government.

This latter function as a special court of errors was probably the most important of the General Court's extralegislative responsibilities. Formal appellate jurisdiction in Massachusetts began with the county courts and, if satisfaction could not be found within the province, ended with the Privy Council in London. Yet the General Court regularly received and considered private petitions whose requests covered the entire gamut of legal redress: granting and setting aside judgments, reopening cases considered legally closed, releasing prisoners from jail, voiding transactions, and disposing of property held in trust by the courts.[7]

---

[7] This catalogue of the General Court's judicial powers is based on an analysis of the rulings on private petitions found in *A&R*, vols. 12–15. See also Massachusetts Archives (State House), Boston, Mass., 53:141–46.

In theory, these quasi-judicial functions represented a carte blanche for the central government's involvement in the lives of the province's citizens. Yet in fact, the General Court viewed its judicial role principally as a nettlesome chore which, as the Court continually lamented, distracted the legislator and burdened an already overworked legislature. More important, the General Court renounced any attempt to establish guidelines for dealing with such petitions. Each was treated separately, seemingly without reference to past decisions and clearly without reference to any reigning ideology.[8]

A similar reluctance characterized the central government's relationship with the province's two hundred–odd townships. By virtue of the charter, the General Court decided which lands to survey, to whom to grant them, and when to allow a settlement to become a full-fledged town entitled to its own voice in the Assembly. In the seventeenth century, a Puritan government had used similar powers to establish stable, contiguous settlements which spread steadily and orderly westward. In the eighteenth century, however, legislators no longer regimented by orthodox notions of community abandoned this goal. The consequence was a crazy-quilt settlement pattern based only upon the inscrutable logic of land speculation.[9]

Once a settlement became a town, its accountability to the General Court diminished only slightly. Yet the Court became involved in local squabbles only after a town's dissident minority appealed for help. The dominant as well as the most troublesome of these quarrels involved the supervision of local taxing procedures. Each provincial tax assigned to every town a fixed per-

[8] A&R, 2:786, 1065; MHJ, 25:71, 32:120, 228.
[9] See, for example, A&R, 14:788–89, and Roy Hidemichi Akagi, The Town Proprietors of the New England Colonies (Philadelphia, University of Pennsylvania Press, 1924).

centage of the total tax bill which the towns then divided among their inhabitants. The catch, of course, was in the local valuation of property, and this apparently depended a great deal on who made up the tax rolls. Sorting out the conflicting claims in one of these cases was not an easy task. And though it was one the General Court faced annually, provincial legislators neither adopted a systematic approach to the problem nor availed themselves of this opportunity to structure economic relationships on the local level.[10]

Complementing the General Court's reluctance to intervene in the governance of Massachusetts' townships was its similar refusal to aid either individuals or communities. Internal improvements were exclusively a local matter, the responsibility of town and county governments. A town hard pressed to maintain its bridges and roads occasionally received special grants of land whose proceeds were earmarked for the specific project. More often, the General Court simply allowed the community to hold a lottery to raise the required funds. Only in times of genuine calamity, usually caused by an outbreak of smallpox, might the General Court bestow modest amounts of direct financial aid or a tax abatement. Commercial privileges to individual entrepreneurs were seldom asked for and rarely granted.[11]

Few provincials conceived of their government as a means to alter the basic structure of society. Eighteenth-century Massachusetts had already turned its back on seventeenth-century precepts, which stressed an ordered community and a central state responsible for controlling all aspects of political, economic, and

[10] *A&R*, vols. 12–15, record the General Court's actions on town petitions. The Massachusetts Archives, particularly vol. 49, has preserved some of the petitions themselves.
[11] See, for example, *A&R*, 3:482–83, 538–39, 888–91, 14:97, 812–17, 15:67–68.

social life. Massachusetts, without reading *Wealth of Nations,* had in many respects become an archetype of the classical economic state. To be sure, no one in the province theorized about a governmental system whose primary responsibility was to protect and preserve the natural processes of economic and social activity. But in the actual operation of their government, provincial politicians evidenced a strong reluctance to play with either the organization of the economy or the structure of society, and felt intuitively that to do so would be unnatural.[12]

The bounds of the political system were limited. Since the central government was little more than a neutral arbitrator charged with the protection of property, the ordinary citizen could not, but more importantly should not, expect to have the government solve his problems for him. And in the most obvious sense he was, as he believed he ought to be, left alone, neither constrained by government restrictions on his private behavior nor assisted in his attempts to secure his or his family's future. But the function of government in the eighteenth century was also to insure the continued existence of the state, taking from each citizen enough of his property to achieve this end. And having provided a barrier against external threats, it was obligated to prevent the strong from violating the rights of the weak and to protect the few from the clamors of the many. No one in Massachusetts doubted the propriety of these obligations. Instead, provincials quarreled over how such obligations were to be met. In these disputes the final arbiter was the General Court, and it rendered its decisions in the form of tax levies, annual budgets, decisions to print (or not to print) more paper money, and statutes governing relations between creditors and debtors,

[12] See Joseph Dorfman, *The Economic Mind in American Civilization, 1606–1865,* 3 vols. (New York: The Viking Press, 1946), 1:111–77.

and indirectly between buyers and sellers, farmers and merchants, and every other class of individuals whose property interests made them part of the provincial economic order. How and why these decisions were made is the story this book tells.

1

The Legislative Task

THE MUTED NATURE OF THE GOVERNMENTAL IMPULSE IN THE eighteenth century marks the most dramatic difference between politics then and now. No less important, however, are differences in the political process itself. Because governmental agencies are now expected to perform complex tasks, most Americans have accepted the institutional complexities which seemingly must accompany the providing of extensive public services. Nowhere is this more obvious than in the legislative arena, which has become a world unto itself, replete with its own rules, symbols, customs, and criteria for success. Even state legislatures, for example, employ systems of seniority, standing committees, and party apparatus to diffuse authority and to stabilize the process by which the legislature renders its decisions and by which it apportions status and power among its members.[1] In the eighteenth century, however, a provincial General Court, burdened with more limited responsibilities, applied quite different concepts of organization to its political tasks.

---

[1] See Nelson W. Polsby, "The Institutionalization of the U.S. House of Representatives," *American Political Science Review*, 62 (1968): 144–68.

In the eighteenth century the Court House dominated central Boston. Three stories high and topped by gilded lion and unicorn, the building housed both the General Court and the town's merchant exchange. To reach the government offices, one entered a side door, ascended a narrow stairway, and emerged in a small foyer separating the House and Council chambers. On the right sat the 28-man Council, in a spacious and well-appointed chamber whose measured dignity matched the stature of the men who regularly assembled there. Across the hall, in a room scarcely larger than the Council's, met the hundred or so men who annually trekked to Boston as the people's representatives. Too hot in the summer and overheated in the winter, the crowded chamber was always in some sort of disarray.[2]

In its own way, what transpired within this Representatives Room matched the disheveled nature of the chamber itself. Formal proceedings were governed by a brief set of rules which the House annually reviewed and adopted. Representatives were to be polite, courteous, and decorous, but beyond prohibiting a member to speak out of turn or wander aimlessly about the chamber, House rules enhanced, rather than restricted, the member's freedom. His right to debate remained unfettered, an almost nonexistent legislative calendar allowed him to discuss whatever interested him, and only a lack of ingenuity or diligence could limit his capacity to introduce amendments and motions.[3]

The Assembly's roster of officers was equally fragmentary. At the beginning of each term, the House appointed four sergeants-

[2] Walter Muir Whitehill, *Boston: A Topographical History* (Cambridge, Mass.: Harvard University Press, 1963), pp. 20–21; Hugh Morrison, *Early American Architecture* (New York: Oxford University Press, 1952), pp. 435–39; Alan Rabinowitz, "The Representatives Room, Town House, Boston" (unpublished architectural detail, 1970).

[3] Massachusetts Archives (State House), Boston, Mass., 283:257–61.

at-arms charged with maintaining House decorum and keeping guard at the chamber's door. Most men assigned this task were experienced but unimportant legislators who, though familiar with House procedures, were seldom troubled by more weighty responsibilities. The clerk played a more important role. Elected by the House and entitled to a moderate income from fees and special grants, he organized the Assembly's records, kept its journal, and supervised the printing of its official records. For more than a decade John White, though never a representative, held the post. By the 1740s, however, the House regularly chose its clerk from among its own members, and the fact that Roland Cotton, a quarrelsome but prominent politician, frequently held the office suggests that some prestige attached to it.[4]

The chief officer was the speaker whose election opened each term. Most incumbent speakers were unanimously reelected, while vacancies often engendered a lively contest among the Assembly's principal members. Once installed, the speaker presided over House sessions, scheduled most business, appointed most committees (frequently chairing the more important), and served as the Assembly's official spokesman. Such power, in itself, was no more extensive than that typically enjoyed by the presiding officer of a legislature. But the speaker of the Massachusetts Assembly shared authority with no one—not with committee chairmen, not with party leaders, not with steering committees. Always the partisan, the speaker normally led floor debates and usually served as one of the administration's major floor managers. When an energetic and skilled legislator occupied the

[4] MHJ, 25:9, 30:7; A&R, 14:95, 175, 220; Clifford K. Shipton, Sibley's Harvard Graduates, 15 vols. (Boston: The Massachusetts Historical Society, 1873–   ), 6:298–304 (hereafter cited as SHG); Thomas Hutchinson, The History of the Colony of Massachusetts-Bay, ed. Lawrence Shaw Mayo, 3 vols. (Cambridge, Mass.: Harvard University Press, 1936), 2:188.

chair, he set the tenor of House proceedings and often determined the thrust and scope of public policy.[5]

Much of the speaker's power derived from his control over a committee system which gave form and substance to the legislative process. In the Massachusetts Assembly there were no standing committees. For each bill, petition, and bureaucratic function the speaker appointed a separate and temporary committee and often, before the House finally resolved the issue, several committees. It was not at all unusual for a major bill to be proposed by one committee, drafted by another, revised by a third, revised again by a fourth, and cast into its final form by a fifth. In the 1756–57 House, when the war against France put added pressures on an already overburdened Assembly, Thomas Hubbard created more than 400 separate committees with more than 1600 individual committee assignments. Even in the 1751–52 Assembly, which met for only 65 days, Hubbard made more than 450 individual assignments.[6]

Ordinarily committees contained a chairman and two to four members. At one time they met over dinner in local taverns at the province's expense. Then in 1741 a House questioned the morality of subsidizing the representatives' recreation and stopped paying tavern bills. By the 1750s most committees met in special chambers in the Court House attic. Even when a free meal and ample refreshments were included, committee work was still a time-consuming chore. Most representatives who served on one committee simultaneously sat on three or four

[5] See, for example, Peter Orlando Hutchinson, *The Diary and Letters of Thomas Hutchinson*, 2 vols. (London, 1883), 2:52; Lyman H. Butterfield et al., *Diary and Autobiography of John Adams*, 4 vols. plus supplement (Cambridge, Mass.: Harvard University Press, 1961, 1965), 1:225–26 (hereafter cited as *JA-Diary*); Cushing to Sawyer, 6 November 1770, *Collections of the Massachusetts Historical Society*, 4th ser. 4 (1858): 357

[6] The drafting of the 1755 excise on rum portrays the committee system at its most complex; *MHJ*, 32:250–73. Chapter 2 below discusses the importance and distribution of committee assignments.

others, each with its own responsibilities, each making its own demands. Occasionally the House recessed to allow more time for committee meetings, though more often the speaker simply ordered delinquent committees to meet and left it up to the members to find sufficient time.[7]

Most committee work dealt with the hundreds of petitions for private bills which annually flooded the House. Once the House agreed to hear a petition, a committee had to be appointed to issue summonses, collect and review the relevant documents, hold hearings at which all parties could exchange recriminations, and then compile a report. Petitions dealing with town disputes consumed even more time. Usually the committee traveled to the town to hold hearings which inevitably became public spectacles. Having sifted through the conflicting claims, the committee then reached a decision that inevitably occasioned a new appeal to the entire House. Local disputes were seldom amenable to rational compromise.[8]

Service on a committee to draft public rather than private bills, while often just as tedious, was usually more rewarding. The Assembly handled routine legislation in much the same way as it dispatched private petitions: a committee was appointed to survey the problem, compile a report, and occasionally draft a bill. Consideration of the few major issues that annually came before the House conformed to a slightly different pattern. The process began with the governor's opening speech, which traditionally urged greater taxes, a balanced budget, and increased

[7] *MHJ*, 19:84, 28:64, 75, 32:333, 337, 33:150.
[8] The heading "General Court, equity jurisdiction" in the index of the 1736–37 journal (*MHJ*, 14:277) indicates the amount of time the House was forced to devote to private petitions. For committee procedures see *MHJ*, 8:353–54, 25:26–27. See James Phinney Baxter et al., eds., *Documentary History of the State of Maine*, 24 vols. (Portland, Me.; State of Maine, 1869–1916), 11:247–50, 253–55, 273–75, 277–80, 284–85, 415–22, 427–41, for the political dispute which convulsed Berwick, Maine, and led to four separate appeals to the General Court.

defense appropriations. Once the House had debated these requests, the speaker appointed the necessary committees, and they ordinarily began their deliberations by simply copying the expiring statute. The committee then wrangled over the precise tax rate or the size of the budget or the number of troops to be garrisoned in a fort. Only infrequently did a committee rewrite a statute or change its style by revising, for example, the basis of tax evaluation or the categories within the budget or the responsibilities of a frontier outpost. More radical changes in long-standing policies were even rarer.[9]

Because it was a temporary work group with limited responsibilities, a committee always remained the creature of the Assembly it served. The House established a committee's procedures, defined its quorum, and prescribed the style of its formal report. Even a committee originally created to investigate specific problems needed the speaker's permission before it could draft remedial legislation. Then, too, the Assembly's right to instruct a committee assured the representatives the ultimate control of it. Technically the speaker in creating any committee gave it a binding mandate. Routine issues needed only brief instructions— ordering a committee, for example, to draft a bill regulating ferries or preserving meadow lands. But tax, appropriation, and currency bills usually went to committees only after the House had specifically established the basic framework of the proposed bill. And when a committee gave an unsatisfactory report, it was simple enough for a member to move for the appointment of a new, presumably more cooperative, committee.[10]

Once drafted in committee, a bill followed a path copied from the procedures of the British House of Commons: three separate

[9] *MHJ*, 26:89; Massachusetts Archives, 119:656–69. The rhythm of legislation was discovered by analyzing all bills introduced during the 1741–42 term.
[10] *MHJ*, 17:26, 35, 18:82, 19:117, 131, 26:40–41, 89, 27:33, 35, 127, 136, 140, 29:50, 121.

readings, engrossment (the act of authorizing the clerk to draft an official copy of a bill), and enactment. There was, however, little else that was parliamentary about House floor procedures. House consideration of a bill was determined in part by the legislative work load and in part by caprice. Scheduling was the speaker's prerogative, checked, however, by a member's right to move for a set time for reading any particular bill and by a tradition of scheduling debate on controversial legislation at least one day in advance. While House rules required a bill to be read in full on three separate days, the Assembly, as often as not, crowded two readings, and occasionally all three, into a single morning. Debate, recommittal, and tabling could come at any time, depending on the whim of the speaker and the mood of the membership.[11]

Engrossment marked the Assembly's initial acceptance of the measure. The engrossed bill next went to the Council, which repeated the same basic pattern: three readings, debate, amendments, and engrossment. The bill then returned to the House for enactment, traveled back to the Council for a second enactment, and then went to the governor for his signature. A bill changed by the Council followed a different route. Considering each amendment separately, the House frequently asked a committee to review the issues involved and occasionally requested the creation of a joint committee or a conference to compromise differences. Technically, neither chamber could alter the purpose or basic framework of an engrossed bill. Yet this custom, like most of the General Court's procedural rules, was ignored at will. With equal ease both chambers tabled engrossed measures only to resurrect them later when alternative proposals failed to

---

[11] The maneuvering surrounding the 1751 tax bill provides a classic example of this flexibility; *MHJ*, 28:15–17, 35–46. See also *MHJ*, 17:35, 96, 28:13, 17.

win enactment. And once both chambers had forged a seemingly acceptable compromise, a shifting majority within one house could reject the bill and insist that the process begin anew.[12]

The flexibility of these procedures was reinforced by an ebb and flow in House attendance. To convene, the House required the presence of forty representatives, and while daily attendance early in a session averaged seventy members, representatives constantly drifted away to plow their fields and tend to their local interests. Theoretically, House rules provided ample machinery for coping with a constantly dwindling membership. Representatives absent without permission were subject to fines and could, by a vote of the House, be summoned by a writ served by a county sheriff. In practice, however, most representatives proved reluctant to vote fines. Consequently massive absenteeism always plagued the House, forcing frequent recesses and occasionally the introduction of controversial legislation to entice the delinquent member back to Boston.[13]

The major challenge facing anyone plotting legislative strategy was to guess which members would be present at any given moment. And since the floor of the House, not the committee room, served as the primary focus of legislative activity, the success of any coordinated strategy depended heavily upon chance. For the House would frequently devote several days to arduous

---

[12] "Legislative Minutes of the Council," Massachusetts Archives, passim; *MHJ*, 17:243, 18:77, 19:144, 147, 26:153, 174, 27:10. Hutchinson, *History of Massachusetts*, 3:66n; Pepperrell to Shirley, 18 November 1748, Baxter, *Documentary History of Maine*, 11:425–26.

[13] "Attendance Rolls," Massachusetts Archives, 49:151, 160, 240, 244, 331, 380, 410, 417, 419, and 441, and 89:1–18; *A&R*, 1:89; Bernard to Jackson, 29 October 1762, 21 January, 23 January, and 1 February 1763, Bernard Papers, Harvard College Library, Cambridge, Mass. For the consequences of absenteeism see *MHJ*, 18:224–25, 19:112, 184, 188. See also *Independent Advertiser*, 4 April 1748.

debate, agree on a final compromise, and then reject the bill when the sudden influx or departure of members altered the division of opinion.

The confusion of the House, moreover, made certain that persuasion, rather than tactical maneuvering, was the only way to defeat or pass legislation. In modern legislatures floor debate serves a variety of purposes. Primarily directed outward—toward the press, or some special interest, or a member's constituency—speeches delivered on the floor allow the legislator to try out new ideas, to advocate new policies, to make and answer political charges, or simply to enhance his public image. But the lobbying and persuasion that influence votes take place chiefly behind closed doors, in committee chambers, cloak rooms, private clubs, or wherever else two legislators meet.

The Massachusetts Assembly was not without its smoke-filled rooms. Within a minute's walk of the Court House were a half-dozen taverns which, along with the small boardinghouses where most representatives lodged, provided sufficiently secretive habitats for political gossip and deals. But whatever happened outside the chamber, it was on the House floor that even the most minute details of legislation were decided. Prolonged discussion was the principal means of influencing decisions. And debate was a deadly serious endeavor intended to change men's minds in order to make decisions possible. For this reason, floor debate was also secret. Legislators were to be free agents, their debates unfettered expressions of their own opinions. To open the doors, the House suggested, would only tend "very much to the obstruction of that freedom and liberty of speech so necessary for the good and welfare of the province." [14]

While House rules thus enhanced a member's opportunity to express his views, custom made certain that debate itself con-

[14] *MHJ*, 6:135. *Independent Advertiser*, 26 December 1748.

formed to eighteenth-century notions of proper decorum. A member was expected to curb his temper and observe the niceties of gentlemanly politeness. James Otis, Jr., learned early that however successful fiery oratory might be in arousing Boston, within the House he had better keep his tongue in check. When he first sat for Boston in the spring of 1761, a friend in the delegation reminded him that the Assembly expected calm, clever speeches, not impassioned oratory. "Mr. Otis," he lamented, "you have great abilities, but are too warm, too impetuous, your opponents though they cannot meet you in argument, will get the advantage by interrupting you, and putting you in a passion." The young lawyer replied, "Well if you see me growing warm, give me a hint, and I'll command myself." Two weeks later the House tested Otis' resolve when Timothy Ruggles, a former speaker of the House, suddenly interrupted him in mid-sentence. Otis began a nasty retort when he felt the tail of his coat tugged by his friend. Scowling, Otis composed himself and resumed his speech. Almost immediately the dean of the House, John Choate, rose to a new point of order, and Otis again felt a slight tug at his coat. His patience gone, Otis hissed to his friend, "let me alone, do you take me for a school boy?", and then delivered a torrent of sarcasm directed at Choate.[15] Otis had been victimized by two master parliamentarians.

Otis suffered little more than momentary embarrassment. John Tyng, another member of the Boston delegation, was not so lucky. In the chair sat Thomas Hubbard, and the issue under discussion was a special grant to the governor. During the course of the debate, Tyng rose to a point of order which Hubbard summarily dismissed. Angered, Tyng retorted, "If the speaker puts a nonsensical question, I have a right to oppose it." Again ruled out of order, Tyng renewed his charge: "The

[15] William Tudor, *The Life of James Otis* (Boston, 1823), pp. 92–94.

speaker has no right to set me down, unless by order of the House." Still not satisfied, Tyng petulantly added, "When I began to speak, I observed the speaker treated me with an uncommon degree or warmth of temper." Within the hour the House had its own answer for Tyng's outburst. Escorted from the House chamber, he was ordered to apologize to both Hubbard and the House.[16] Tyng refused to serve penance and did not reappear on the House floor for the remainder of the session.

Even when decorum was maintained, most floor debates were grueling and heated. The House considered controversial measures paragraph by paragraph, sentence by sentence, and, if need be, word by word. A debate could begin in the morning, resume after the dinner break, and then continue into the early morning hours. And, as often as not, the representatives would repeat the pattern later in the week when the bill came up for engrossment and then again when the House considered enactment. The cadence and tenor of debate, then, determined the pace of legislation. It was not always a long process. Routine business, particularly private petitions, ordinarily engendered little discussion. Even some potentially controversial issues passed with only limited debate. And in times of genuine crisis, the House, putting aside its natural fondness for prolonged controversy, could, with remarkable efficiency and near unanimity, approve bold, even controversial measures. But such precipitate action was rare, the normal pattern being to debate, discuss, and haggle interminably.[17]

Climaxing each debate was some kind of vote. Often the speaker simply sensed the will of the majority, tabling motions which lacked support, scheduling business for convenient times,

[16] *MHJ*, 33:127–28.
[17] *MHJ*, 26:17, 29:109, 33:141. Cf. Hutchinson, *History of Massachusetts*, 2:332–33.

and appointing desired committees. Individual members could, and did occasionally, demand formal votes, and engrossment and enactment of bills did require some formal expression of approval. But whether such approval was in the form of voice votes, a show of hands, or an unrecorded tally is not known. The one exception to the anonymous quality of House voting was the roll call. Initiating a formal vote required a motion from the floor and majority approval. The speaker then ordered the clerk to call the roll, beginning with Boston's four representatives, proceeding through each county delegation, and ending with the normally absent member for Sherburne. Once the vote was announced, the ayes and nays were recorded in the official journal.[18]

In part the Assembly's fluid procedures simply reflected the absence of standing committees and the unregulated nature of floor activity. Yet House procedures were equally a product of a second uniquely eighteenth-century phenomenon. In Massachusetts all the evils of bad government were attributed, indirectly if not directly, to parties, those secret cabals which sacrificed the public good upon the altar of private gain. Thomas Fleet, for two decades the editor of the *Boston Evening Post,* spoke for an entire society when he boasted:

Although I have lived in this town upwards of *twenty-seven* years, I have never been of any *company,* clan or party, either in church or state, but wherever I have had a right to speak or act, have always done it with openness and freedom, according to my *own* judgment, and not that of *others,* which may be one reason why I have so few hearty friends at this time. I have always endeavored to behave as a good subject and a good neighbor,

[18] [James Allen], *A Letter to the Freeholders of Boston* (Boston, 1749); Bernard to Jackson, 1 January 1763, Bernard Papers; [James Allen], *A Letter to a Friend in the Country* (Boston, 1740); *MHJ,* 27:195.

rendering to all their dues, and hope I have been among those that *be quiet in the land.* I have indeed expressed myself in a free, open, undisguised manner, as becomes an *honest* man.[19]

The absence of organized public associations bent on winning political office was responsible for much of the fragmentation which characterized politics in Massachusetts. Alliances among politicians did exist, but they were invariably small, close-knit, and ephemeral. The political ethic, having damned parties as conspiracies, placed an implicit limit on coordinate action. Coalitions, when they formed, were not only small but covert, because the participants could admit neither to themselves nor to the community at large that greater political influence demanded a pooling of resources and a coordinated strategy. Political action was thus atomized. Politicians, no less than the voters who placed them in office, remained independent, being neither disciplined nor organized by the exigencies of party politics. In the Assembly the people's representatives went about their tasks unfettered by party responsibilities, without a party position to cleave to, but also without the advantages coordinated action yields in a political arena.

The absence of parties imposed certain conditions on House procedures. Most modern legislatures depend on party organizations to set the pace and tenor of proceedings. Responsibility for mustering quorums, disseminating policy positions, and canvassing the membership falls to party whips and conference leaders. Legislative parties not only enunciate policy which their members either adopt or reject, they also help establish the procedural context within which legislatures work. In the eighteenth century, however, only a legislature's rules and precedents could order the workday. In Massachusetts, the absence of

[19] *Boston Evening Post,* 6 October 1740.

party organization simply aggravated the disorder created by the Assembly's already permissive procedures.[20]

The Assembly coped with this problem by negotiating the contents of every proposed piece of legislation on the House floor. Ordinarily negotiations opened when the speaker appointed a committee to consider an issue, and they intensified when the House read the bill for the first time. In the ensuing debate, the representatives voiced their objections, listened to the committee's explanations, and further defined the measure that would satisfy their demands. The speaker then appointed a new committee to revise the bill. Once redrafted, the bill was again debated and not infrequently recommitted. And so it went. The process continued until a draft commanded a majority.

The pattern was not invariable. Some bills were debated before being sent to committee. Sometimes, too, the bargaining did not begin until the bill's third reading or until after engrossment when the bill returned to the House for enactment. Similarly bills could be engrossed, denied enactment, and then reconsidered when efforts to find a better compromise failed. And occasionally the House wrote four or five bills on the same subject and then appointed a committee to amalgamate them into a single draft. But whatever the variations, the basic procedure remained essentially the same: the committees initiated and the membership responded until enough representatives were satisfied that the current draft was the best they could pass.

With only slight modifications, the same negotiating process reconciled differences between House and Council. Major legislation initiated by one chamber was usually altered in the other. Amendments were added, whole clauses struck out, and oc-

---

[20] Cf. Stanley M. Pargellis, "The Proceedings of the Virginia House of Burgesses," *William and Mary Quarterly*, 2d ser. 7 (1927): 73–86, 143–57.

casionally entirely new bills substituted. At crucial points in the bargaining, joint committees were often appointed to break deadlocks and to compromise major differences. Each chamber, by the changes it suggested and the amendments it rejected, let it be known what was negotiable, and out of the welter of proposals and counterproposals gradually emerged a compromise acceptable to a majority in each chamber.

The success of these negotiations depended on two factors. First, unlimited access to the House floor allowed representatives a free, often turbulent exchange of opinion. The second, and more important, factor was the flexibility permitted by the absence of standing committees. A committee unwilling or unable to report a bill demanded by the majority could either be reorganized or replaced altogether by a new, and presumably more responsive, group of representatives. Nothing prevented the speaker from reassigning the same men who drafted a bill to the task of making (or not making) the proposed alterations. Yet, for the most part, the speaker appointed committees whose composition mirrored the political persuasions of the majority of the moment. As a consequence a committee was never able to say: This is the only bill we will draft, take it or leave it.[21]

Although made possible only by the absence of standing committees and well-developed procedural rules, the negotiating process was a kind of specialized procedure for defining acceptable legislative behavior. Similarly, the custom of revising old legislation rather than drafting new compensated in part for the lack of experienced legislators and a system of standing committees. More important, perhaps, floor debate, though it often embroiled the entire House, was ordinarily dominated by

---

[21] See, for example, the maneuvering surrounding the 1751 currency act; *MHJ*, 27:181–234.

a handful of Assembly leaders. In his *Biographical Dictionary,* John Eliot, who had little admiration for Thomas Hutchinson, at least gave the latter his due as a compelling debater and in the process portrayed the role men like Hutchinson often played within the Assembly:

> In the House of Representatives . . . [Hutchinson] acquired great reputation. He had the charms of oratory beyond any man in the Assembly. There was equal fluency and pathos in his manner; he could be argumentative and smooth. . . . [In 1746] he was chosen speaker of the House; but had the same influence among the members as when he led in their debates.[22]

Yet the fact remained that every representative enjoyed equal access to the House floor. And even the rawest back-bencher, when sufficiently disgruntled, could take to the floor to voice his demands or disrupt the orderly flow of legislation.

From our own perspective, the Assembly's procedures quickly take on the quality of a vast phantasmagoria in which nothing ever remains the same. What rules existed were either changed or ignored at will, and few of the procedural arrangements we now consider essential to efficient decision-making had yet come into being. Nor were the participants themselves oblivious to the attendant confusion. Thomas Hutchinson, for example, believed that the Assembly, for all its pretensions, was a most unparliamentary institution. "The House," he lamented, although occasionally objecting

> to motions and proceedings which come before them as not being in parliamentary form, yet are not strict in conforming to some of the most useful rules of Parliament. A bill or motion is not only referred from one session to another, but a bill, after rejecting upon a second or third reading, is sometimes taken up and passed suddenly the same session. They have an order of the

---

[22] John Eliot, *A Biographical Dictionary* (Boston, 1809), p. 272.

House, that when any affair had been considered, it shall not be brought before the House again the same session unless there be as full a House as when it was passed. . . . But even this rule, like many other of what are called standing orders, is too frequently by votes, on particular occasions, dispensed with, which lessens the dignity of the House.[23]

More prosaic commentators worried instead about the cost of prolonged legislative sessions. To many outsiders, verbal duels seemed wasted, beside the point, and expensive, because the representative was being paid to bask in the resonance of his own oratory. Daniel Fowle once caustically asked who else but the province's elected statesmen would

protract a warm debate for 8 or 10 days about the *situation* of a *C—rt House,* as if they had no business of importance before them, but to wait upon the return of an express, *viz. that the government of* New York will do nothing, and then very gravely bring on a long debate, whether they will *do nothing themselves.*[24]

Sometimes the politicians who sat through these debates seemed no happier about the disarray. In 1748 a Council, still exhausted from the experience of sitting 165 days the previous term, suggested that reform could no longer be delayed:

Whereas the frequent and long sessions of this Court occasion a great charge to the province, and a great damage to many of the members . . . in their private affairs: And the Board being of the opinion, that there be many things in the usual proceedings and transactions of the Court that might be altered, so as to save much time and charge, and yet the public not in the least injured thereby, nor private persons fail of that relief which they seek to this Court for in their exigency.[25]

But once having appointed a joint committee, the Court shelved procedural reform for another term.

[23] Hutchinson, *History of Massachusetts,* 2:336.
[24] *Independent Advertiser,* 2 May 1748.
[25] *MHJ,* 25:71.

Probably the most telling criticism of the Assembly's procedures came from William Shirley, who, more than most politicians, demanded a rational, ordered legislative system. The governor was concerned not so much with the Assembly's procedures per se as with the incoherence an unregulated approach to legislation had created in the province's statutes. The cluttered nature of the statute books, he suggested, was obvious to all who bothered

> to cast their eyes over the province law books, and examine into the number of acts made for repealing, altering, amending, examining, or revising, not only single acts, paragraphs, or clauses of single acts, but for the explanation and alteration of some clauses, or even sentences, and the repealing of others, contained in several acts of different natures, all promiscuously blended together in the same explanatory act.[26]

As long as the Assembly resisted procedural reforms, the statute books would reflect the disorder of the legislative process itself. The House, of course, paid for its flexibility in institutional inefficiency. But in the eighteenth century, an Assembly facing a limited number of problems could afford a confused approach to legislation.

[26] *MHJ*, 30:190.

2

The Social Prerequisites
of Power

THE CLUTTERED NATURE OF THE LEGISLATIVE ARENA NOTWITH-
standing, the Massachusetts House of Representatives was
a successful deliberative body. In part the negotiating
process itself compensated for the confusion encouraged by the
Assembly's permissive procedures. Because most decisions
emerged from bargains struck on the House floor, each member
was able to use legislative activity to achieve goals important
both to himself and his community. Consequently most representatives had a vested interest in a functioning legislative system, one that could render decisions and reconcile differences.

A second and probably more decisive factor, however, was the
skill and efficiency of the Assembly's leaders. They derived their
institutional power from their control of the Assembly's ad hoc
committee system. About a dozen men in all, these principal
members wrote most fiscal legislation, were the Assembly's official spokesmen, and occupied those positions within the House
most likely to provide personal gain. A slightly larger group of
sub-leaders spent most of their time drafting minor legislation
and reviewing private petitions. At the pyramid's base were the

Assembly's back-benchers, by far the largest but the least active group of representatives.[1]

In durable political systems, leadership is always the specialty of the few. For a variety of motives and with varying results, a handful of men provide the order and organization successful decision-making requires. Thus there was nothing unusual about either the size or the responsibilities of the Assembly's leadership. The dozen or so men who controlled the Assembly's committees played much the same roles that cabinet ministers and coalition managers played in the eighteenth-century House of Commons or that committee chairmen and party leaders play in modern legislatures.

Ordinarily a legislature recruits its leaders from among its most senior members. Whether the institution utilizes a formal seniority system or not, membership in the group which dominates the body comes only after an apprenticeship has been served —an apprenticeship which allows the neophyte to acquire the necessary legislative skills and to establish his acceptability to those already in power. In the eighteenth-century Virginia House of Burgesses, for example, power and influence were monopolized by those who, in addition to bearing illustrious family names, had spent considerable time learning the intricacies of the legislative system. A new member, whether destined for leadership or not, spent his early years in the Assembly working his way up the seniority ladder of one of the five standing committees. While not all committee chairmen were the most senior committee members, most were men who had long records of legislative service and who had proved their worth to the dominant members of the establishment—the Robinsons, Randolphs,

---

[1] For the statistical analysis on which this discussion of leadership is based, see the statistical appendix.

Pendletons, and Lees who considered the House of Burgesses their special domain. Even Thomas Jefferson served six years before becoming a leader. And during that period, brief only in comparison with what other men were required to wait, he served the apprenticeship expected of all young men.[2]

Leaders in the Massachusetts House experienced a remarkably different introduction to legislative power. In 1753 James Bowdoin, then only twenty-six, began his first term as a representative for Boston. The grandson of a French immigrant and the son of an industrious father who had amassed a major mercantile fortune and served on the Council, Bowdoin had entered his father's counting-house upon graduation from Harvard in 1745. Three years later he married Abigail Erving, daughter of the provincial councilor, and took his place in the first ranks of Boston society. Thus Bowdoin was no ordinary freshman representative. The son of a prominent father, the son-in-law of an equally imposing political figure, he enjoyed all the symbols of status and prestige that eighteenth-century society could bestow.[3]

Bowdoin's rise in the House was equally spectacular despite his noticeable lack of political experience. On his first day in the Assembly he received two prized appointments: first as part of the ceremonial delegation which announced the election of a new Council; and second as a member of the committee responsible for ruling on a disputed election. During the next two months he helped draft the bill for the governor's salary, served on two joint committees, was responsible for writing a minor piece of legislation, and participated in the auditing of the commissary general's accounts. By the Assembly's third session, his apprenticeship was over. Now a full-fledged leader, he served

[2] Jack P. Greene, "Foundations of Political Power in the Virginia House of Burgesses, 1720–1776," *William and Mary Quarterly,* 3d ser. 16 (1959): 485–506.
[3] *SHG,* 10:514–20.

on the committee which drafted a new schedule of custom-house fees, chaired a committee reviewing a major private petition, and worked on two joint committees. At the close of the term he received his most important assignment, a place on a special committee investigating apparent deficiencies in the collection of a variety of excise duties. For the next two years he continued to move up within the ranks of major House leaders before being elevated to the Council in 1757.

Bowdoin was the youngest and probably one of the more gifted House leaders, but his experience was scarcely unique. Of all the major leaders who sat in the Assembly between 1740 and 1755, nearly 90 percent began their legislative careers at the top of the Assembly's political hierarchy. Hence, in the Massachusetts Assembly, the height to which a representative rose was, in fact, determined by who he was when he entered the House rather than the length of his service or quality of his work once a member of the Assembly. In short, a House leader was extraordinarily visible, as if he wore a chevron on his sleeve identifying him as a man to be reckoned with, as a politician who, on the basis of his standing in the community at large, was entitled to power and influence.

Among the more conspicuous attributes distinguishing the leader from the back-bencher was the location of his constituency. The eastern shore, a narrow strip of towns running from Newbury in the north to Barnstable in the south and including all the province's mercantile centers, elected less than one-fourth of the Assembly's membership and yet contributed more than half of the Assembly's leaders. These maritime towns were the centers of a flourishing and far-flung trading economy. From their wharves, provincial ships set out for every port open to British bottoms; and on their endeavors ultimately depended the fate of the entire provincial economy. While fewer than 10 percent of the colonists were directly involved in trading enterprises, it was Massachusetts' foreign and inter-American commerce which provided the necessary outlets for domestic products and supplied the luxuries most colonists seemed incapable of doing without.

Within the House, the men who represented these trading towns and who presumably spoke for the merchant community accounted for nearly half of the Assembly's major leaders. Boston alone contributed 28 percent of these leaders, and between 1740 and 1760, Bostonians occupied the speaker's chair three out of every four years. Not all of those who sat for mercantile communities were merchants, but most were. They were men like Thomas Hutchinson, James Allen, Thomas Hubbard, Thomas Foster, John Tasker, and the Brownes of Salem—men who owed both their livelihoods and prominence to either their own or their father's mercantile endeavors.

One other distinct group of men with similar constituencies was particularly likely to belong to the leadership. While the Connecticut Valley (Hampshire County) contributed a proportion of the leadership equal to its share of the total membership, within the county's delegation a handful of men stood out—Israel Williams, Oliver Partridge, John Worthington, Joseph Dwight, Joseph Hawley. These were the valley's river gods, the holders of vast tracts of land and the monopolizers of Hampshire County offices. Wealthy, proud, headstrong, they were as likely a collection of political oligarchs as were to be found in Massachusetts.[4]

Yet despite immense local power, they played a curiously ambivalent role in provincial struggles over patronage and public policy. Only two things seriously concerned them: military

[4] Robert J. Taylor, *Western Massachusetts in the Revolution* (Providence: Brown University Press, 1954), particularly chap. 2 and p. 33. See also *SHG*, 5:96–105, 7:56–66, 8:301–32.

affairs, for which they had a genuine aptitude; and the politics and distribution of power within the valley. Among themselves they could fight over political spoils with a gusto befitting feudal barons. Hampshire County was their preserve, and they remained the final arbiters of what the provincial governor and General Court could and could not do within the valley.

The performance of the valley's political magnates within the House reflected their general unwillingness to become enmeshed in the intricacies of provincial policy-making and the responsibilities of legislative leadership. Half the time the House operated without the presence of a Hampshire County delegation.[5] But when actually in Boston, the county's political leaders were accorded all the deference to which their positions entitled them. Within the House these men exercised an influence proportional to the effort they were willing to expend.

The representatives from the rest of the province's constituencies were conspicuous for their failure to become House leaders. Better than 65 percent of the House sat for the small farming communities which made up the bulk of the province's townships and which contained most of the province's inhabitants. The majority of these representatives were farmers or small tradesmen, men who owed their livelihood to the small, seemingly prosperous farms which dominated the countryside or to the small businesses essential to every farming community. Despite their numerical superiority, less than 10 percent of these men ever became House leaders. In the final analysis, the Assembly's yeomen lawmakers—men whose outlook and general economic situation differed little from those who elected them to the House—accorded, rather than received, political deference

[5] "Attendance Rolls," Massachusetts Archives (State House), Boston, Mass., 49:151, 246, 244, 331, 386, 410, 417, 419, 441, 18:1–18. Hutchinson to Williams, 1 February 1748–9, Williams Papers, Massachusetts Historical Society, Boston, Mass.

and allowed the Assembly's Hutchinsons, Hales, and Choates to use the House as a springboard for increased political power.

The nature of a leader's constituency was not the only attribute distinguishing him from the rank and file. Three-fourths of the Assembly's leaders were also members of the provincial judiciary. In the eighteenth century, the men who sat on the province's courts fulfilled functions which have long since been absorbed by other local institutions. These justices not only heard civil and criminal cases, but also governed the province's eleven counties. Appointed judges, not elected officials, assessed and dispensed county taxes, surveyed local highways, granted licenses covering the right to retail everything from snuff to alcohol, and generally determined the level and scope of local activity. For most citizens, it was the county court and not the provincial government which represented governmental authority and which was most often thought to be verging on arbitrary and oppressive rule.[6]

Service on the bench did not necessarily make a representative a House leader. Slightly more than half the justices of the peace elected to the House became back-benchers. Nevertheless, seven out of every ten House leaders doubled as provincial justices. The importance of judicial experience also suggests a more subtle characteristic of the Assembly's leadership. In a political system in which few positions conferred power and responsibility, the province's judges held a preeminent place. Their offices were not only marks of political achievement, but also symbols of their own social importance. Thus, to some extent, their status within the Assembly corresponded to the social deference they enjoyed in the community at large.

[6] Taylor, *Western Massachusetts*, pp. 26–33; Robert J. Taylor, ed., *Massachusetts, Colony to Commonwealth: Documents on the Formation of Its Constitution* (Chapel Hill: University of North Carolina Press, 1961), pp. 51–89.

A third characteristic distinguishing leaders from nonleaders more directly reflects this connection between social deference and legislative status. About 10 percent of the Assembly were graduates of Harvard or Yale. Among these men, 60 percent became House leaders. In sharp contrast, less than 15 percent of those without college experience belonged to the leadership.

This marked tendency of the House to recruit its leaders from the ranks of those who had a college education admits of a variety of interpretations. The most obvious is that in a province in which most men lacked a grammar school education, having attended Harvard or Yale increased one's status. New England's insistence that education and a learned clergy were essential to the right ordering of society and the proper practice of religion endowed these two institutions with a special stature. Harvard, founded in the first decade of settlement, contributed most of the men who staffed the province's pulpits and filled her professional classes. By the middle of the eighteenth century, the College was also educating an increasing number of the province's political and economic leaders.[7]

The social backgrounds of those who journeyed to Cambridge to receive a public education further illuminates the stature of the institution and the prestige attached to her graduates. Of the 59 men who sat on the Council between 1740 and 1755, 26 had attended Harvard and 36 sent their sons there. Almost half of Harvard's graduates were the sons of prominent political leaders, professional men, successful merchants, large landowners, and ministers. Among the province's social notables, whether they

---

[7] See Samuel Eliot Morison, *The Founding of Harvard College* (Cambridge, Mass.: Harvard University Press, 1935) and *Harvard College in the Seventeenth Century*, 2 vols. (Cambridge, Mass.: Harvard University Press, 1936); Robert Middlekauff, *Ancients and Axioms* (New Haven: Yale University Press, 1963); Franklin Bowditch Dexter, *Biographical Sketches of the Graduates of Yale College* (New York, 1885).

intended their sons for the ministry or not, a Harvard education was often considered a proper beginning for boys who were destined to lead lives at least partially devoted to public service.

Not all Harvard graduates came from the gentry. Indeed one out of every two students were members of the province's middling majority. Most of these sons of successful farmers, small businessmen, and artisans—for whom a college education was both a source of pride and a considerable sacrifice—became ministers or learned a profession. But among this group there were also the John Adamses and the Thomas Hubbards, for whom a college education was a springboard to both fame and fortune.

Despite the status conferred by attending Harvard, the relationship between a college education and being a House leader was probably the product of a more direct link between social prestige and political influence. When a boy entered Harvard, he was given a class rank initially compiled by the college steward and later cast into official form by the president and faculty. A great deal depended on where a boy was placed. For the next four years the order in which he ate, recited, and marched in formal processions was determined by his class standing. In the seventeenth century, these rankings were based on the student's probable distinction and usefulness to society, and reflected intellectual promise as much as relative social standing. By the second quarter of the eighteenth century, however, ranking was almost wholly based on social distinction or what a 1770 Overseers' report called "the supposed dignity of families." The system used after 1723 divided each class into three groups. The first included, in descending order, the sons of the province's governor, lieutenant governor, councilors, and justices of the peace. The second category contained the sons of university graduates and was dominated by those with minister fathers. The third group, which contained half or more of each class, included everybody else.[8]

Despite the system's mechanistic overtones, it did produce class lists accurately reflecting the relative social standing of Harvard students. Boys whose fathers were not prominent political figures but were still wealthy or important men were usually accommodated by the timely discovery of a near relative who possessed the proper qualifications. Or the president and faculty would make an exception in order to give a boy ranking commensurate with his family's social position. General John Winslow, worried over his son's placing in the class of 1753, wrote to President Holyoke urging that proper note be taken of his family's eminent position, even though the general was not a high-ranking civil officer:

> As I am bound to sea and rank in our way is looked upon as a sacred thing and it is generally allowed that the sons of the New England Cambridge are placed according to the degrees of their ancestors, I have therefore put in my pretensions for my son, beginning with the country in which we breathe.

To buttress his case, the general then catalogued the accomplishments of the Winslow family. His father Isaac "had the honor to have the first place in both civil and military affairs in the County of Plymouth . . . and until he resigned was president of the Council of this province." For himself, Winslow pointed out that "from my early days I have been entrusted in the public affairs of the county and province until 1740 when I had a company in the unfortunate expedition against Cathergenia and have had since two commissions of the same rank under his majesty and entrusted with the command of the second

[8] Morison, *Harvard in the Seventeenth Century*, 1:58–64; Clifford K. Shipton, "Ye Mystery of Ye Ages Solved, or, How Placing Worked at Colonial Harvard and Yale," *Harvard Alumni Bulletin* 57 (1954): 258–59, 262.

garrison in North America which is my present station." [9] The General's pleas were not in vain: Holyoke placed young Winslow second in the class.

Just as a distinguished genealogy guaranteed the Harvard freshman a place at the head of the line, so, too, it promised a public career of equal distinction. If a representative had ranked in the top half of his Harvard class, he had an 80 percent chance of becoming a House leader. Indeed he belonged in the House, just as he did in the community at large, to a small, readily identifiable group of social notables, men who had inherited social prestige and hence political power.

[9] Winslow to Holyoke, 20 October 1749, *Proceedings of the Massachusetts Historical Society*, 2d ser. 9 (1895): 6.

3

The Professional Style

WHEN JOHN ADAMS HAD BEEN IN WORCESTER FOR SIX MONTHS, he told a friend, "This whole town is immersed in politics."[1] And so it was; indeed, so was every provincial community. Whenever two provincials gathered, talk inevitably turned to the oddities of politics and the foibles of politicians. Yet, for all his gossip, the average provincial seldom engaged in political activity. He had little desire to hold office; his attendance at town meetings and participation in provincial elections was sporadic; and when he did join in political campaigns, he rarely lent more than his moral support to the cause.[2]

This lack of political involvement was peculiar to neither Massachusetts nor the eighteenth century. Today few citizens ever become politically active. Most do not know the names of their local representatives. Only a hearty few are familiar with either the organization or the leaders of their political party. And almost no one outside the political organization attends precinct

[1] Adams to Webb, 12 October 1755, *Microfilms of the Adams Papers,* reel 343.
[2] Robert E. Brown, *Middle Class Democracy and the Revolution in Massachusetts* (Ithaca: Cornell University Press, 1955), pp. 21–99. See also petitions of Medway and Topsfield to the General Court, Massachusetts Archives (State House), Boston, Mass., 46:137, 358.

meetings, works for the nominations of candidates, or performs any of the trivial tasks that politics normally entails. Perhaps wrongly, most citizens assume that the government will muddle through without their active participation. What is evident, too, is that most citizens assume that their activity can make little difference. The machine, the boss, the nebulously defined clique that monopolizes the political apparatus, is somehow beyond his reach, the average citizen believes.

There is, however, one significant exception: the citizen whose immediate interests are suddenly threatened by his government. In response to decisions to bulldoze a park or change local zoning requirements or deplete school budgets, some citizens become amateur activists. They write letters to their representatives, organize protest committees and demonstrations, and show a new interest in the electoral process and the selection of candidates. Frequently these protests are successful because most politicians, intent on preserving their political base, adjust their policies in order to accommodate these suddenly aroused citizens. And once the crisis has passed, these citizens disengage from politics, leaving the government to the professional politician.[3]

We know, of course, a good deal more about political attitudes now than about attitudes in the eighteenth century. But there seems little reason to doubt that then as now political participation generally conformed to the pattern described above. There is, moreover, a limited amount of direct evidence testifying to the constancy of these attitudes. In Boston, spring elections for representatives to the General Court attracted an average of 480 voters. Yet the turnout over a twenty-year period (1735–1755) ranged from a high of 700 voters in 1748 to a low of 240

[3] See, for example, Robert A. Dahl, *Who Governs?* (New Haven: Yale University Press, 1961), particularly pp. 225–26, 277–310; Robert E. Lane, *Political Life*, rev. ed. (New York: Free Press, 1965); Angus Campbell et al., *The American Voter*, abr. ed. (New York: Wiley, 1964), pp. 49–64.

in 1737. These fluctuations simply reflect an ebb and flow of political interest and involvement within the capital. In times of crisis, the Bostonian turned out, suffering whatever inconveniences a morning spent at Faneuil Hall entailed. The rest of the time he complained, protested, and criticized without ever feeling compelled to take action.[4]

In Lynn, a small farming and fishing community fifteen miles north of Boston, town meetings ordinarily attracted fewer than 150 citizens, and most elections were decided by less than one-third of the town's eligible voters. Then in March 1741, Lynn's formerly apathetic citizens turned out in droves to defeat politicians who had controlled the town for more than a decade. The issue was the Land Bank, and the town's voters removed from power every politician suspected of being opposed to the paper money scheme. In June, the town's inflationist majority extended its vendetta to include Lynn's two representatives to the General Court. Benjamin Lynde, Jr., recorded the results of the election: "Representative meeting mustered on all sides 347 voters. Gardner had 182; Flint, 179; Mr. Lee, 161; B. Browne, 142; so the Land Bank still prevailed."[5]

The most dramatic example of an apathetic electorate suddenly being galvanized into action came thirteen years later in Braintree, a thriving farming community southwest of Boston. The Assembly had enacted a special rum excise which Governor Shirley refused to sign unless a majority of the province approved the tax. Reluctantly the House had printed the measure and asked the towns to consider it at their summer meetings. In Braintree, the selectmen included the bill in the warrants

---

[4] Boston, Mass., *Report of the Record Commissioners of the City of Boston*, 39 vols. (Boston, 1881–1909), 12:165, 192, 219, 256, 276, 294, 14:17, 45, 72, 93, 115, 148.

[5] [F. E. Oliver], ed., *The Diaries of Benjamin Lynde and of Benjamin Lynde, Jr.* (Boston, 1880), p. 162.

MERCHANTS, FARMERS, AND RIVER GODS • 42

issued for the August 19 meeting. The town frequently had trouble mustering enough citizens to convene a meeting, and on this occasion only 59 residents appeared at the meetinghouse. After a heated debate, the excise was endorsed by a 30 to 29 vote. A month later, a special meeting attended by 200 angry citizens rescinded this endorsement, deciding instead that the excise was "inconsistent with our rights and privileges as Englishmen."[6]

Braintree also illustrates a second similarity between political action then and now. Today governments function because in every community there are a handful of men who genuinely enjoy the game of politics and for whom political action is not a sacrifice of precious time. These activists enjoy political participation. They are full-time, professional politicians who give the community a stable, functioning, and usually responsive government.[7]

Obviously, Braintree's government never required the efforts of a coterie of professional politicians. But within the community, a handful of activists did make most decisions. Some were men like John Adams' father, a successful farmer who frequently served as selectman. Others were local tradesmen and part-time lawyers. Finally there were a few country squires, like Josiah Quincy, who dabbled in local politics while maintaining their business interests in Boston. These men, perhaps two dozen in all, effectively ran the town. Among themselves they competed for power with remarkable fervor, negotiating, planning, scheming, building alliances, and occasionally making appeals to the electorate in their battles to gain more personal power.[8]

This same pattern was repeated on the provincial level. But

[6] Samuel A. Bates, ed., *Records of the Town of Braintree* (Randolph, Mass., 1886), pp. 335–38; *Boston Weekly News Letter*, 19 September 1754.
[7] Dahl, *Who Governs?*, pp. 305–25.
[8] See chap. 4 below.

those who dominated the central government were professional politicians—councilors, principal judges, military commanders, and House leaders, in all about 150 men. For some of these leaders, politics and public service actually constituted distinct careers, and in this sense they can properly be labeled professional politicians. But they were also professionals because the attitudes and values they exhibited were peculiarly a product of the roles they played within the political arena.

One index of the distinctness of these attitudes was the cynicism with which many citizens viewed their leaders—not so much as individuals, but rather as a class of men. In Massachusetts, the target of political exhortation was inevitably the same: the politician who in public mouthed pious platitudes and then in private exploited a virtuous people for personal gain. Probably the most effective master of such rhetoric was Daniel Fowle, a contentious newspaper editor with little use for politicians in general and none at all for William Shirley, the province's governor, who displayed a professionalism few provincials could either match or appreciate. When Shirley, with the support of the Assembly's principal leaders, sought to retire the province's paper currency, Fowle asked:

> What is government, but a trust committed, by all or most, to one or a few, who are to attend upon the affairs of all, that everyone may with the most security attend upon his own? A great and honorable trust, but too seldom honorably executed: those who possess it having it often more at heart to increase their power than to make it useful, and to be terrible rather than beneficent. . . . Honesty, diligence, and plain sense are the only talents for the executing of this trust, and the public good is its only end. As to refinements and finesses, they are often only the false appearances of wisdom and parts, and oftener tricks to hide guilt and emptiness; and they are generally mean and dishonest; they are the arts of jobbers in politics who, playing their own

game under the public cover, subsist upon poor shifts and expedients; . . . [they are] small wicked statesmen who make a private market of the public and deceive in order to sell it. . . . Honesty and plainness go always together, and the makers and multipliers of mysteries, in the political way, are shrewdly to be suspected of dark designs.[9]

Yet in decrying the "makers and multipliers of mysteries, in the political way," Fowle had simply caricatured the obvious in terms every provincial understood. To the outsider, the world of the professional was indeed mysterious, employing as it did its own rules, language, and measures of success. The importance of this professional approach to political action is uniquely reflected in a letter from Jeremiah Gridley, a leading lawyer and legislative leader. Dated February 1757, his letter describes an Assembly session which considered the demand made by Lord Loudoun, then British commander in America, that Boston quarter some of his troops.

This morning the General Court . . . was adjourned . . . and thank God I am at home again. It has been a long and busy session . . . as I was obliged to attend courts of law at intervals and at the same time not to be absent when any thing of moment to the General Court was transacted. . . . After his Lordship's message to the Council . . . was sent to the House, several of the members seemed to be determined upon an inquiry into the right of quartering: I endeavored to divert it as much as possible but thought all in vain. At least knowing their incapacity to determine such a point, [I] moved, if the House *would* proceed upon it, that the members who had begun the motion might be appointed a committee to consider it and report. This stopped their career, and in a short time the House asked to . . . [quarter] the recruits at the Castle. . . . I was glad to prevail upon them thus far. The Council instead of acting upon the vote appointed Mr. Hutchinson and the chief justice [Stephen Sewall] a com-

[9] *Independent Advertiser*, 2 February 1748–9.

mittee to be joined with one of the House to consider what was required. I was appointed chairman of the House's committee on this part and we met. . . . Mr. Hutchinson and the chief justice had . . . drawn up a report, the substance of which was a protest against his Lordship's demand of the government, asserting their rights as Englishmen by charter to raise and appropriate moneys as they thought proper, seeming to yield at the same time to a due proportion for the necessity of the king. I instantly opposed the report, I incurred the displeasure of Mr. Hutchinson and the chief justice. The chief with great warmth and sputter began to catechize me about English rights. I acquainted him that he misunderstood the question, that Lord Loudoun knew as well as he that he could not demand quarters of the legislature. . . . I told him his report tended to nothing but to bring the right of quartering into question.[10]

In the end Hutchinson relented, and the Council passed the Assembly's resolution. It sidetracked the issue of quartering, while still providing housing for Loudoun's troops.

In attempting to avoid a constitutional crisis, Gridley exemplified the professional's traditional distaste for ideological polemics. Yet in its own way, Hutchinson's willingness to use constitutional rhetoric to achieve pragmatic goals was equally professional. Committed to increasing the province's military budget, Hutchinson would have had the General Court protest Loudoun's impolitic demand for quarters—thus satisfying the province's sense of constitutional independence—while also acknowledging "a due proportion for the necessity of the King," a euphemism for justifying Loudoun's future requests. Equally revealing were the targets of Gridley's scorn: the back-benchers' "incapacity to determine such a point"; and Sewall's most unprofessional behavior, his "great warmth and sputter."

[10] Gridley to McAdam, 2 February 1757, Loudoun Papers, Henry E. Huntington Library, San Marino, Calif. See also ibid., Hutchinson to Loudoun, 16 and 25 March 1757.

James Otis, Jr., despite his own volubility, expressed a similar impatience with men who could not control their emotions. In a letter to his father, the younger Otis recounted a verbal duel between James Allen and John Tyng, two Boston representatives noted for their quick tempers. Allen, more than any politician of his generation, typified the professional who either could not or would not play the game by its established rules. Something of a demagogue, Allen was blessed with a gift for sarcastic invective which periodically reduced him to political impotency. In 1748, while leading the campaign against currency redemption, he had assaulted Governor Shirley with such verbal abuse that the House, egged on by Hutchinson and the elder Otis, had expelled Allen and thus greatly eased the passage of the currency bill.[11] Young Otis' letter, dated September 1750, is as follows:

> Among all the news what is marvelous in everybody's eyes is the following. Mr. John Tyng being indebted to Mr. Allen . . . Johnny . . . comes with six hundred pounds old money in [paper] bills and very sanctimoniously emptied his pockets. But the grand seignior told him he would not touch them; he would have the [silver] dollars; Johnny you'll easily believe was thunder struck . . . [and] told him that he was out of character to demand dollars, he being so professed a friend to bills etc. . . . But Allen claims silver he must pay. Tyng went off hoping it was the effect of passion, as he says, though he might hope it was the juice. He came in today with his bills but was as peremptorily refused as at first. He therefore went and got the . . . silver . . . to the utmost farthing. Mr. Tyng took his discharge and after he had got it safe in his pocket he began to let drive and they parted with scoundrel, rascal, villain, and sot, the only proper compliments

[11] SHG, 6:159–64; George Richards Minot, Continuation of the History of Massachusetts-Bay (Boston, 1798), p. 104; [James Allen], A Letter to a Friend in the Country (Boston, 1740); Boston Evening Post, 20 January 1755.

that ever passed between them, and continue to hate one another as heartly as either of them ever served the D-v-l.[12]

Allen and Tyng, interestingly enough, were the only two representatives expelled from the House. And both expulsions came when the offender threatened a project particularly important to the administration.

How different was John Adams' appraisal of James Otis, Sr., who, in a quarter-century of service in the Assembly, occupied every position of authority the House could bestow including the speakership in 1760. After spending a pleasant afternoon accompanying Otis to Barnstable, Adams observed: "He is vastly easy and steady in his temper. He is vastly good humored and sociable and sensible. Learned he is not. But he is an easy, familiar speaker. He gave me many anecdotes both of his law and politics." [13]

Such commentaries suggest the broad outlines of the attitudes characteristic of the professional's world. Although provincial politics were richer if more volatile because of men like Allen and Tyng, real power belonged most often to men like Otis, who muted ideological differences, curbed their tempers, and preferred the quiet of the dinner table to the clamor of the public arena. Most of the professional's life was devoted to such sociability, to dealing with men and opinions. It was a world in which feelings and emotions played special roles, because personal contacts and understandings were the primary mode of activity. While the professional pursued goals he thought consistent with the society's moral principles, he distrusted the enthusiasts who cast all issues in terms of good and evil. While he

[12] Otis to Otis, 10 September 1750, Otis Papers, Massachusetts Historical Society, Boston, Mass.

[13] *JA-Diary*, 1:227.

respected the electorate's potential power and capacity for political mischief, the professional was happiest when political decisions were left to men like himself. And as a professional he expected his rewards to match his endeavors. In return for providing the expertise and skill which a functioning government required, he wanted personal power, political advancement, and suitable financial rewards.

Although painfully aware of the politician's uniqueness, most provincials simply lamented how seldom "exalted parts, great improvements, consummate discretion, and unfeigned honesty unite in one person." [14] Occasionally, however, political writers were more explicit about the suspect connection between the leader's status as a professional and his role as a policy-maker. One Boston pamphleteer, seeking support for the reelection of two Boston representatives, contrasted the baseness of most politicians with the virtues of his own candidates, whose

> tender regard to the people . . . warded off that great evil, an impress—who honestly endeavored to answer the intentions of their constituents . . . [and] who had ability and influence sufficient to . . . have taken off the greatest part of the load of taxes unjustly lying upon us—gentlemen, who though they had so considerable an influence in the late virtuous and happy administration, have yet not so much as asked a court favor for themselves, but on the contrary, have discountenanced every species of bribery and corruption, and in some good measure repaired the honor and credit of the government.[15]

This 1760 election pamphlet, which failed to salvage the careers of the two men in question, raised a pair of related but distinct questions which the colonists themselves rarely bothered to separate. The first was the alleged existence of widespread politi-

[14] *Independent Advertiser*, 8 May 1749.
[15] *To the Freeholders of Boston* (Boston, 1760), pp. 1–2.

cal corruption. The second was the more subtle and complex question of legitimate political rewards and the way in which the professional's interest in patronage and preferment determined his stands on political issues.

The most notorious political scandal in the quarter-century before the Revolution involved Thomas Clap, militia colonel, House leader, and judge on the Plymouth County Court of Common Pleas. In 1760, a group of Clap's Scituate constituents charged the good colonel with eighteen separate counts of misconduct. Embarrassed by the charges levied against one of its own, the House reluctantly assembled the various principals and spent two days listening to their well-rehearsed tales.[16]

Apparently Clap's troubles began in the spring of 1751, when Abiezar Turner, a local farmer about to be brought before Clap's court, asked for some legal advice. Turner wanted bail releasing him from custody while his case was heard. Clap arranged the matter, but demanded a fee, suggesting that since Turner had been spared the cost of hiring a lawyer it was only right that such a sympathetic judge should receive part of what Turner might have otherwise paid. Obviously relieved, Turner was only too happy to oblige. Nine months later, however, Turner returned with a more vexing problem. His widowed mother had haled Samuel Holbrook into court, charging him with fathering the child she was then carrying. Too late, Turner realized the rashness of her action. Whether she won or lost, the poor woman became liable for court fine and church censure. Remembering that Clap had been helpful once before, Turner and a friend quietly approached the judge. Could he arrange it so that Mrs. Turner was not tried for fornication? Or, if this was not possible, could he guarantee the minimum fine? Turner

---

[16] *Boston Evening Post,* 28 May 1760; *A Reply to Col. Clap's Vindication* (Boston, 1760); Thomas Clap, *An Answer to . . . a Reply* (Boston, 1761).

later claimed that in return for £4, Clap had promised to quash any indictment. But not fully trusting the judge, Turner had insisted on signing a promissory note which he delivered to a third party until Clap fulfilled his bargain. In 1760, Clap admitted that Turner had indeed approached him, but only to inquire how much the fine might be. In a spirit of neighborliness, Clap offered to receive £4 from Turner with which he would pay the fine, even if the sum required should be greater. Clap's version, however, never fully clarified the need for elaborate negotiations or the holding of the £4 in escrow. At the last minute, Turner decided not to trust the judge, and his mother's timely discovery that she was, in fact, not pregnant ended the imbroglio.

In 1755, Clap's military office offered the opportunity for financial remuneration. As a militia colonel busily recruiting for the Crown Point expedition, Clap had been approached by Thomas Hobart. Although interested in a commission, Hobart had mistakenly signed up with Colonel Brown's regiment, in which there was no opening for an officer. Understandably, Brown had refused to release Hobart unless a suitable replacement was found. Clap, then recruiting for Colonel Turner's regiment, in which there was a vacancy for an ensign, suggested an amicable compromise. Colonel Brown received one of Clap's recruits. Colonel Turner accepted Hobart. Hobart got his commission, and Clap received eight dollars and two gold crowns paid in three equal installments. Clap never denied receiving the money, and Hobart later testified that for his commission "and some other kindnesses . . . [I] rewarded Col. *Clap,* according to his pleasure, and never to this day find any fault with him on that account." [17]

Two years later, Clap's recruiting practices took a different

[17] Clap, *An Answer,* p. 11.

turn. With the sudden resignation of one of his recruits, Clap found his regiment a man short. The captain of the affected company quickly filled the vacancy with John Smith, who, on the night of April 22, appeared in Clap's living room for formal induction. At this point the captain suggested antedating Smith's enlistment to March 22, thus saving the inconvenience of returning a month's pay to the provincial Treasury. What happened to the money is unclear, but Smith swore he never saw a penny of it.

For years these tales had been common gossip in Scituate, but not until 1760 was the House asked to declare Clap's various activities "unjust, partial and oppressive." After the hearing, the House resolved that the colonel was indeed guilty but recommended neither his indictment nor his dismissal from the Assembly. The Council refused to concur in the Assembly's reprimand, and there the case officially ended—almost.[18]

Charging that the Assembly's mild rebuke had passed only because "the principal members had gone home," Clap took to the press to vindicate his name, persuading the *Boston Evening Post* to devote most of one issue to presenting his side of the case.[19] His foes, in return, issued a pamphlet which both substantiated and gave wider circulation to the charges against the colonel. Clap contributed one more pamphlet to the controversy, repeating the charges and countercharges already made. In the meantime, Scituate's voters had rendered their own verdict. In May 1760, Clap sought and won reelection to the House.

Whether or not Clap was guilty of petty graft is almost beside the point. What is important is that in a society in which men used the slightest pretext to levy charges and countercharges, Clap was the only major figure to be formally accused

---

[18] *MHJ*, 36:158, 190, 194, 216, 257–58.
[19] *Boston Evening Post*, 28 May 1760.

of accepting bribes. It is, of course, easier to levy charges of illicit activities than to disprove the existence of political corruption. But there is simply no evidence that corruption was widespread. Nor are there any indications that either bribery or graft influenced political decisions. Despite the litany against the politician's proclivity for graft, political corruption in Massachusetts was apparently both petty in nature and restricted in scope. Clap was probably neither more nor less corrupt than many other politicians. But the contentious colonel had made enemies, and when they moved to oust him, they resurrected the tales of his past misdemeanors.

Provincial pamphleteers were on more solid ground when they focused on the relationship between the professional's pursuit of legitimate political rewards and his stands on questions of public policy. The eighteenth century, of course, was the age of the placeman. In England, patronage welded together parliamentary majorities, united ministries, won elections, and determined the composition of the civil service, the military establishment, and, to a lesser extent, the Church. "As a rule," Richard Pares has suggested, "friends and political influence stuck to the fingers of every man who had ever handled any high office from which patronage depended."[20] Although English politics often appeared tawdry and sordid, there was little that was either covert or patently illegal about the uses of patronage. Men of affairs simply granted that the politicians were entitled to suitable financial remuneration. If a few isolated voices cried reform, few Englishmen thought it practical to alter either the way in which political rewards were distributed or the role patronage played within the English political system.

[20] Richard Pares, *King George III and the Politicians* (Oxford: Clarendon Press, 1953), p. 80.

Although it was 3000 miles away, Massachusetts was always tangentially involved—and sometimes deeply enmeshed—in the English patronage system. The chief link was the royal governor, whose appointment symbolized his ability to obtain English political connections and whose policies were invariably influenced by the twists and turns of London politics. For a provincial merchant community tied to English credit and allied with England's mercantile establishment, a familiarity with London's current political configurations was crucial since it often meant the difference between prosperity and ruin. More important, the patronage system, albeit on a smaller scale, was replicated in Massachusetts.

Patronage politics within Massachusetts was merely English politics writ small, with two essential qualifications. First, the political rewards available in Massachusetts were not only less lucrative than those available in England, they were, by comparison, minuscule. The chief patronage plum was the naval office—a post which carried a moderate income from fees, an opportunity to dispense minor jobs in the customs service, and some personal status. It was, as Governor Bernard suggested, "the principal of the governor's limited patronage and worth all the rest." [21] What Bernard dismissed as the rest—and what most colonists considered excessive—was his right to commission militia officers and nominate judges and civil servants. In all there were less than 300 important patronage positions: county officers, militia colonelcies, and judgeships. The aggregate value of government contracts, land grants, and special bonuses was equally limited. But as William Douglass, the colony's reigning political commentator, noted, while "we have few places of any considerable profit in the governor's gift . . . a great many small farms

[21] Bernard to Pownall, 2 March 1761, Bernard Papers, Harvard College Library, Cambridge, Mass.

well leased out may be equivalent to a few great farms." [22]
Clever and resourceful men could substantially improve their
financial status from government service, and a few even managed to live exclusively on it.

The second qualification, and one which better reveals the
nature of politics in a colonial political system, involves the
qualitative difference between English and provincial patronage.
Primarily a redistribution process, the English system rewarded
and reclaimed a fixed supply of offices, sinecures, and contracts,
which often guaranteed the recipient an income regardless of
how much or how little he worked. But in Massachusetts there
were no sinecures, no pensions, no fixed incomes. Political rewards were special opportunities for, but not guarantees of,
increased wealth, security, and prestige. Land, the most tangible
sort of largess available, was only as valuable as the recipient's
ability to make a profit out of a potential resource. Military commissions, which usually involved recruiting bonuses and supply
contracts, were boons only to sharp bargainers who could also
convince reluctant farm boys that glory and destiny lay in answering the call to military service. Even a justice of the quorum
sessions, the lowest patronage post that provided an income,
could realize the potential of his office only by diligently attending most sessions of his court.[23]

Still, for the clever politician, these rewards did provide opportunities that hard work, luck, and considerable ingenuity
could convert into substantial financial returns. After Indian
raids had resumed in the Connecticut Valley in the spring of

[22] Douglass to Colden, 20 November 1747, *Collections of the Massachusetts Historical Society*, 4th ser. 2 (1854): 172–77. The best index of the amount of
patronage available is William H. Whitmore, ed., *The Massachusetts Civil List
for the Colonial and Provincial Periods, 1630–1774* (Albany, 1870).
[23] See, for example, John J. Waters, *The Otis Family in Provincial and Revolutionary Massachusetts* (Chapel Hill: University of North Carolina Press, 1968),
pp. 61–109.

1748, Governor Shirley ordered a defense force recruited out of the militia and made Joseph Dwight the campaign's commander. In order to raise the necessary force, Dwight needed to offer an attractive enlistment bounty. And once recruited, the men had to be paid. Dwight solved the first problem by offering as bonuses the muskets the province had provided. Technically the guns were to remain the property of the government and were to be returned once the regiment was mustered out. But Dwight assured his men that a grateful province would never reclaim the guns.[24]

Dwight's solution to the money problem was more ingenious. Shirley, as commander in chief of the province's militia, had issued Dwight £6,000 in drafts on the royal Paymaster General in London. But the drafts would be redeemable only after the campaign had ended and after the governor's accounts had been audited. Dwight, if he hoped to raise an effective fighting unit, needed to pay his men at the time of their service. To do this, he issued bills for £6,000 sterling on his own signature which he sold for province bills to Edmund Quincy, a Boston merchant and friend. Dwight paid his troops with the proceeds. To cover the notes bearing his signature, Dwight used the Paymaster General's notes to borrow £6,000 sterling from an English merchant. Quincy then sold the English notes in Boston for provincial bills. Dwight and Quincy's profit came from their ability to sell the English notes at a premium price to local merchants who needed specie to satisfy their London accounts. Dwight later justified these complicated transactions when Shirley threatened to hold up clearance of the Paymaster General's notes:

> Now I pray your excellency to consider whether the advantage of the crown in punctually paying off at a good rate men of such loyal, generous, and good dispositions will not outweigh that of

[24] *SHG*, 7:59–61.

saving a few 4ds with the discouragement and loss of such a temper in the king's subjects, whereby it will be rendered impracticable upon any the best concerted measures (be the emergency what it will) to raise the like number of brave men in New England.[25]

Though more spectacular than most, Dwight and Quincy's scheme typified the way in which military contracts, land grants, schemes to increase immigration and spur domestic industry mingled personal gain with public service. Although they often castigated the politician for enriching himself while performing these tasks, most colonists implicitly accepted the system's inherent practicality. Since politicians inevitably sought personal gain, the task was not to interdict their ambitions, but rather to harness them, to rationalize the distribution of rewards in order to minimize corruption and maximize the efficiency of the government. Thus government officials received little or no salary and instead earned most of their income from fees and commissions, which always entailed the actual performance of a public duty. Political rewards in Massachusetts were essentially incentives whose value was directly proportional to the individual's initiative, endeavor, and, in some measure, his skill and success in carrying out his public responsibilities. If Dwight and Quincy stood to gain from their currency manipulations, that gain came from their resourcefulness in equipping and paying an army intended to provide military security to the western frontier.

This reciprocal relationship between public service and personal rewards also provided the ethical framework within which the politician could justify his own personal gains. The professional, no less than the political outsider, was the product

---

[25] Dwight to Shirley, n.d., James Phinney Baxter et al., eds., *Documentary History of the State of Maine,* 24 vols. (Portland, Me., 1869–1916), 11:390–91. Great Britain, *Journal of the Commissioners for Trade and Plantations from January 1741–2 to December 1749* (London, 1931), pp. 466–67.

of a moral environment which stressed hard work, honest endeavor, and a virtuous life. If he no longer adhered to the tenets of orthodox Puritanism as enunciated by John Cotton and enforced by John Winthrop, he was still a Puritan in the larger sense of the word: public service remained a sacred trust and calling which, among other things, demanded adherence to a code of religious morals. However irrelevant the colonists' commitment to a moral code might appear to modern observers, it did affect political policies and influence politicians. When Charles Chauncey told the province's assembled rulers that they should "promote the *general welfare* and *prosperity* . . . by encouraging . . . industry, frugality, temperance, chastity, and the like moral virtues," he not only enunciated orthodox doctrine, he defined the criteria of good government in terms most politicians readily accepted.[26] For this triad of industry, frugality, and probity both justified and helped delineate legitimate political rewards. To her politicians America appeared to be a vast, underdeveloped continent which only hard work would convert into a strong, thriving adjunct to the British empire. But the realization of this program required much: importing new settlers, building up the domestic economy, and removing the French. The responsibility for achieving these goals naturally devolved upon them, for, as politicians, they were the men who had the capital to risk and who could provide the skills, leadership, and resourcefulness the great project required. That they should personally benefit from the industry, frugality, and capital so liberally invested in improving the province seemed only right.[27]

[26] Charles Chauncey, *Civil Magistrates Must Be Just* (Boston, 1747), pp. 44–45.
[27] See, for example, Winslow to Waldo, 29 October and 7 December 1749, Massachusetts Archives, 53:428–29, 454–55; Winslow to Waldo, 26 January 1749–50, Baxter, *Documentary History of Maine,* 12:39–40; Otis Little, *The State of Trade in the Northern Colonies* (Boston, 1749).

Whatever the moral justification, political leaders sought personal gain with a remarkable fervor. Just how serious they were about patronage and preferment is suggested by a letter Joseph Hawley wrote Israel Williams in the fall of 1754. Since the death of John Stoddard in 1748, the Connecticut Valley had witnessed a lively struggle for political supremacy. With a war against France imminent, Shirley arranged a temporary agreement dividing the valley's military patronage. Hawley, however, repudiated this arrangement once he discovered that not he, but Ephraim Williams would be given the remaining major's command. To Israel Williams, Hawley proposed a conference with Oliver Partridge and Ephraim Williams to arrange a more satisfactory compromise. "Otherwise," Hawley continued,

> it seems to me all our separate designs and projections will be likely to prove abortive. . . . You sir and Major Ephraim concert what you think proper and labor it with the governor and he will plea with the whole Court. Colonel Partridge schemes something different perhaps which he will labor with the governor and House. I am privy to neither scheme and perhaps if the first of my hearing thereof should be in the House, neither may appear perfectly agreeable; and although I am a person of but small consideration yet if providence should etc. order it that I should be in the House when those matters should be considered, if there appears sinister designs interwoven in the plans, it will be no difficult matter to prevent their taking. I don't think that in my private capacity I am of much importance as to such matters but as a member of the House it is possible I may be, for I have always spoke my mind in the House and sometimes have been heard.[28]

Hawley's message was clear: he would delay military appropriations until his own political demands were met.

[28] Hawley to Williams, 3 October 1754, Williams Papers, Massachusetts Historical Society, Boston, Mass.

Still, Hawley's letter was atypical—not in the sentiments it expressed, but in the fact that it existed at all. The province's politicians seldom wrote to one another, and when they did, their communications were ordinarily brief, often cryptic, references to appointments to be kept or broken, past and future political favors, and a host of equally trivial items. Perhaps a fear of his letters going astray and later being used to embarrass him kept the politician from committing himself in writing. But his reluctance to fill his letters with political gossip probably had a simpler explanation. Politics, then as now, was essentially an oral art. The tavern, boardinghouse, legislative chamber, and private parlor were the natural milieu of the politician, not because he craved secrecy, but rather because he thrived on the amiable sociability such surroundings offered. For the politician, the political system was a network of personal arrangements and understandings, often developed with little conscious thought and almost never solemnized by even informal written agreements. The absent political leader might have to be told of the major events occurring during his absence, but only an oral account, preferably from another politician he understood and trusted, would allow him to evaluate the events he had missed.[29] There was, in short, little reason to write letters.

There does, however, exist one tantalizing description of the politician's private world. In 1770 John Adams served a single term in an Assembly already rent by issues of constitutional authority and the rights of man. Despite the magnitude of events and his own habit of dissecting the men and institutions with which he dealt, Adams recorded few of his impressions except to note occasionally, "This week has been taken up in the hurry of the Court, and I have not been able to snatch a moment

[29] See, for example, Hutchinson to Williams, 19 January 1754, Williams Papers.

to put down any thing." Toward the end of his term, however, Adams did find time to record in detail an evening spent with some of his more important colleagues.

> Dined at the honorable John Erving's, with Gray, Pitts, Hancock, Adams, Townsend, J. Erving, Jr., G. Erving, Boardman. We had over the nominations of Nat. Hatch to be judge of the Common Pleas, and Ed. Quincy to be a Justice of the Quorum, and H. Gray's story of a letter from a repentant Whig to him.
>
> *H. Gray.* "The General Court is a good school for such conversation as this"—i.e. double entendre, affectation of wit—pun—smut, or at least distant and delicate illusions to what may bear that name.
>
> Gray said he could sometimes consent to a nomination when he could not advise to it. And says he, I can illustrate it to you Mr. Hancock. Suppose a young gentleman should ask his father's consent that he should marry such a woman. . . . The father says I can't advise you, to have a person of . . . her character, but if you have a desire, I won't oppose it. You shall have my consent. Now Mr. Hancock I know this simile will justify the distinction to a young gentleman of your genius.[30]

As Adams suggests, whatever the nature of influence within the professional community, interpersonal relationships played a dominant role. In fact, men presumably had influence in proportion to their ability to observe those norms of professional behavior that politicians thought important. To understand why, one only has to remember that the professional belonged to a remarkably close-knit community, a specialized group of men with remarkably similar social backgrounds and political interests. Four times a year these leaders congregated in Boston for General Court sessions, and often the community was reunited when county courts met or when the Superior Court rode circuit. Because contact was frequent and ordinarily

[30] *JA-Diary,* 1:358, 2:1.

informal, those who did not fit were simply excluded—and those not invited to supper had no voice, not at least within the community itself.[31]

Hawley's letter to Williams illustrates a second probable determinant of influence within the community: the importance of political rectitude. Hawley faced a trying dilemma. He wanted the major's command, and yet to receive it he had to do battle with Williams, one of the Connecticut Valley's most senior and venerable river gods. Much of the self-effacing tone of the letter stemmed from Hawley's attempt to disguise his own ambition. Williams was a senior statesman, a respected leader long past his political apprenticeship. Hawley, on the other hand, was just beginning his career, and, though no less ambitious and probably more talented, he could ill afford Williams' lasting enmity. To avoid this pitfall, Hawley attempted a flank attack, suggesting a conference involving Williams, young Ephraim, and Oliver Partridge, who in every sense was Williams' equal. As gentlemen, Hawley hoped, they would negotiate their differences over a quiet glass of Madeira in the best tradition of eighteenth-century politics.[32]

If all else failed, Hawley was prepared to use every resource at his disposal. By bringing the issue up in the House, he would transform a quarrel over preferment into a major legislative imbroglio. How often such tactics were employed is difficult to tell. The Assembly's constant wrangling over military strategy suggests such maneuvers were not uncommon, though in part this wrangling also reflected the rank and file's impatience with high taxes and large draft calls. Given the stress placed upon group solidarity and conforming behavior, however, it seems

[31] See Oliver, *The Diaries of Benjamin Lynde;* both Lyndes kept detailed records of their dining partners when they were in Boston and when Superior Court business took them to a county seat.
[32] Robert J. Taylor, *Western Massachusetts in the Revolution* (Providence: Brown University Press, 1954), pp. 13–24; see also Ernest Francis Brown, *Joseph Hawley* (New York: Columbia University Press, 1931).

likely that overt blackmail was less prevalent than might be imagined. United on issues creating political largess, the professional community preferred to cut up the pie in the privacy of a tavern or the seclusion of the governor's mansion.

Equally important and unfortunately just as veiled was the leadership's influence over the Assembly's rank and file majority. What little evidence we do possess comes primarily from the limited number of roll calls the House published. They suggest that the back-bencher was seldom so intimidated that he abandoned his own preferences for those of the leadership, perhaps because on some key issues the leadership itself was seriously divided. Votes dealing with the basic structure of the economy— issues on which a conservative political aristocracy might have achieved its greatest solidarity—did not unite the leadership. But a roll call involving either political spoils or support for a governor responsible for dispensing patronage usually enjoyed the leadership's nearly unanimous support. Probably the most revealing vote called for the sending of additional troops to Crown Point in 1755. Unhappy with the prospect of increased draft calls, a third of the rank and file voted against the resolution. In sharp contrast, the leadership voted 16 to 1 to send more troops and thus for the increased military commands and contracts an expanded war effort entailed.[33]

The rank and file could of course win any vote on which they were sufficiently united. Unfortunately the back-bencher always faced a limited choice: he could either adopt or reject what an Assembly committee proposed. True, he could continue to reject propositions until a bill contained the features he desired, but seldom did he actually draft legislation. This suggests that, in part, the leadership's power and influence derived from its control of the Assembly's legislative machinery. In a highly institu-

[33] See the statistical appendix.

tionalized legislature, this control of the committee system in itself might have allowed a united leadership to dictate most policy choices.

Yet the provincial Assembly was not highly institutionalized, and on only select issues was the leadership actually united. This, in turn, points to a second, more subtle source of a leader's institutional power and influence—his ability to give concrete form to ideas favored by a rank and file majority. In this present context, it becomes useful to recall part of Jeremiah Gridley's account of the 1757 session. After Loudoun's request for troop quarters "was sent to the House, several of the members seemed . . . determined upon an inquiry into the right of quartering. . . . At least knowing their incapacity to determine such a point, [I] moved . . . that the members who had begun the motion might be appointed a committee to consider it and report. This stopped their career, and in a short time the House asked to . . . [quarter] the recruits at the Castle." [34]

Legislative proposals came in all shapes and sizes. Some expressed only broad, often intuited needs, while others were remarkably explicit, couched in immediately applicable terms. The back-bencher understood what he wanted: an inflationary economy and military retrenchment. Yet translating these goals into specific legislative decisions required a special talent which could shape the final decision as much, if not more, than its initial formulation. For example, a dozen expedients could encourage inflation. To choose among them was to determine which specific sectors of the economy benefited most.

The House leader enjoyed personal power and influence because he alone could translate general goals into specific policy choices. While he could not persuade the back-bencher to abandon prior policy commitments, the leader could subtly bend

---

[34] Gridley to McAdam, 2 February 1757, Loudoun Papers.

these commitments to his own interests. Whether or not this phenomenon characterized all political deference patterns is difficult to determine. In smaller farming communities, political rectitude rather than specialized expertise probably determined who enjoyed power and influence. In major population centers like Boston, however, leaders did apparently convert expertise into actual power. At election time, city voters chose among rival leaders, basing their choices on the candidates' policy stands, personal charm, and proven ability. The provincial voter was nobody's fool. Desiring neither personal power nor a tyrannical government, he settled for an amiable compromise: he would tolerate political leaders who neither oppressed him nor allowed political chaos to reign. He might grumble that all politicians were inherently corrupt, but when called upon to make viable choices, he opted for an efficient political system, one controlled by professional politicians.

In the seventeenth century, a government's primary responsibility was to preserve domestic tranquillity by maintaining the prerequisites of a static society. John Winthrop put it as bluntly as anyone when, in preparing to lead his company of Puritans ashore, he reaffirmed that "God Almighty in His most holy and wise providence has so disposed of the condition of mankind, as in all time some must be rich, some poor, some high and eminent in power and dignity, others mean and in subjection." The first lesson men drew from such axioms was the indivisibility of community responsibility, economic power, and social status. To be preeminent in one realm, by definition, was to be preeminent in all; those who possessed dignity and power also possessed sufficient wealth to justify such status. But that was not all. Equally important, the virtues one sought as well as the vices one avoided differed according to one's place in the social firmament. Those "rich and mighty" were to exercise "love, mercy, gentleness, and temperance" so as "not to eat up the poor," while "the poor and inferior sort" were to practice "faith, patience, and obedience" so as not to "rise up against their superiors and shake off their yoke." [35] What Winthrop promised the colony's inferior sort, however, was not only subservience but the security of knowing one's obligations, the limits of one's deference, and the restraints placed on those entitled to exercise the awesome power vested in a Puritan government. It was, as with every aspect of Puritan thought, a contract, a setting forth of conditions that guaranteed stable, effective social organization.

For half a century Winthrop's notion of a hierarchical society knit together by contract characterized social relations in Massachusetts. Only slowly did doubts appear, and then not so much concerning the hierarchical nature of society as the distribution of power and status within the community. Winthrop had envisioned a rural society, but it was the colony's merchants who came to possess great wealth. And having inherited a constitution which made religious salvation a prerequisite for political privileges, the colony's second generation gloomily discovered that some men of wealth and social status stood outside the established church and hence outside the councils of government. Thus changes were made. In 1686 England, with important backing from the colony's growing merchant community, revoked Massachusetts' original charter, which had made the colony responsible for its own form of government and all but immune to outside pressures. Next came six years of near chaos

---

[35] John Winthrop, "A Model of Christian Charity," in *The Puritans,* ed. Perry Miller and Thomas H. Johnson, 2 vols. (New York: Harper and Row, 1963), 1:195. See also Bernard Bailyn, "Politics and Social Structure in Virginia," in *Seventeenth-Century America,* ed. James Morton Smith (Chapel Hill: University of North Carolina Press, 1959), p. 91.

during which England attempted to combine Massachusetts in the all embracing dominion of New England. Finally, in 1691, the crown issued a new charter transforming Massachusetts into a royal province. The religious qualification for suffrage was replaced by a means test, which had the unintended effect of making most adult males eligible to vote. Disputes and divisions in the once monolithic religious establishment became more open and eventually irreconcilable. And shaken by two decades of conflict capped by the travesty at Salem, the nature of the government itself changed, shedding its activist role. By the middle of the eighteenth century, the province was content to regulate its currency, defend its frontier, and divide up the spoils of office among its growing community of professional politicians.[36]

Despite such changes, Winthrop's concept of an ordered, mutually dependent society remained, albeit in somewhat muted form. Men still enjoyed ordered lives, paying and receiving the deference their status dictated, incurring and discharging the responsibilities important in a close-knit community bent on preserving an internal consensus about the goals and purposes of society. And in the provincial political arena, power, wealth, and status remained synonymous, while those accorded deference continued to discharge their responsibilities in terms largely derived from Winthrop's notion of a social contract. Men entitled to influence were expected to restrain their lust for power. But they were also to provide effective leadership. They were, in short, to become experts in the art of government.

On the provincial level the supplying of this expertise became

[36] See particularly Perry Miller, *The New England Mind: From Colony to Province* (Cambridge, Mass.: Harvard University Press, 1953), and Bernard Bailyn, *The New England Merchants in the Seventeenth Century* (Cambridge, Mass.: Harvard University Press, 1955).

an increasingly complex task. The sheer growth of the province doubled and then doubled again the demands placed upon government and hence on the province's gentry. More judges, more militia officers, more legislators were needed to discharge the central government's responsibilities. The integration of the Massachusetts economy with England's economy created further complications, as did the colony's growing role in the defense of the American continent. By the middle of the eighteenth century, the art of government required the skill of a professional, someone capable of performing politically complex tasks.

The growing complexity of colonial government does not wholly explain why, in the process of discharging its social responsibilities, Massachusetts' governmental elite transformed itself into a community of professional politicians. Probably a second factor was the increasing influence English practices and customs had on the colony's politics. In Winthrop's eyes, Massachusetts had been as distinct from as it was superior to the mother country. England was the mammon God had ordered to reform or submit to His vengeance. This was to be Massachusetts' mission—to be, in Winthrop's phrase, a "city upon a hill," a beacon of reform lighting the way to righteousness and fealty to God's edicts. The first dissenters from this notion had come from Boston's growing merchant community. Indeed the merchant's dissatisfaction with Winthrop's Boston derived in no small measure from the obvious disparity between the growing power and influence of England's mercantile establishment and the merchant's limited role in Puritan Massachusetts. So the merchant cultivated friendships with and learned to imitate his London counterpart. Thereafter even those politicians not drawn from the merchant community quickly followed suit. In manner, style, and custom, provincial politics took on a decidedly

English hue. Judges appeared in scarlet robes and wigs as befitted their offices. Pamphleteering—when not limited to gross plagiarism—religiously followed the English model. And the introduction of accomplished English politicians like Samuel Shute and William Shirley as royal governors hastened the transformation. To ape men of Shute and Shirley's stripe—men tempered in the intricate business of patronage politics, English-style—was to assume the attitudes and values of the professional politician.

Perhaps one additional factor encouraged the professionalization of provincial politics or at least influenced the particular kind of professional ethic which emerged in Massachusetts. A political professional is more than a servant of the people he governs, though he is that, too. Above all he serves his own interests, reasoning that, if he is true to his calling, what is good for him also benefits those who have accorded him power. At the same time the professional in politics recognizes that society is composed of groups that compete for advantage. This understanding that groups can legitimately compete in the political arena—that there are, after all, both winners and losers—moderates the professional's enthusiasm for absolutes. To him, political decisions are, in their very essence, compromises, melds of separate points of view in an attempt to approximate the common good. More than that, political decisions are always temporary, reflecting nothing more than a momentary distribution of power. Given a change in circumstances, a realignment of coalitions, or simply another opportunity to decide the question, what is policy one day can be discarded the next with neither loss of face nor diminution of the authority attached to that decision. While as an individual the professional can conceive of a single standard of truth—of a political absolute—seldom can he afford to hold out until enough of his colleagues similarly define the common good. Professionals need not agree, but they must work together.[37]

In Winthrop's Massachusetts, men were not supposed to have interests separate from those of the community. There was but one common good: the deciphering, enactment, and enforcement of God's edicts. The watchword was not compromise but con-sensus—the basic belief of the entire community that what the government did in the name of all was for the undeniable good of all. Bound together by the language and symbol of the covenant, the Puritan community saw in its central government the visible embodiment of the commonwealth's organic unity. Some men might be farmers and others merchants, but such labels marked separate callings rather than distinct and competing interests. There was, after all, but one church polity, one true form of government, one just price for the entire community. And if rightly calculated, such decisions were to be eternal, the continuing reflections of God's greater truth. To be sure, Puritan Massachusetts had its share of self-seeking leaders. Yet men who prospered from discharging their political responsibilities were suspect, in their own eyes as well as those of the community. It is probably no coincidence that John Winthrop required several special grants of land from the General Court simply to maintain the economic status he had carried with him to Massachusetts.

As long as such ideas prevailed, as long as they played an important role in defining legitimate behavior, the growth of a professionalized political ethic was retarded. Such ideas persisted into the eighteenth century, resulting in both political and ideological turmoil. The first three decades of the new government—from the issuance of the new charter in 1691 until 1726, when

---

[37] Guy E. Swanson, *Religion and Regime: A Sociological Account of the Reformation* (Ann Arbor: University of Michigan Press, 1967), pp. 29–30.

the king issued an explanatory charter reaffirming the prerogatives of the province's royal governor—witnessed the bitterest of
quarrels over the nature of Massachusetts' constitution as well
as the initial experiments with a paper currency. When Shirley
entered the governorship in 1741, he remarked to the Duke of
Newcastle, "I am sensible . . . that I am now entering upon the
government of a province where Colonel Shute quitted the chair
and Mr. Burnett broke his heart through the temper and opposition of the people." [38] Shirley, however, would demonstrate that
Massachusetts was governable after all, partly because he was
the most professional of politicians, and partly because the province's leadership had itself absorbed the importance of professional behavior, had at last abandoned Winthrop's strictures
against self-serving politicians and his definition of good government as one committed to unchanging standards of conduct and
policy.

Only a handful of men explicitly celebrated this transformation of values. Probably the most vibrant voice belonged not to
a political leader, but rather to a man of the pulpit, to John Wise,
the burly minister from rural Chebaco parish, defender of John
Proctor before the judges of Salem, and lampooner of Massachusetts' most venerated ministerial family. Wise's message was
simple: let men be themselves, let them compete, let them seek
their selfish interests, because we know from experience that
men will eventually find compromises which approximate the
common good. In 1721 Wise applied such reasoning to the question of a paper currency. His answer was a private land bank
which drew its directors from every sector of the economy and
thus harnessed private and selfish interests for the public good.
He was remarkably explicit about just where such men should

[38] Shirley to Newcastle, 23 August 1741, Charles Henry Lincoln, ed., *Correspondence of William Shirley,* 2 vols. (New York: Macmillan, 1912), 1:40.

come from precisely because he, better than most, understood the kinds of special interests then competing for economic advantage.

> I shall just point at such men as are proper in this case: landed men . . . great merchants who (though worth many thousands) keep the main of their personal estate stirring in a way of trade and merchandise, both in their own and other countries; also such other gentlemen, men of great estates and of great wisdom, who though they keep up a very considerable trade and merchandise, yet let out much at interest, and as their gains this way are less so also is their risk; there is a sort of wise and very prudent men that are a kind of *amphibious* beings who live in both elements, land and water; these are eminently qualified as members for a private bank. And also rich farmers and mechanics, men of character and influence (according to their sphere) in the places where they live. The main of these men must belong to our *metropolis* and other seaports and towns of trade, and others to be dispersed through the province. A convenient company of such persons so qualified and incorporated, I do imagine, shall be capable to carry on a bank of credit with greatest advantage, with an immense good and benefit to the public.

Such a bank would work because the directors in compromising their own diverse interests would seek what was best for all of Massachusetts. They would be "men of differing functions, and their own interests, as well as honor, wisdom, and honesty will oblige them always to steer right and do well for other men; for if they hurt others, they hurt themselves." [39] Wise held no fear of a professionalized political leadership as long as the composition of such an elite mirrored the separate and competing interests of the people being governed.

Wise discarded traditional definitions of community and

[39] [John Wise], *A Word of Comfort to a Melancholy Country* (Boston, 1721), pp. 34. See also [John Wise], *Vindication of the Government of New England Churches* (Boston, 1717); Miller, *From Colony to Province*, pp. 288–302, 317–19.

consensus. For the most part, however, the political rhetoric of the eighteenth century clung to these ancient axioms. On the local level particularly, provincials still settled disputes by achieving a consensus based on principle rather than effecting a compromise among competing interests.[40] Even in the provincial political arena, men resisted announcing divisions over questions of policy. One reason so few roll-call votes were published in the eighteenth century was that to list the ayes and nays was an explicit admission that a sizable minority of the Assembly could dissent from the dominant belief as to what was right and proper policy. Perhaps what finally forced the printing of a vote was the majority's desire to label as apostate those who broke faith with the idea of a common will. The forces which impeded the development of explicit political coalitions in the eighteenth century similarly testify to the enduring appeal of the Puritan definition of society as a covenanted community seeking that action which would benefit the total society. Political rhetoric still condemned competition as well as the seeking of individualized rewards. Indirectly, at least, this traditional approach to questions of policy reinforced the idea of a stable social order in which a community's natural elite rightly exercised political, social, and economic power. To a considerable extent the professional owed his own prominence to such notions. More important, perhaps, the principal contributors of political rhetoric were themselves politicians. Those who decried self-seekers in a political way more often than not were professionals seeking and representing special groups in much the same manner as those they condemned.

This disjunction between practice and rhetoric meant that the professional ethic was itself covert. Success in politics thus de-

[40] See particularly Michael Zuckerman, "The Social Context of Democracy in Massachusetts," *William and Mary Quarterly*, 3d ser. 25 (1968): 523–44.

manded an implicit denial of the primacy of consensus in the provincial political arena, implicit in the sense that the professional dared not announce, as Wise did, a new political order in which public policy was a matter of mediating among competing interest groups. But the professional was expected to put this idea into practice, to shy away from absolutes, to learn and practice the intricacies of patronage politics.

Learning to walk such a tightrope was no simple matter. The rhetoric was the product of the socializing process every colonial experienced—the learning of values, of ways to perceive what he experienced, of the proper symbols to be employed in understanding how society was organized. The professional ethic he acquired as the son of a distinguished family. Just as other youths came to believe that leadership was the responsibility of the social notable—a responsibility he was welcome to as long as he fulfilled the community's expectations of what a leader should be and do—sons born into the gentry came to want and expect political power. The family experiences which made him a seeker of power also equipped him to perform his political role. Family life, dominated by a political father and populated with important relatives and friends, taught the socially prominent youth the nature of the political arena, its special language, customs, traditions, and, above all, its professional ethic, so at variance with announced principles of political organization. Since this was a cultural experience available to few outside the gentry, political prominence remained synonymous with social standing. Put simply, there were few ways to become an insider —a professional—without being born one. There were no minor offices to instill the requisite values or offer an introduction to greater political power. Even the local activist who sat in the Assembly became something of an amateur when confronted with the complexity of the legislative process. Out of necessity as well as conviction he deferred to the professional, who was often younger but always more willing and better equipped to exercise political power.

These professionals were not modern politicians in knee breeches and powdered wigs. Their ideas about the proper role of government and lack of partisan attachments marked them as products of an eighteenth-century political culture. Yet along a scale of political development these provincial leaders had more in common with their Yankee sons than with their Puritan fathers, largely because in mid-eighteenth-century Massachusetts, expertise and the ability to behave professionally had come to rival inherited social status in determining who joined the governmental elite. The politics of deference still held sway, but the transition to the politics of party had begun.

4

John Adams, Upstart

BETTER THAN MOST, JOHN ADAMS UNDERSTOOD HOW NOTIONS
of social deference and experiences drawn from family
life mixed in the political arena. Among those inequalities
which gave some men in Massachusetts special influence over
the course of events, he noted in 1787, the most obvious was
wealth. "It will not be denied that among the wisest people that
lives there is a degree of admiration, abstracted from all depend-
ence, obligation, expectation, or even acquaintance which ac-
companies splendid wealth, ensures some respect, and bestows
some influence." The second inequality was the advantage enjoyed by those inheriting famous names which, by insuring "an
habitual national veneration for their names, and the characters
of their ancestors described in history, or coming down by tradition, removes them further from vulgar jealousy, and popular
envy, and secures them in some degree the favor, the affection,
and respect of the public." Yet Adams also understood that
neither wealth nor inherited social prestige in themselves fully
explained why the gentry dominated eighteenth-century politics.
For, he continued, "the children of illustrious families [also]
have generally greater advantages of education and earlier op-

portunities to be acquainted with public characters and informed of public affairs than those of meaner ones, or even those in middle life." [1]

Yet Adams was himself an exception, a son of the province's middling majority who nonetheless made himself a professional politician. What Adams wanted out of life was simple enough. "Reputation," he told himself again and again, "ought to be the perpetual subject of my thoughts and aim of my behavior. How shall I gain a reputation! How shall I spread an opinion of myself as a lawyer of distinguished genius, learning, and virtue." [2] His concept of reputation betrayed a vanity which characterized Adams' entire life. Yet for all of his grandiose pretensions, he wasted little time longing for exotic riches or quixotic fame. He contemplated and sought very real goals, a preeminent position within the legal profession, a prominent voice in political affairs, an opportunity to stamp his imprint on his own times.

Adams' story is worth telling in some detail for, unlike those social notables with whom he eventually shared political power, Adams had failed to inherit an intuitive grasp of the nature and prerogatives of leadership. Rather, this farmer's son schooled himself in the art of political action. The painfully self-conscious record of this schooling, preserved now in a loosely organized diary, offers a unique insight into the kinds of lessons most leaders absorbed simply because they were who they were.

Despite considerable social mobility, eighteenth-century Massachusetts was not a society in which men rose from rags to riches. Families improved their status gradually, over several

---

[1] John Adams, *A Defence of the Constitutions of Government of the United States of America*, 3 vols. (Philadelphia, 1787), 1:110–11.
[2] *JA-Diary*, 1:78. All biographical information has been drawn from the editorial notes accompanying the diary and autobiography unless otherwise noted.

generations, until those who emerged among the province's social elite were not so much outsiders as newcomers. Certainly the three most spectacular success stories conformed to this pattern. Thomas Hancock was the son of a Harvard-trained country pastor; Thomas Hubbard's father was a successful mechanic, a blacksmith of sufficient means to afford a home on Fort Hill and enough status to join the Ancient and Honorable Artillery Company; and John Adams was the eldest son of a prominent and prosperous farmer, a militia officer, nine times a selectman, and for more than a decade a deacon in Braintree's north parish church. At his father's death, Adams noted, "almost all the business of the town [was] managed by him for twenty years together." [3] What the Braintree Adams lacked was social status, and this the deacon intended his eldest son to acquire.

In the eighteenth century two paths led to social upgrading. The more spectacular, as well as the more difficult, was an advantageous marriage. The second path led to Cambridge and what in the eighteenth century was called a public education at Harvard. When he was sixteen Adams enrolled in the class of 1755.[4] His college career was not very noteworthy except that here, apparently, he began regularly to keep a diary. At his commencement Adams was approached by a representative from Worcester, the principal town in a largely frontier region in the center of the province, and asked to become the community's new schoolmaster. Adams quickly accepted.

Keeping school in the eighteenth century frequently served as a temporary occupation for Harvard graduates not committed to the ministry and yet uncertain as to just where their future lay. After nearly a full year in Worcester, Adams was no closer to a decision than he had been when he accepted the position.

---

[3] Ibid., p. 1n. For Hancock see chap. 8 below; for Hubbard see *SHG*, 6:490–95.
[4] Ibid., 3:257–58.

In a letter to his classmate Charles Cushing, he evaluated the various callings open to a young man of his inclinations. Obviously the path of least resistance was still the ministry. In his senior year he had won a Hollis scholarship intended for young men preparing for ministerial careers. Nevertheless he had accepted the schoolmastership and thus given himself a momentary respite from a decision he increasingly dreaded. "I am as yet," he told Cushing, "very contented in the place of a school master. I shall not therefore very suddenly become a preacher." And yet the pulpit, he was sure, was his eventual destination, not out of choice, but resignation, not out of an inward call to serve God and His community, but in search of the scholarly and contemplative life. A divine, Adams told Cushing and thus reassured himself, "has more leisure to inform his mind, to subdue his passions, few temptations to intemperance, . . . an opportunity of diffusing truth and virtue among his people." All this was possible as long as he could avoid "the decrees of councils or the sentiments of fathers" and instead rely on "the dictates of his mind . . . [and] spend his time in the improvement of his head in knowledge and his heart in virtue." [5]

What else might he do? He could, he supposed, become a physician, although he lacked the necessary "skill and ingenuity." Or, and this was the calling which came first to mind, he could become a lawyer. Because the letter was as much to convince himself as to inform Cushing of the merits of the ministry, Adams catalogued the drawbacks of the legal profession. A lawyer starts more quarrels than he resolves; he spends his time "fumbling and raking amidst the rubbish of writs, indictments, pleas, ejectments"; he impoverishes others that he might enrich himself; and he ends up "pleading dry and difficult cases

[5] Adams to Cushing, 1 April 1756, *Proceedings of the Massachusetts Historical Society* 46 (1913): 412.

[which] have very few charms in my eye." True, a legal career was "an avenue to the more important offices of the state, and the happiness of human society is an object worth the pursuit of any man. But"—and this was the "but" Adams constantly saw himself encountering—"the acquisition of these important offices depends upon many circumstances of birth and fortune, not to mention capacity, which I have not, that I can have no hopes of being useful that way." [6] Adams would retreat to the ministry because he lacked the social prerequisites of a political career.

He knew well his world of social distinctions. While prosperous farmers like his father played key roles within Braintree, they were not the town's social notables. That role was reserved for the Quincys, a family of Boston merchants and country squires who, for more than two generations, had quietly presided over Braintree affairs. Patriarch of the family and occupant of the mansion at Mount Walaston was John Quincy, twelve times speaker of the House of Representatives, provincial councilor, and, after 1764, Adams' grandfather-in-law. Only slightly less imposing was cousin Josiah who, along with his brother Edmund, had amassed a fortune in trade before retiring to rural Braintree. These were the men who counted in Braintree, who knew the governor, who quietly supervised local affairs, who visibly embodied the importance of social standing in rural Massachusetts.[7]

Harvard was Braintree and the Quincys writ large. Every time Adams entered the dining hall, recited in class, marched in a formal procession, he was reminded just who he was—a boy in the middle, bright and energetic and yet clearly different from those at the head of the line. The premier spot belonged

[6] Ibid., p. 411.
[7] *SHG,* 5:444–49, 8:463–75, 13:285–89, 478–88.

to his friend Charles Cushing, son of the provincial councilor. Behind Cushing came Henry Appleton, whose father was a member of the Harvard Corporation, William Browne, descended from the Winthrops and heir to one of the province's great mercantile fortunes, Phillip Livingston of the New York Livingstons, and John Wentworth, scion of the New Hampshire governor.[8] Here Adams' education began. Along with Winthrop's lectures on natural philosophy, which Adams copiously tried to recapture in his diary, he absorbed the details of a hitherto unknown world. And in the end he emerged from Harvard with a set of ambitions which transcended even his father's desires for his eldest son: he wanted a career no less distinguished and important than the careers of his friends Cushing and Wentworth.

Adams also emerged from Harvard with a new status of his own. In Worcester he quickly joined the social circle which dominated both town and county—not so much as an active partner, but as a pleasant and educated addition to the community's small set of informed and animated men. Mid-century Worcester belonged to the Chandlers—to John, Sr., county magnate, provincial jurist, militia colonel, and to his sons John, Jr., and Gardiner, who, while still in their thirties, received militia regiments of their own, no mean feat even in an age of patronage politics. Chandler adjuncts and friends rounded out Adams' new circle: Timothy Payne, the judge's son-in-law and representative to the General Court; James Putnam, the county's principal barrister and another Chandler son-in-law; Nathan Willard, town physician; and two ministers, Ebenezer Thayer and Thadeus Maccarty.[9]

Out of this mingling with men of prominence and power

[8] *SHG*, 13:512.
[9] *JA-Diary*, 1:2n.

Adams' decision slowly emerged. In August of his second year in Worcester he put aside thoughts of the pulpit and began to study law with James Putnam. Despite Worcester's reputation as a frontier backwater, Putnam possessed a thorough, if not gifted, legal mind. Adams would have never traveled to Worcester to read law with a rural barrister. But he could neither have afforded nor probably been able to obtain a clerkship with a leading member of Boston's bar—as did his neighbor Samuel Quincy, who clerked for Benjamin Pratt. Whatever Putnam's drawback in terms of status and prestige, he more than satisfied young Adams. Indeed so totally absorbing was his apprenticeship that Adams all but abandoned his diary. For two years—in fact for the last time in his life—Adams kept his own counsel, temporarily free of the compulsion to dissect himself and those about him.

When the apprenticeship was over, Adams returned to Braintree. In his autobiography he suggests that he left Worcester because to stay and survive meant accepting an invitation to join the nascent opposition to the Chandlers' paternalistic rule. Adams later recalled that "as the Chandlers were worthy people and discharged the duties of their offices very well, I envied not their felicity and had no desire to set myself in opposition to them, and especially to Mr. Putnam who had married a beautiful daughter of that family and had treated me with civility and kindness." He also remembered that he feared for his health in Worcester where "the air . . . appeared to be unfriendly to me to such a degree that I panted for wont of the breezes from the sea and the pure zephyrs from the rocky mountains of my native town."[10] What Adams really panted for was a larger stage on which to try his talents; and Braintree provided this. The town itself was without a professional lawyer, but that was only a

[10] Ibid., 3:269–70.

small part of its attraction. In Braintree, Adams could establish his practice in friendly surroundings, make his reputation there before attempting to practice before the county courts in either Boston, Plymouth, or Bristol. In Worcester, no matter how successful, he would have remained a country lawyer, unknown to the Gridleys, Otises, and Pratts who dominated the Boston bar. In Braintree, Adams at least stood a chance of achieving the reputation he now craved.

Adams returned to Braintree in the fall of 1758. At twenty-three he had every reason to be pleased with himself, having already parlayed a Harvard education, a genuine gift for the law, and an ambition to make something of himself into a reputation as a bright and promising young man. True, he was still young John Adams, but now that was enough to gain him entry into the small group which passed for an elite in rural Braintree. Yet he was also far short of his goal. If, as he had told Cushing two years earlier, a legal career was to lead to the more important offices of state, he had yet to compensate for the "many circumstances of birth and fortune" his own status denied him. Admitted socially into the company of his betters, he had yet to learn to be comfortable with those he wished to emulate.

Shortly after his arrival in Braintree, Adams provided a revealing glimpse of the problem he knew he faced. In his diary he composed a letter to his friend and classmate John Wentworth, now a merchant in Portsmouth, New Hampshire, and preparing for his inevitable role as a principal leader of the colony his family controlled almost as a fiefdom. The letter itself is remarkable primarily for its lack of inhibitions. From salutation to closing paragraph, Adams let his pen run wild, confessing his admiration and envy for Wentworth's prospects, bemoaning his own meager hopes for success and his belief that only the benevolent auspices of his friends promised advancement. The letter is worth quoting at length since it provides a vivid contrast to Adams' usual, more circumspect approach towards those he felt to be socially superior.

Mon Ami,

My letters for the future will come to you, not from a school house but from the cell of an hermit. I am removed from Worcester to Braintree where I live secluded from all the cares and fatigues of busy life in a chamber which no mortal visits but myself except once in a day to make my bed. . . .

Here no idea of a lady, of diversions, of gay life, business, or of pleasure ever enters. Here I read, smoke, think, and sleep. Old Roman lawyers and Dutch commentators are my constant companions. What ample provision have I here accumulated for lasting felicity! The only thing I fear is that all my passions, which you know are the gales of life, as reason is the pilot, will go down into an everlasting calm. And what will a pilot signify if there is no wind.

To prevent this I must entreat you to redouble your letters which always raise a full gale of love, sometimes almost a tempest of emulation and sometimes a breeze of envy, and will be sufficient . . . to waft the vessel, though she is not the best of sailors, with full speed along the voyage. But what and where is the port of my destination? In sincerity I am afraid to tell you. Tis however a harbor where every vessel may ride securely. A harbor in which, though tempests rage around and thunders roll above and earthquakes shudder beneath, neither the vessel, her cargo, or her crew ever receive any damage.

But to be plain, I am beginning life anew. . . . I have mentioned studies, I find myself entering an unlimited field. A field in which Demosthenes, Cicero, and others of immortal fame have exulted before me! A field which encloses the whole circle of science and literature, the history, wisdom, and virtue of all ages.

Shall I dare to expatiate here in full career, like the nobler animals that range at large, or shall [I] blindly, basely creep, like the mole or the weasel? Tell me.[11]

The letter was never sent. Instead Adams composed a second, more circumspect draft, conveying the same hope, in more subtle and less risky terms, that Wentworth had not forgotten him.

> I resume with pleasure my long neglected pen . . . to inform you that I am still alive and well; that I am removed from Worcester to Braintree where I expect to live and die; and although I have for a long time neglected to write you, I have never forgot to think frequently of you and to wish you all the happiness that you deserve; no small quantity truly!
>
> The perpetual rotation of things in this world is such that we are obliged·by shifting our theatre of action frequently to shift our friends, to drop at once a whole company that we loved like our own souls and to contract with a set entirely new. Thus when I left this place I left behind me one set of friends and by removing to Cambridge acquired a new one, a set that no accident will ever be able to make me forget; although by removing from that place to Worcester I was (with pain enough) separated from them. . . . Whether I shall ever remove again I know not and don't much care, but whether here or elsewhere I shall always love my friends old and new, and shall wish sincerely for a resumption and an endless continuation of that correspondence with you which was, while it lasted, one of the most considerable pleasures of my life.[12]

This use of the diary to say in private what he dared not confess in public became a standard feature of Adams' attempt to strike a balance between youthful enthusiasm tinged with self-doubt and the more controlled and sophisticated self-assurance he saw in those who epitomized all that he sought. His approach to court cases was the same. The first drafts of his pleadings

[11] Adams to Wentworth, n.d., ibid., supp., pp. 64–65.
[12] Adams to Wentworth, n.d., *New England Historical and Genealogical Register* 5 (1851): 414[6].

suggest not so much the learned advocate as the college debator over fond of implausible flourishes of rhetoric. Each succeeding draft became more precise, more given to the details of the case and less concerned with broad principles of social organization. Only after he had internalized the style and composure of the bar's leading practitioners would Adams dispense with first drafts in his diary.[13] This was also true of his social and political relationships, but this kind of internalization took longer, was more difficult and considerably more painful.

Adams was sure of just two things: himself and the fact that success would be the product of his own endeavors. In Braintree he learned the rudiments of husbandry his father had neglected to teach him. When in Boston he sought out those who could tell him about commerce, shopkeeping, shipbuilding, and whatever else contributed to the province's economy. When he was not observing, he read. By the time he was thirty, Adams probably knew more academic law than all but a handful of the province's lawyers. When his first writ demonstrated an unfamiliarity with the almost unintelligible intricacies of provincial law, he made himself an expert on that subject, too. His inquisitiveness became a standing joke among his contemporaries. At one point Robert Treat Paine teasingly asked if Adams intended to be a sage. Upset by Paine's mockery, Adams silently fumed, "Oh! P. has not penetration to reach the bottom of my mind. He don't know me. Next time I will answer him, a sage, no. Knowledge enough to keep out of fire and water is all that I aim at." [14] Adams probably never fully realized how aptly he had described himself or how much knowledge he would feel himself compelled to absorb before claiming the rewards due him.

---

[13] See, for example, *JA-Diary*, 1:136–38, 192–93.
[14] Ibid., p. 52.

He was sure, however, that scholarship offered him one—
and perhaps his only—entry to the Boston bar. To be more than
a simple country lawyer Adams required a patron who would
sponsor his membership. In October 1758 Adams made his way
to Boston, where he slipped quietly into the Court House to
observe the Suffolk County justices in session. He knew almost
no one, and the few familiar persons he did spot ignored him.
That night he accompanied Samuel Quincy to a small gathering
where he "saw the most spacious and elegant room, the gayest
company of gentlemen and the finest row of ladies that I ever
saw. But the weather was so dull and I so disordered that I
could not make one half the observations that I wanted to make."
The next day Adams made his approach to Jeremiah Gridley,
dean of the bar. What Adams later remembered most was
Gridley's "conscious superiority." Primed to plead his case for
admission to the bar, Adams was dumbfounded at Gridley's
ready acquiescence in the project. Next Adams was subjected to
a rapid fire discourse on methods of legal study followed by an
equally brisk lecture on the virtuous life a young lawyer should
lead: pursue the law—not fame; read widely; marry late; and
forego idle company. Formalities completed, Gridley departed
for court with Adams in tow.[15]

Once sworn, Adams was on his own. First on the agenda was
rooting out Braintree's pettifoggers part-time, unschooled lawyers adept at drawing the writs which bulked large in any rural
practice. The town was full of such men, but only Ebenezer
Thayer truly threatened and hence fascinated Adams. A tavern
keeper and local politician as well as a part-time lawyer, Thayer
was the man Adams had to replace as Braintree's chief source of
legal advice. Convinced his first task was to wean away Thayer's

[15] Ibid., pp. 54–55.

clients, Adams began a campaign to secure the men who were in positions to recommend legal counsel. He rode out to see Moses French to ask the newly named constable to serve a writ. Afterwards a self-satisfied Adams recorded the success the journey had brought. French "told me he was not yet sworn, but was obliged to me for coming to him, and would be glad to serve me at any time, and would now rather than it should be any damage to me. Thus he was pleased, I hope secured. Men are only secured by falling in with their inclination, by favoring their hopes, clearing their prospects." [16]

Eventually Adams decided to confront Thayer directly, to humiliate him if possible, and thus to destroy him. For a year he nurtured this obsession. Thayer was watched, countered, and at last bested. With as much relief as triumph, Adams kept score in his diary.

> This is the third time I have been before Major Crosby with Thayer. The first time he was . . . for John Spear. That action was demolished. The next time he appeared for Nathan Spear against Eph. Hunt and John Vinton. Those actions were demolished. The last time he appeared for Bayley against Niles, White, Hayden, etc. These actions were all demolished. Thus I have come off pretty triumphantly every time and he pretty foolishly. Yet I have managed none of these cases in the most masterly manner. I see several inadvertent mistakes and omissions. But I grow more expert, less diffident, etc. I feel my own strength. I see the complacent countenances of the crowd, and I see the respectful face of the justice and the fearful faces of petty-foggers more than I did.[17]

Braintree was the scene of his exploits, but Boston continued to be the center of his ambitions. A secure local reputation would

[16] Ibid., p. 85. See also ibid., pp. 136-37.
[17] Ibid., p. 193.

provide the young lawyer with a great deal. He could hope to succeed eventually to his father's place in town affairs. A militia commission would be his if he desired one. No doubt he would become a justice of the peace and take his turn as Braintree's representative to the General Court, thus helping to swell the largely rural, back-bencher majority. Adams wanted more. It was all right to sit for Braintree. John Quincy had done so and become speaker of the House. But the difference between Samuel Niles, Braintree's current representative, and John Quincy was the difference between the local activist who became a back-bencher and the professional who became a leader.

Adams' professionalization began with the traumatic interview with Gridley. Adams had been struck by the old lawyer's self-command, his brusqueness, the awe he so obviously induced. Later, as Adams watched Gridley move among the close-knit circle of lawyers, Adams became aware of his patron's shortcomings, his uneasiness, his unwillingness to disguise the contempt he often felt towards his inferiors. Timothy Ruggles, on the other hand, possessed the quiet command of a man who knew how to get what he wanted. Adams had met Ruggles in Worcester as a friend and ally of the Chandlers. Now he renewed this acquaintance in Boston as he watched Ruggles reign over both the bar and the House of Representatives. His "grandeur," Adams thought, was the product of the "quickness of his apprehension, steadiness of his attention, the boldness and strength of his thoughts and expressions, his strict honor, conscious superiority, contempt of meanness. . . . People approach him with dread and terror." Ruggles appeared as proud and lordly as Gridley, but he concealed it better, and this made him more popular. What was "easy and natural" in Ruggles was "stiff and affected" in Gridley. Still, Gridley's was the greater legal mind. To Adams, his words seemed to "pierce and search, have something quick and animating. He is a great reasoner and has a very vivid imagination." [18]

Adams filled his diary with dozens of these thumbnail sketches of leading lawyer-politicians. And always his purpose was the same. From each he expected to learn what contributed to greatness and what detracted from reputation. Just as he had learned to harness his imagination, so he became a consummate master of the art of imitation. There was no mystery involved. Adams understood full well what he was about.

> The principle in nature is imitation. . . . How naturally we imitate, without design or with, modes of thinking, speaking, acting that please us! Thus we conform gradually to the manners and customs of our own family, neighborhood, town, province, nation, etc. At Worcester I learned several turns of mind of Putnam, and at Boston I find myself imitating Otis, etc. But q[uery], who will learn the art soonest and most perfectly, he who reads without a design of extracting beauties or he who reads with? The last undoubtedly. . . . I learned with design to imitate Put's sneer, his sly look, and his look of contempt. This look may serve good ends in life, may procure respect.[19]

As Adams grew more confident in his role as a learned counsel, he paid increasing attention to the political dimensions of his ambitions. Along with its other functions, the diary now became something of a casebook on the practical art of politics. Like most New England towns, Braintree in 1758 was dominated by a handful of men, the Quincys, the town's justices of the peace, important tradesmen, and a few prosperous farmers like Adams' father. But again it was Ebenezer Thayer who held center stage. Already a deputy sheriff and captain of the militia, the wily tavern keeper now angled for the selectmanship held by Adams' father and for Niles's seat in the Assembly.

[18] Ibid., p. 83.
[19] Ibid., p. 84.

Thayer made his move in April of Adams' first year home. At a town meeting held during a spring snowstorm, he defeated the elder Adams' bid for reelection. Adams' father raged. His defeat was a base political trick made possible only by the storm, which persuaded three-fourths of the town's voters that it was no night for politics. Thayer had triumphed only because his "crew of debtors and laborers" had suddenly found themselves in the majority. And he knew full well that only these circumstances had compensated for his "meanness of soul and insignificancy in the town." The younger Adams, having watched his father vent his anger, filed another lesson in his diary. "The point was carried, not by merit, nor by real popularity, but by mean and clandestine artifice and plotting." [20]

Though he couched his observations in moralistic terms, Adams was obviously impressed by Thayer's adroitness in the rough and tumble of town politics. With morbid fascination Adams later watched his father, Thayer, and James Bracket auction off a forfeited farm. "Let me remark the management of the sale and the behavior of persons, especially of Thayer and Bracket, watch his treatment of people and their treatment of him." And when he could, Adams collected opinions of Thayer, usually from men like Samuel Niles who were the objects of Thayer's intrigues. "Mr. N. has the worst opinion of Thayer's morals. He detests the base methods of debauchery and lying and duplicity." Josiah Quincy was no less explicit. "Eb. Thayer," Quincy told the impressionable Adams, was "the worst of men . . . a conspirator against his country . . . a Cataline." [21]

This gem Adams collected in the comfort of the Quincy drawing room. How well Adams knew the Quincys before going to Harvard is unclear. Upon his return to Braintree, however, he

[20] Ibid., p. 82.
[21] Ibid., pp. 93, 97–98, 216.

joined the small circle which revolved around the Quincy household. And here, as Quincy rambled on, Adams completed his political education. It was Quincy, playing the role of a surrogate father, as well as a potential father-in-law, who opened up the world of professional politics to the young upstart, who taught Adams the language of political action, the ins and outs of patronage politics, the pitfalls to be avoided when securing friends and building alliances. Quincy transmitted not knowledge so much as a particular style, the way to tell a good story, the importance of social amiability, of moderation, of cool judgment as opposed to rash action. Sometimes in his diary Adams would make explicit those lessons implicit in Quincy's rambling discourses. More often Adams simply absorbed, as Quincy's own sons had absorbed, the style and attitudes of this rather contentious squire. After a long evening in the Quincy drawing room he would note simply, "Spent the evening and night at the colonel's in ill natured, invidious remarks upon Eb. Thayer and morals and General Court." [22]

Although a generation and an obvious difference in status separated them, Adams was remarkably at ease with Quincy. Such was not always the case with men of Quincy's standing. In Worcester, Adams had always felt uncomfortable with the Chandlers, afraid that his own eagerness to impress others would betray him, make him seem foolish and awkward. Then he had confessed,

> When in company with persons much superior to myself in years and place, I have talked to show my learning. I have been too bold with great men. . . . I have foolishly aimed at wit and spirit . . . but instead of shining brighter I only clouded the few rays that before rendered me visible. . . . I now resolve for the future . . . never to say an envious thing concerning governors, judges,

[22] Ibid., p. 132.

ministers, clerks, sheriffs, lawyers, or any other honorable or lucrative offices or officers, never to affect wit upon laced waistcoats or large estates or their possessors, never to show my own importance or superiority by remarking the foibles, vices, or inferiority of others.

An evening spent with the colonel invoked no such inhibitions, largely because Quincy was less than the complete professional. He was in fact something of a bungler and consequently enjoyed less power and influence than his wealth and status should have earned him. Adams was aware of and amused by the colonel's shortcomings. He increasingly held Quincy up to the kind of standards he had first learned in the Quincy drawing room and during his forays into Boston. He would listen to Quincy exclaim, " 'I value not the governor's favors more than this pinch of snuff in comparison of my honor and my duty to my town,' " and then write in his diary, "these reiterated protestations in favor of honesty, goodness, patriotism, or rather these verbal pretensions . . . raise suspicions and jealousies. Too much talk, prate. . . . He praises himself as much as other people censure him. . . . Does he believe what he says?" The fickleness of Quincy's political prejudices was equally a source of amusement. After the colonel had devoted an entire evening to raging against the governor's neglect of his talents for important office, Adams summed up his impressions of Quincy's political prowess.

Colonel's friendship is not worth a wise man's seeking, nor his enmity worth fearing. As long as you flatter his vanity, gratify his avarice, or favor his ambition you will be a great genius, an honest man, a good man, in short you will be everything; but as soon as you obstruct any of his views you will be a silly man, a knave, in short everything that is bad. While the governor, as he thought, had a great opinion of him, the governor was wise, learned, industrious, etc., but when he found the governor despised him, the governor had no principles, was guided by self interest.

Quincy knew the rules of the game, but his play left something to be desired. Thus with him Adams was able to practice his wit, to perfect his style, to unbridle his curiosity and ask all the probing questions he would have liked to ask the Chandlers or Gridley or Ruggles or the other men whose good impression of himself Adams thought too vital to be compromised by impertinence.[23]

By the spring of 1760 Adams was ready for a major enterprise of his own. He was neither a prude nor an abstainer, but in his search for a cause with which to ignite an apathetic populace Adams declared war on Braintree's dozen taverns. That Eb Thayer owned a small rum shop in the middle precinct only made Braintree's drinking habits a more appealing target. After the elder Adams' defeat the previous year, his son had become increasingly critical of the role local taverns played in the political canvass. Thayer's supplanting of Niles as representative in May of 1760 confirmed Adams' worst suspicions. In taverns, he knew now, "the time, the money, the health, and the modesty of most that are young and of many old are wasted; here diseases, vicious habits, bastards, and legislators are frequently begotten." For a year Adams preached the gospel of temperance. In his diary he vented his righteousness in draft essays he neglected to send off to be published. Within the town he set out in search of other sound-thinking, sober citizens who similarly understood the evils of unregulated taverns that dispensed sin and blasphemy in equal portions. But it was the effect that free rum had on otherwise enlightened voters which formed the crux of the young crusader's message.

[23] Ibid., pp. 37, 81–82, 93–94.

The number of these houses have been lately so much augmented, and the fortunes of their owners so much increased, that an artful man has little else to do but secure the favor of taverners in order to secure the suffrages of the rabbles that attend these houses, which in many towns within my observation makes a very large, perhaps the largest number of voters. The consequence is that these offices and elections, which all the wisest legislators of the world in humble imitation of God and nature have allotted to probity and understanding, may in time, I dare not say have already become the gratuity of tipplers for drams and sops! Good God! Where are the rights of English men! Where is the spirit that once exalted the souls of Britons and emboldened their faces to look even princes and monarchs in the face.[24]

By May 1761 Adams succeeded in welding together a coalition strong enough to amend Braintree's tavern regulations. The new laws, more concerned with a just price for rum than a decrease in the quantity consumed, were duly put into effect. Adams thus secured his first political victory. The importance of the crusade, however, was not its apparent success but its obvious ineffectiveness. Braintree's drinkers scarcely batted an eye at the new regulations, and Eb Thayer continued to reap both financial and political rewards from his tavern under his law offices. In later life Adams recounted the lessons learned. "I only acquired the reputation of a hypocrite and an ambitious demagogue by it; the number of licensed houses was soon reinstated. Drams, grog and sotting were not diminished. . . . You may as well preach to the Indians against rum as to our people." [25] The crusade against the taverns was the work of a gifted political amateur. Adams' next project would bear the stamp of the professional.

Adams' father died in the late spring of 1761. The young lawyer, in addition to his expanding legal practice, now found

[24] Ibid., pp. 130, 191.
[25] Ibid., p. 130n.

himself the owner of considerable property and the head of a family prominent in local affairs. At the same time, Thayer announced his intention to resign as deputy sheriff. Adams seized this opportunity to enter the political arena once more, this time to secure the post for his brother Peter.

If ill-disguised enthusiasm and righteous dogmatism marked the crusade against the taverns, the campaign for the deputy sheriff's post was handled with considerably more finesse. Adams began by quietly enlisting those who bore a grudge against Thayer and his party. Niles was the first recruit. Quickly added were the town's other leading anti-Thayerites, Joseph Crosby and Joseph Palmer. These men, whom Adams had first met in Quincy's drawing room, formed the nucleus of a politically potent faction. Still Adams did not rest easy. Thayer, he feared, would hear of the project and not resign. Or, his inexperience would betray him. "Intrigue and making interest and asking favors," he told himself, "is a new employment. . . . I'm un-practiced in intrigues for power." And when not uneasy over possible failure, Adams fretted over the decay of his own morals: "I begin to feel the passions of the world. Ambition, avarice, intrigue, party, all must be guarded." [26]

Anxiety only spurred his endeavors. Once the local justices had been secured, the center of the campaign became Stephen Greenleaf, the county sheriff. Adams played on Greenleaf's vanity and encouraged the old man to talk of Thayer's failings and slights, both real and imagined. To insure victory, Adams had his allies suggest that if Peter Adams was not given the post, local constables would serve John Adams' writs, thus reducing Greenleaf's income from fees. Adams had touched all the sheriff's weaknesses, "his interest, his vanity, his honor." In sight of victory Adams marveled at the efficiency of his attack

[26] Ibid., p. 217, 216.

which "was not much disguised or concealed, yet it was so silently conducted that . . . the grand adversary never once suspected it." [27]

Peter Adams' installation as deputy sheriff marked the end of John Adams' political apprenticeship. Within Braintree he was a full member of the small group which dominated the town's political life. More important, he was now prepared to take advantage of the opportunities his expanding law practice and growing reputation provided. If he needed visible proof of just how far he had come since leaving Harvard, he received it the next June. At Basse's, a popular tavern just outside Braintree, Peter Oliver offered to take Adams part way to Taunton, where Adams was to try a case before the Bristol County court. As they rode along in Oliver's ornate coach with its gaudy coat of arms and scarlet outriders, the flamboyant aristocrat and the intense young lawyer made a strange pair. Oliver represented all that was traditional in provincial politics. The scion of a wealthy and distinguished political family, he was a judge of the Superior Court, a member of the Council, and one of the handful of men then running Massachusetts. Yet between the two men existed the bond which transcended whatever differences their social backgrounds had once created. They were both professionals, public men who understood, because they shared, the perspectives of the politician. As they journeyed through the Massachusetts countryside, talk naturally turned to politics. Oliver gossiped about Timothy Ruggles' election as speaker of the House, the increasing interest provincial lawyers were showing in House affairs, and the ravings of James Otis, Jr., the young firebrand determined to make good his boast to "throw the province into flames" because his father had not been made chief justice.[28]

[27] Ibid., p. 217.
[28] Ibid., p. 226.

In the winter of Adams' first year in Braintree he had entered one of those reflective periods which would become an Adams characteristic. In his diary he set before him the paths to the reputation he sought. It is, as with so much of the diary, a remarkable passage both for its candor and its clear perception of the world he sought to make his own.

> Shall I make frequent visits in the neighborhood and converse familiarly with men, women, and children in their own style on the common tittletattle of the town and the ordinary concerns of a family, and so take every fair opportunity of showing my knowledge in the law? But this . . . would take up too much thought and time and province law.
>
> Shall I endeavor to renew my acquaintance with those young gentlemen in Boston who were at college with me and to extend my acquaintance among merchants, shopkeepers, tradesmen, etc., and mingle with the crowd upon change, and traipse the town house floor with one another in order to get a character in town. But this too will be a lingering method and will require more art and address, and patience too, than I am master of.
>
> Shall I, by making remarks and proposing questions [to] the lawyers at the bar, endeavor to get a great character for understanding and learning with them. But this is slow and tedious and will be ineffectual, for envy, jealousy, and self interest will not suffer them to give a young fellow a free generous character, especially me. Neither of these projects will bear examination, will avail.
>
> Shall I look out for a cause to speak to, and exert all the soul and all the body I own, to cut a flash, strike amazement, to catch the vulgar? In short shall I walk a lingering, heavy pace or shall I take one bold determined leap into the midst of some cash and business? That is the question. A bold push, a resolute attempt, a determined enterprise, or a slow, silent, imperceptible creeping. Shall I creep or fly.[29]

Adams eventually traveled all four paths. He became an expert

[29] Ibid., p. 78.

at the kind of small talk which bound together rural communities like Braintree. He was no less adept at cultivating important friendships. By the time he was thirty he enjoyed a substantial reputation as a legal scholar. And in the end he found his cause to speak to—not Braintree's drinking habits and the suspect role tavern keepers played in local elections, but the larger question of the political rights and liberties that eighteenth-century Americans assumed they enjoyed in perpetuity. In a very real sense the Stamp Act made John Adams, brought him the reputation he craved and the power he sought. Yet he would have achieved prominence whether or not England had sought to reorder her empire. He would, no doubt, have made the journey to Boston to legislate on behalf of the province. And once in the Assembly he would have joined with that body's other professionals, sharing both the responsibilities of power and the rewards of political leadership.

During the height of the Stamp Act crisis, after Boston had twice witnessed riots, had watched her courts closed, her government and economy brought to a standstill, he happened across Samuel Adams on his way to a meeting of the Monday night club. Upon his cousin's invitation Adams joined the gathering where he found:

> Otis, Cushing, Wells, Pemberton, Gray, Austin, two Waldos, Inches, Dr. Parker—and spent the evening very agreeably, indeed. Politicians all at this club. We had many curious anecdotes about governors, councilors, representatives, demagogues, merchants, etc. The behavior of these gentlemen is very familiar and friendly to each other, and very polite and complaisant to strangers.[30]

They were, as Adams reminds us, "politicians all," professionals bent on preserving a political status quo which guaranteed them the opportunity to govern their own province.

[30] Ibid., p. 270.

5

Jonathan Belcher and the Politics of Crisis

I N THE SUMMER OF 1756 THE EARL OF LOUDOUN TOOK COM-
mand of a British-American expeditionary force then garrisoned in the mud at Albany. Though scarcely a brilliant
soldier, Loudoun at least understood what was required: an
effective army raised and supplied by local governments. Thus
would the French be repelled; and thus would Loudoun, in partnership with the colonies' royal governors, reaffirm the efficacy
of British authority even here on the outskirts of the empire.
Loudoun was no more successful than those who had preceded
him; and by November he knew where to lay the blame. "The
truth is," he told the Duke of Cumberland, "governors here are
ciphers; their predecessors sold the whole of the king's prerogative, to get their salaries; and till you find a fund, independent of
the province, to pay the governors, and new model the government, you can do nothing with the provinces." [1]

Loudoun's image of the colonial governor as a cipher has been
a curiously persistent one. The eighteenth century, most have
agreed, witnessed the decline of the governor's constitutional

[1] Loudoun to Cumberland, 11 November 1756, Loudoun Papers, Henry E.
Huntington Library, San Marino, Calif.; Stanley M. Pargellis, *Lord Loudoun in
North America* (New Haven: Yale University Press, 1933), pp. 42–44.

prerogatives and the concomitant rise of the real power of the colonial legislature and particularly of the lower house. There was a gradual, yet perceptible and irrepressible shift of authority away from the governor and toward the Assembly until that institution, through its control of public finances, exercised a veto over most aspects of public policy.[2]

Yet for Massachusetts, at least, this focusing on the decline of the governor's constitutional prerogatives raises a number of disturbing paradoxes, not the least of which is the provincials' own concern with what they considered the governor's almost dictatorial powers. And when one catalogues the power the governor retained, instead of the authority supposedly lost, one sees a certain plausibility in such fears. With the exception of its annual May session, the General Court met, adjourned, and dissolved at the governor's command. Every legislative act required his signature. Councilors, although elected by the General Court, required his consent before assuming office; and even the election of a Speaker of the House was subject to his veto. With the consent of the Council he staffed the province's law courts and appointed most county officials. Finally, the governor remained commander in chief of the provincial militia with authority to commission and promote all militia officers. Few modern constitutions, even those intended to reinforce executive authority, provide greater opportunities to exert executive leadership than did the Massachusetts charter.[3]

[2] See, for example, Leonard Woods Labaree, *Royal Government in America* (New Haven: Yale University Press, 1930), and Jack P. Greene, *The Quest for Power: The Lower Houses of Assembly in the Southern Royal Colonies, 1698–1766* (Chapel Hill: University of North Carolina Press, 1963). For a critique of Greene's argument see John M. Murrin, "The Myths of Colonial Democracy and Royal Decline in Eighteenth-Century America: A Review Essay," *Cithara* 5 (1965): 53–68.

[3] *A&R*, 1:1–23; William Douglass, *A Summary, Historical and Political of the . . . Present State of British Settlements in North America*, 2 vols. (London, 1760), 1:472–73.

A second paradox is suggested by the nature of the Assembly itself. In general, political systems which are not highly institutionalized enhance, rather than decrease, the importance of executive authority. For a legislature to compete effectively with a chief executive it must become an efficient locus of power, one capable of both initiating and executing complex policy decisions. Lacking this ability, the Massachusetts House of Representatives could only respond to proposals suggested by better-organized political units, in this case by an administration dominated by a single personality.[4]

A third paradox, reflected in the professionalism of the province's local leadership, similarly warns against discounting the governor's political prerogatives. Most of what the professional sought the governor controlled: military commissions, civil appointments, and access to British officials who could dispense even more liberal rewards. While the Assembly's backbenchers did often seek to curb the governor's ability to dispense political largess, the Assembly's leaders were almost unanimous in support of a status quo which left the governor's patronage powers unimpaired.

Yet the image of a governor rendered constitutionally impotent has endured, largely because so many royal governors were sadly ineffective. As a result, British authority in America was, as Loudoun laments, significantly impaired. Where we have erred, however, is in attributing these failures to a constitutional weakness or decline in the office of governor and to a purposeful quest for power on the part of a popularly elected Assembly. The alternative, I think, is to abandon constitutional categories of analysis altogether, substituting in their stead criteria which

---

[4] Nelson W. Polsby, "The Institutionalization of the U.S. House of Representatives," *American Political Science Review* 62 (1968): 144–68; James Sterling Young, *The Washington Community, 1800–1828* (New York: Columbia University Press, 1966), pp. 157–210.

better reflect the dilemmas inherent in executive authority. What we must do in effect is ask a new series of questions: what resources, informal as well as formal, were at the governor's disposal, what strategies did he employ in converting these resources into actual influence, and finally, what obstacles, both internal and external, threatened either his policies or his political status?

Jonathan Belcher was almost a caricature of the New England Yankee: arrogant, vindictive, often impetuous despite a most solemn belief in rational action and calculated maneuver. Yet Belcher was also one of the proudest fruits of the New England experiment, a merchant prince and congregational elder, influential politician and would-be literary muse as well as a member of the Harvard class of 1699, an accomplished world-traveler, and Massachusetts' first Mason.[5] Upon graduation from Harvard, Belcher had become something of a dilettante who nevertheless remembered that in New England successful careers were made of more substantial stuff than modish dress and imposing airs. Sent to Europe by an indulgent father, he had visited the continent's traditional attractions as well as the Court at Hanover (where, he reported later, he was "entertained by the Princess Sophia . . . as if she had been my mother").[6] Returning to Massachusetts in 1706—just in time to wed Mary Partridge, daughter of the late lieutenant-governor— he spent the next two years in his father's counting-house before again sailing for Europe and a second timely visit with the good Sophia.

By 1716 Belcher was sufficiently established in Massachusetts to invest £500 in the successful campaign to make Samuel Shute

[5] *SHG,* 4:434–50.
[6] Belcher to White, 27 December 1704, *Publications of the Colonial Society of Massachusetts* 20 (1920): 97.

governor. Two years later Belcher won election to the Council, an auspicious beginning for a man who, though nearly forty, had never held elective office. Tagged an administration man, Belcher lost his seat in 1720, sat again in 1722 and 1723, and then spent the next two years in forced retirement before returning to the Council in 1726. Shortly thereafter Belcher underwent something of a metamorphosis, the first of several which would mark his political career. As long as Shute occupied the governor's chair, Belcher remained a cautious supporter of fiscal conservatism and the royal prerogative. In 1728, however, he celebrated the appointment of a new chief executive by forging an alliance with Elisha Cooke, the venerable Boston physician who commanded the inflationist majority within the House. Dispatched to London as the Assembly's special agent, Belcher renewed his acquaintances among the Hanoverians and again became an American fixture at Court. At this point the governorship again became vacant. To the province's surprise and delight Belcher was named governor of both New Hampshire and Massachusetts in June 1730.

The following August he delivered his inaugural. Paraphrasing the Old Testament, Belcher reminded the assembled legislators, "Pleasing is the sight, while I behold and say, *ye are my brethren: ye are my bones and my flesh;* and I have no interest separate from your true and real interest." But there was also a quiet detachment to the speech, a subtle reminder that, although a provincial himself, his commission and his intention to discharge his new obligations faithfully had somehow set him apart. They might all be New Englanders, but it was the "miserable state of your bills of credit" which debased the economy and eroded public faith in private property. Such problems, he declared, would be met jointly, he acting in his official capacity as a royal governor and the legislators in theirs as representatives of the province. He was in Massachusetts to govern fairly, but firmly. With respect for the proper spheres of authority, "the king's honor and service" would be protected, and the natural result would be the "substantial happiness of this province." [7]

Throughout his governorship, Belcher would project this public image of the perfect colonial governor, one jealous of the king's prerogatives, faithful to his instructions, and committed to restraining an impetuous Assembly. Privately, however, Belcher would assume a different guise. He was, or so he thought, a politician who weighed carefully the consequences of every stand he took. He had convinced himself, and now hoped to persuade others, that his political campaigns always preserved his maneuverability, so if circumstances changed he could easily bend with the wind. And rather than constitutional arguments and ultimatums, his private political style would depend on the resolute wielding of his powers of appointment to bring him the victories he sought. [8]

Capable of remarkable self-deception, Belcher never saw the paradoxical nature of these self-images. When writing to London he actually became the kind of governor he pictured himself as being, one committed to the right ordering of the provincial constitution so that the governor was the king's representative in fact as well as name. At the same time, his letters to political allies and friends stressed his appreciation of political realities and a willingness to compromise whenever discretion became the better part of valor. Understandably, many accused Belcher

---

[7] *MHJ*, 9:238-40.

[8] My analysis of Belcher's political personality is based on his speeches and messages to the General Court (*MHJ*, vols. 9-18, passim), his reports to London, found in Great Britain, K. G. Davies, ed., *Calendar of State Papers, colonial series, American and West Indies* (London: Her Majesty's Stationery Office, 1872-   ), and his surviving letter-books, largely published in *Collections of the Massachusetts Historical Society*, 6th ser. 6 (1893) and 7 (1894), hereafter cited as Belcher Papers, vols. 1 and 2 respectively.

of playing a double game, of announcing his loyalty to the cause of prerogative authority and yet refusing to pay the price such loyalty demanded. But in his own mind Belcher perceived the issue quite differently. With a perfectly clear conscience he could cite the speeches made and the ultimatums delivered as evidence of his faithfulness to the king. With equal conviction, he could approve of legislation which patently violated his instructions and then congratulate himself for having avoided prolonged controversy and political acrimony.

This ability to compartmentalize his mind masked yet another unpleasant facet of Belcher's political personality: he was equally incapable of playing either of these self-defined political roles. In a prolonged constitutional controversy, he simply lacked staying power. Too often what he labeled compromise was nothing less than capitulation. At the same time, Belcher lacked the temperament for political maneuver. No matter how carefully he weighed the alternatives, no matter how clever and resourceful he thought himself, at heart Belcher was an impulsive politician who had little patience and less finesse.

Impulsive men can become successful politicians. Despite their lack of style, their restless energy and drive occasionally allow them to succeed where more cautious and calculating men fail. Typically, Belcher commenced his governship with an assault on the civil list. Arguing that the appointment of a new governor terminated all local commissions, he made fifty-one new appointments. In Suffolk County alone, he replaced half the Inferior Court of Common Pleas and nineteen justices of the peace. In his hands the governor's power of appointment became an awesome weapon with which to reward friends and punish enemies. Politicians who earned his distrust or incurred his animosity were stripped of their influence and reduced to political spectators. This policy was not without its successes.

Under Belcher the Council enjoyed less freedom than ever; and a professional community constantly reminded of the governor's inherent power initially produced few leaders willing to sacrifice their places for the dubious honor of having challenged a determined chief executive.[9]

Belcher's approach to legislation was scarcely more subtle. He avoided fiscal controversy by putting few restrictions on the printing of paper money. On other issues he communicated his requests in formal speeches and messages which constantly reminded the representatives that as royal governor he was responsible for securing legislation conforming to his instructions. When the House balked, he seldom took the initiative in arranging a compromise. Rather he simply reiterated his demands and then waited for the House to produce a more amicable solution. He failed, of course, to create a reservoir of goodwill. But then, he had no need to, or so it seemed. Like every governor, he had a limited number of friends in the House who could keep him apprised of developments. The Assembly's other leaders, dependent upon him for the rewards they sought, kept their opposition within bounds. The Assembly's rank and file, pacified by continued inflation and awed, perhaps, by the governor's display of obstinacy, voted substantially what Belcher wanted.[10]

In January 1735 Belcher described the success he believed had been wrought by his policy of intimidating the Assembly and threatening the professionals. Referring his son to an account of the Assembly's just-concluded session, he noted,

[9] William H. Whitmore, ed., *The Massachusetts Civil List for the Colonial and Provincial Periods, 1630–1774* (Albany, 1870); Thomas Hutchinson, *The History of the Colony and Province of Massachusetts-Bay*, ed. Lawrence Shaw Mayo, 3 vols. (Cambridge, Mass.: Harvard University Press, 1936), 2:281, 286–87n; John A. Schutz, *William Shirley, King's Governor of Massachusetts* (Chapel Hill: University of North Carolina Press, 1961), pp. 5–37.

[10] See, for example, *MHJ*, 9:331–32, 335, 347–48, 353–54, 387–88, 10:99, 104, 170, 213, 300, 412–16.

you will see what passed in this Assembly at their last sitting, which has been one of the most quiet for 18 years past. Cooke is shrunk into an old Indian squaw. D[u]m[me]r takes pains to get Wilks out of his agency, but the governor's interest is so good with the Assembly that nothing of that nature will be done. I think the getting of an act for establishing so large a bounty on the raising of hemp will give me considerable credit and honor with the Ministry, who have recommended it hither so often as a thing of vast advantage to the crown, but never could get it done. Indeed the country is now so easy that the Assembly are ready to do almost any thing I propose to them. I have got Mr. Wilks a grant of £500 sterling and of £800 . . . [in Massachusetts] money.[11]

If he had been more perceptive, Belcher might have also noted that the influence he boasted of was as much a product of circumstance as it was of his own political resourcefulness. When he assumed the governorship, the province had already witnessed three decades of constitutional turmoil. With a New Englander presiding over the government, Massachusetts had welcomed an excuse for a respite from controversy. In return for new emissions of paper, the Assembly had even stopped insisting on levying taxes and granting appropriations by special resolve rather than by formal acts which the Privy Council could review. Belcher had also benefited from his 1728 alliance with Cooke, who had temporarily abated his attacks on prerogative authority. And when the alliance later collapsed, Cooke's own tragic decline had already ended his ability to harass the governor. After 1735, however, these circumstances counted for little. A new opposition emerged, the Assembly became increasingly less tractable, and the professionals, while still wary of the governor's power of appointment, became more willing to challenge the chief executive.[12]

[11] Belcher to Belcher, 6 January 1734-5, Belcher Papers, 2:181.
[12] A&R, 2:690-95, 701-03, 707-11, 744-46; Hutchinson, *History of Massachusetts*, 2:284-87; Schutz, *Shirley*, p. 21.

The causes of Belcher's difficulties were a complex blend of circumstance, England's shortsighted monetary policies, the opportunism of the political leaders who vied for power in the late 1730s, and Belcher's insistence on disciplining every maverick who seemingly threatened his administration. Provincial governors inevitably alienated some political leaders. Even if there had been enough patronage to satisfy routine demands, those leaders who were denied important policy roles would still have sought power. The challenge facing any governor was to convince dissatisfied politicians that future preferment might come only if their opposition remained within acceptable bounds. Belcher, perhaps, frustrated the ambitions of more politicians than did most chief executives. Yet it was the anger, rather than the size, of the opposition that posed a threat for the governor. By 1736 the ranks of the disaffected included a growing number of important men who, besides distrusting the administration's intentions, had come to fear Belcher personally.

Belcher's problem was created by an insistence on answering every threat, real or imagined, with a personal vendetta. Opposition was unacceptable since it could only result from personal animosity toward the governor. He had once thought highly of William Shirley, an English lawyer who had arrived in Massachusetts in 1731 and now hoped to replace Belcher as governor. While the English lawyer angled for support in London, Belcher wrote to his son, "Sh-r-ly is in the dregs of poverty, with a large family, and is as mean, false, ungrateful, and perfidious as any instance I have met with, but in short this world is full of such creatures." Indeed someone was always abusing him. During the early years of his administration, David Dunbar, the royal Surveyor-General of the Woods, and Cooke had been the villains. In 1734 Belcher told his brother-in-law,

I come now to what you mention about Colonel Dunbar and Mr. Cooke. All the plague and trouble I have ever had in New Hampshire is entirely owing to the former, and the same to the latter in the Massachusetts, and the breaches are now so wide, and their malice so rancorous that it's not possible to think of a reconciliation. No. I must defend myself as well as I can, and while I am a good governor for the king and to the people, I hope the rage and revenge of two such persons won't hurt me.

By 1739 his opinion of Robert Auchmuty was no higher. Belcher had helped make Auchmuty judge of the Vice Admiralty Court, but now the good judge, principally for his support of Shirley, was deemed "a most finished Irish villain. . . . And when I had done him all the services in my power, then he began to return my goodness in the vile, ungrateful manner in which he now behaves." [13]

Another of the creatures constantly plaguing the governor was Samuel Waldo, whom Belcher once suggested, "the infernal dungeon can hardly produce an equal to . . . for pride and rancorous malice." Waldo, a Maine timber baron with British contracts to cut masts for the royal navy, was one of the few merchants who did not benefit from Belcher's lax protection of the king's forests. When Waldo complained to London and began stirring up opposition within the province, Belcher challenged the merchant's claims to some valuable Maine real estate. Surveying the effect of this campaign, Belcher noted that his attack "would entirely overset" Waldo and "make him clap his tail between his legs, and leer home like a dog, as he is." [14]

It was not merely that Belcher used vituperative language. The province's political rhetoric was always strong and earthy.

[13] Belcher to Belcher, 19 May 1740, Belcher Papers, 2:301. Belcher to Partridge, 20 April 1734, ibid., p. 37. Belcher to Coran, 29 October 1739, ibid., p. 232.
[14] Belcher to Belcher, 19 May, 1740, ibid., p. 301. Belcher to Coran, 20 November 1739, ibid., p. 246.

But Belcher's habit of casting opponents in stark, demonic terms inevitably corrupted his judgment of other men and made conciliation next to impossible. Thus systematically Belcher denied himself the maneuverability every chief executive required. Every opponent became an enemy, and after a while there were few members of the political community he could turn to for support. He would no more forget past wrongs than he would conciliate men he had already punished. In 1737, while Shirley's campaign to oust him gained momentum, Belcher foolishly purged Paul Dudley from the Council. Dudley was the son of a former governor, a member of the Superior Court, and a conservative who might have been expected to support Belcher's program of currency reform. But Dudley was nearly as difficult as Belcher. Proud, willful, and important, Dudley probably resented the fact that Belcher, instead of himself, had been named governor in 1730. In 1738 Dudley failed to win election to the Council, and then the following year the judge, who had never before sought a seat in the Assembly, won election as a representative from his native Roxbury. The House quickly compounded Belcher's embarrassment by making Dudley speaker, and when the governor vetoed this election, House votes put Dudley on the Council. Belcher again barred Dudley from the Council, but now the old judge, with new memories to embitter him, sat as an elder and respected member of the Assembly.[15]

Belcher's vendetta against Dudley involved a second danger. Not only did the judge have important provincial allies, he was also a client of the Walpoles. Again denied a place on the Council, Dudley protested to Horace Walpole, who in turn asked Belcher to explain his conduct. Walpole's letter signaled a further deterioration of the governor's position in London. With Shirley seeking the aid of the Duke of Newcastle, the continued good-

[15] *SHG,* 4:44–53; *MHJ,* 17:4, 5, 7, 8.

will of the Walpoles was crucial. For six months Belcher delayed replying, and not until January 1740 did he finally face up to the task. Belcher opened his defense with a detailed review of the quarrel. As he told the story, Dudley owed his entire political career to Belcher's good offices. Using his influence with Governor Shute, Belcher had first secured the appointment of Dudley's brother as sheriff of Suffolk County and had then recommended Dudley for the Superior Court. Two years later the always obliging Belcher had worked for Dudley's reelection to the Council and, when Dudley began opposing Shute, had even prevailed upon the governor not to remove the judge from his offices. And how had Dudley repaid these kindnesses? He had helped defeat Belcher's own election to the Council, "entirely forgetting how kindly and free from the least private view I had got him and his brother into places of profit and honor." With Belcher in the governor's chair, Dudley had again changed his comportment and petitioned not to be removed from his offices. Belcher, against his better judgment (for he "had no reason to believe [Dudley] . . . a man of truth, but of the vilest ingratitude"), had allowed him to remain on the bench and to take a seat on the Council. For five years, or so Belcher claimed, he had tolerated Dudley's incessant attacks on both the administration's programs and the king's honor, hoping that "this ungrateful man . . . would come to his senses and see his folly and ingratitude." Then in 1737 Belcher had reluctantly vetoed the judge's election to the Council and, when Dudley had shown no sign of repentance, had been forced to repeat this prudently administered punishment two years later. Belcher closed his attack by exposing Dudley's present schemes: "In this last session of the Assembly, in his debates and votes in that House, [he] has been full of opposition to his majesty's royal orders to his governor respecting the drawing in of what moneys were necessary for the support of the king's government and for the defense of his people." Belcher should have expected nothing less. Dudley had little to lose by openly defying the governor. Already denied further patronage and increasingly the target of bitter personal attacks, he saw little prospect of a compromise or any bargain which would be mutually advantageous.[16]

The vendetta against Dudley typified the dilemma Belcher had created for himself. The province's professional politicians, even those who had yet to feel the sting of Belcher's personal anger, could no longer trust the governor. Their own futures and strategies depended upon a rational political order in which men were allowed to change their minds and to form new alliances when circumstances changed. More important, perhaps, Belcher had simply become too erratic and volatile. Shirley summed up these fears when, after an interview with Belcher, he wrote Waldo that the governor "talked to me so insolently about your affairs . . . and talked in such a manner that if you had heard him, it would have galled you to the heart, as it did me. . . . He threatens you very much; and in short he must be got out, or I don't see how you can return with any comfort for the rest of your days." [17]

Even without the professionals' growing distrust of Belcher to aid him, William Shirley was a formidable opponent. He had been a prospering lawyer and rising London politician when the 1720 crash had all but wiped out his inheritance. For the next ten years he had manfully struggled to maintain his standard of living against a rising tide of debts and a constantly growing family. Then in 1731, on the advice of solicitous friends and

---

[16] Belcher to Walpole, 21 January 1739–40, Belcher Papers, 2:264–68. See also *New England Historical and Geneological Register* 35 (1881): 28–32; *MHJ*, 17:217.
[17] Shirley to Waldo, 9 May 1739, *American Historical Review* 36 (1931): 357.

with the kind assurances of the Duke of Newcastle that he would receive an important political office in America, Shirley had embarked for Massachusetts, where he found life pleasant, not a little dull, and most unrewarding. Despite Newcastle's repeated promises, preferment had never come. Then in 1736 Shirley became counsel to Samuel Waldo, thus opening a breach between himself and the governor. But by then Shirley knew that his own political future depended on winning the governorship for himself.

Well known in London, related to Newcastle, trusted by most provincial leaders, reserved, clever, ambitious, Shirley possessed all the qualifications that the task of toppling Belcher required. His personal agent was his wife Frances, whom he had dispatched to London in 1736 when his hopes for preferment seemed darkest. In 1739 Shirley also sent Waldo to London to reinforce contacts among English merchants and to help document the case against Belcher. Waldo's reward for the time and money he so liberally invested in the enterprise was to be the lieutenant governorship when that post became vacant. Finally Shirley enlisted the aid of John Thomilson, a London merchant with extensive New Hampshire connections, who was seeking the governorship of that colony for Benning Wentworth. Thomilson contributed his time, his English influence, and £1000 to help cover expenses.[18]

For the campaign to succeed, Newcastle had to be convinced that Belcher was in fact expendable. To this end, Shirley marshaled an impressive case. David Dunbar, then in London, personally presented the evidence documenting Belcher's failure to enforce the Forest Laws. Thomilson, who was also the New

[18] Schutz, *Shirley*, pp. 3–42; Jere R. Daniel, "Politics in New Hampshire under Governor Benning Wentworth, 1741–1767," *William and Mary Quarterly*, 3d ser. 23 (1966): 78–85.

Hampshire Assembly's official agent, convinced the Board of Trade that Belcher had unfairly sided with Massachusetts over a disputed boundary between the two colonies. Shirley even directed his wife and Waldo to insinuate among English churchmen that Belcher had discriminated against Anglican interests in America. Finally, Shirley suggested that Waldo might remind London of the animosity and dissension Belcher had already injected into provincial politics. Newcastle listened to Frances Shirley's pleas, weighed Shirley's case against Belcher, and counseled more patience. Then, because of fluctuations within English politics itself, Newcastle changed his mind. With the dissolution of Robert Walpole's political support and his own emergence as a leader of a faction favoring war with Spain, Newcastle was ready to move against Belcher. Shirley was to discontinue his campaign against the governor while the province mobilized for a new war in the Caribbean. Once a military victory had been achieved, Newcastle promised to redistribute imperial patronage.[19]

The contest for the governorship might have been settled as Newcastle proposed had not England's insistence that Massachusetts return to a specie currency created a more encompassing and complex crisis. In 1730 the Board of Trade had drafted two new instructions governing the use of bills of credit as a paper currency. Henceforth, the Board had ordered, no more than £30,000 could be emitted in any calendar year. Furthermore, the province was to retire on schedule all notes then outstanding. In effect, England had informed Massachusetts that after 1741,

[19] See note 18 above and Shirley to Waldo, 15 April and 9 May 1739, *American Historical Review* 36 (1931): 350–60; Newcastle to Shirley, 5 April 1740, Charles Henry Lincoln, ed., *Correspondence of William Shirley*, 2 vols. (New York: Macmillan, 1912), 1:17–20.

the year the last emission was then scheduled for retirement, the province would have to do without paper money.[20]

The province's experiments with paper money had really satisfied no one. The government had issued notes, tried a dozen expedients to maintain their value, and still the paper currency had depreciated. Yet the province's inflationists continued to argue that the problem was not too much but too little paper. Only massive emissions of paper, they argued, would spur the province's lagging economy by increasing local production and thus ending the chronic trade deficit. It was to appease these inflationists that Belcher had ignored his instructions and sanctioned the emission of nearly £120,000 in 1733 and 1734. Not until 1737 was the governor able to make some progress towards meeting England's demands. Then the elder Thomas Hutchinson secured passage of a bill issuing £29,000 in a new series of notes (christened "new tenor," each worth four "old tenor" bills) which, for the first time, were nominally backed by gold and silver. More important, the House also granted a tax of £45,000 old tenor to redeem past emissions. But still outstanding were more than £200,000 old tenor which, if Belcher was to obey his instructions, Massachusetts had to retire in the next four years. So things stood when William Shirley launched his campaign for the governorship.[21]

In January 1739 Hutchinson drafted and was probably responsible for House passage of an ingeniously conceived compromise which, by sidestepping Belcher's instructions and amalgamating the major demands of both inflationists and hard

[20] Leonard Woods Labaree, ed., *Royal Instructions to British Royal Governors,* 2 vols. (New York: D. Appleton Century Co., Inc., 1935), 1:220–21; Belcher to the Lords of Trade, 7 November 1737, *A&R,* 2:844–45.

[21] *A&R,* 1:690–93; 701–03; 707–11; 744–46, 2:844–45. Shirley to the Lords of Trade, 24 January 1742, Lincoln, *Correspondence of Shirley,* 1:95–98.

money advocates, promised more lasting relief. The province would issue £60,000 in new tenor notes to select investors who would repay the province in specie, the first half coming due in 1744 and the remainder in 1749. The inflationists would be quieted with a fresh supply of paper currency. Those men with access to specie, primarily Boston's leading merchants, would enjoy noninterest loans from the government. And with £60,000 in new tenor notes pumped into the economy, the government could retire at least some of its old tenor notes in partial compliance with England's repeated demands.[22]

The compromise, however, landed Belcher in a quandary. In normal times he could have consented to the measure, confident that the Privy Council and Board of Trade, while protesting, would not have overturned his decision. But the campaign to unseat him had stripped him of maneuverability, because signing the measure would simply substantiate the charges that he systematically ignored his instructions. Instead, Belcher forwarded the proposal to London with his recommendation that it be accepted as an expedient compromise. Four months later Boston learned the measure's fate. The Board of Trade had solicited the advice of English merchants trading with New England who, rather than a subscription of £60,000, suggested sanctioning less than £40,000. And rather than redeeming the notes in 1744 and 1749, the merchants maintained the province should retire the first third in 1742, another third in 1745, and the remainder in 1749. Finally the merchants asked the Privy Council not to approve any measure until the General Court retired all old tenor notes. In Massachusetts the merchants' report ended any hope of a compromise. Within the House the inflationist majority repudiated every attempt to modify the

[22] *MHJ*, 16: passim, 17:141–44. See also [Hugh Vance], *Some Observations on the Scheme Projected for Emiting 60,000 £* (Boston, 1738).

£60,000 subscription and in June sent Belcher a new supply and tax bill which not only ignored the 1741 deadline, but actually increased the amount of paper in circulation. When Belcher vetoed the measure, the House adamantly refused to enact a more conciliatory and less inflationary bill.[23]

The year 1739 also marked the broadening of the monetary crisis into a major public issue. In part the proposed subscription excited increased public awareness. Across the province men who considered paper money a boon grew restless, while Boston voters who viewed the £60,000 subscription as too deflationary, defeated the reelection bids of three representatives who had supported the compromise. In the press both sides argued the merits of paper money, the morality of inflation, and the future of a province which habitually imported more than it exported. In June the House invited concerned citizens to submit proposals for achieving by private means what England had prohibited the province from achieving as public policy. The following September John Colman presented his plan for a Land Bank.[24]

Colman's scheme was simple enough. Since the government would no longer print paper money, private citizens would have to supply the necessary currency. To achieve this goal, Colman and his partners proposed issuing £150,000 in paper notes secured by land mortgaged to their Bank. On paper the plan not only promised an end to the monetary crisis by insuring an adequate money supply, it also promised to bolster an ailing economy. By making land, the province's major resource, convertible into cash, the Bank would spur the growth of local industry,

[23] *MHJ*, 16:213–14, 254, 17:141–44, 194–95; Great Britain, *Journal of the Commissioners for Trade and Plantation from January 1734 to December 1741* (London, 1930), pp. 272–75.

[24] Peter Orlando Hutchinson, ed., *The Diary and Letters of Thomas Hutchinson* 2 vols. (London, 1883), 1:49–50; Boston, Mass., *Report of the Record Commissioners of the City of Boston*, 39 vols. (Boston, 1881–1909), 12:219, 225–27; *MHJ*, 17:79.

thus making Massachusetts less dependent on English manufactures and less likely to run a trade deficit. The Bank was
not the only plan for ending the crisis, but it was the best supported and the most inflationary. And it did capture the imagination of those provincials who suspected that hard money
was merely a plot for enriching the merchant and keeping the
farmer in perpetual debt.

The directors of the enterprise, however, were themselves men
of means. Colman, the public spokesman for the Bank, was
a Boston merchant who had led a similar attempt to establish
a private bank in 1714. Three other prominent merchants—
William Stoddard, Samuel Watts, and Peter Chardon—joined
Colman on the board. The remaining directors, while less wealthy,
were equally prominent men: Samuel Adams, a successful
brewer and political figure in Boston; Robert Auchmuty, a
leading lawyer-politician currently supporting Shirley's campaign to oust Belcher; George Leonard, a Bristol iron manu-
facturer; Thomas Cheever, a mill owner in Lynn; and John
Choate, a leading lawyer in Essex County whose wealth was
primarily tied up in land. The last place on the board belonged
to Robert Hale, who, along with Choate and Watts, would
provide the political leadership the Bank required.[25]

Thomas Hutchinson later noted that "the principal merchants
in the province abhorred the project," and by and large he was
right. For three decades the bulk of the province's merchants
had railed against the evils of paper money and ridiculed its
promise of economic development. When England had at last
insisted that Massachusetts retire its paper currency, the merchants
had hoped that the province would again have a frugal government, balanced budgets, and a specie currency. Now the Land

[25] George Athan Billias, "The Massachusetts Land Bankers," *University of Maine
Studies,* 2d ser. no. 74 (April 1959), pp. 17–31.

Bank threatened these hopes. Publicly these merchants damned the Bank as merely a more insidious form of the soft money panacea typically favored by the province's poor and unsuccessful. Privately Boston's trading community set out to insure that the Bank would never issue a note. Supported by English merchants, the province's principal traders pressured Belcher and the Board of Trade to prohibit the Bank's incorporation and to force the General Court to observe the 1741 deadline for retiring the paper currency. Then to increase their bargaining position within the province, a score of Boston's merchants countered with a proposal of their own: a Silver Bank which would issue paper notes redeemable in silver at the end of fifteen years. More a tactical ploy than a serious undertaking, the Silver Bank promised neither easy money nor an expansionist economy.[26]

The monetary crisis, now compounded by the rival banking schemes, created a political climate which boded ill for men in power. The currency issue forced the entire province to take sides, and once they had committed themselves, few men were inclined to concede the good intentions of the opposition. As tempers grew short and the debate became harsh, the possibility of reaching an amicable compromise grew increasingly remote. The previous June the House had passed and Belcher had vetoed a supply bill increasing the money supply by £25,000 new tenor. The governor had informed the General Court that the bill blatantly violated his instructions, to which the House replied:

> Wherefore this House apprehend it their duty to adhere to the bill until there be discovered in it some inconsistence with the *Royal Charter*, which is the only rule of legislation. . . . Therefore this House earnestly move that the bill as it has been framed and passed, may be consented to by your excellency, that so his

[26] Hutchinson, *History of Massachusetts*, 2:300; *An Account of the Rise, Progress, and Consequences of the Land Bank* (Boston, 1744), pp. 18–20. *Publications of the Colonial Society of Massachusetts* 4 (1910): 147–63.

majesty's government here may be supported, and the utmost perplexity and distress to this people prevented.

Four days later Belcher had rendered his own interpretation of the Assembly's message. "Your language," he told the representatives, "can . . . [mean] nothing less than this: if the treasury may not be supplied just in such a manner as you judge proper, then the public faith plighted for calling in such a number of bills at this time shall be violated." Belcher had then closed with an ultimatum of his own: "That you may no longer delay the support of the king's government, you may depend I shall not give my consent to any bill of the nature you have now laid before me." [27]

If Belcher had possessed a sense of humor, he might have enjoyed the irony of his dilemma. Resolution of the crisis now offered one, and probably the only, hope of thwarting Shirley's campaign for the governorship. A dramatic legislative victory reducing the amount of paper in circulation and continuing to move the province toward a specie currency would demonstrate his effectiveness and increase his standing among English merchants. If he could do this while simultaneously ending the threat posed by the Land Bank, Newcastle might seriously reconsider removing a governor so obviously in control of his government. Belcher's campaign to achieve these goals is worth considering in some detail, for it illustrates the political resources at the disposal of the governor. Of equal importance, the campaign also demonstrated the resources available to men like Robert Hale—the professional politician who commanded the Assembly's inflationist majority.

Belcher faced two major tasks. He had to prevent the Land Bank from circulating notes, while simultaneously convincing the House to grant sufficient taxes to retire £200,000 old tenor

[27] *MHJ*, 17:104, 112–13.

notes. To achieve this latter goal Belcher simply continued the policy which had, or so it seemed, been so effective in the past. Again and again he replied to Assembly motions by threatening reprisals and insisting that the House observe the 1741 deadline. Answering obstinacy with obstinacy, he attempted to cow the House into submission just as he had previously forced the representatives to accept the elder Hutchinson's program of gradual devaluation. But now Belcher's career hung in the balance. With the electorate clamoring for more paper and the professionals tolling the last hours of his administration, the governor was powerless to make good his threats.[28]

Belcher's approach to the Land Bank was more circumspect and initially more successful. Perhaps hoping that the Bank would die either of natural causes or of a surfeit of merchant opposition, Belcher did little. Even when both Banks asked for the government's endorsement in March 1740, Belcher continued his public silence, apparently content to let the Council champion the cause of sound money. The first round went to the Silver Bankers when the Council secured the creation of a joint committee which condemned the Land Bank's "slender . . . foundation" and its "tendency to depreciate the bills of credit already circulating, and consequently to endamage his majesty's good subjects as to their properties." The committee went on to recommend the immediate suspension of the Land Bank and asked the Silver Bank not to issue notes until May. When the Assembly voted to suspend both Banks temporarily, the Council concurred. Momentarily, at least, Belcher's strategy of publicly ignoring the Bank was producing the desired results.[29]

In May the Land Bankers swept the provincial elections, and Robert Hale, returning to the House after a year's absence, took

[28] See, for example, *MHJ*, 18:197–98, 215–17.
[29] *MHJ*, 17:260.

command of the Assembly's inflationist majority. Forced to contend with the Council's adamant refusal to sanction the Land Bank, Hale devised an alternative, though admittedly less satisfactory, strategy. House defeat of a motion condemning the Land Bank would have to be deemed an adequate endorsement, and accordingly on June 20 the House voted 37 to 59 to defeat a motion prohibiting the Land Bank from issuing its notes. For the rest of the session Hale and his faction successfully blocked every attempt to reconsider the question. On September 12 the House again refused to agree to a joint committee to investigate the two banking schemes, and a week later the Land Bank issued its first notes while a group of angry and frustrated Boston merchants publicly announced they would not accept the Bank's paper.[30]

With the House still adamantly refusing to levy new taxes and with the Land Bank's notes in circulation, Belcher changed tactics. In November, while the General Court was in recess, he and the Council (sitting as his advisory board) issued a proclamation outlawing both banks and ordering every government official, on pain of dismissal, not to receive the notes of either one. The proclamation was a calculated risk. At best its constitutionality was dubious. Further, the threat to dismiss government officials would work only if the professionals never called Belcher's bluff. To reinforce the legitimacy of the order, the Silver Bankers disbanded their scheme. Understandably the Land Bankers did their best to demonstrate that the proclamation need deter no one. Five days after Belcher delivered his ultimatum to the province's professional politicians, Hale, Choate, and two other Land Bank directors resigned as justices of the peace. Still Belcher persisted. On November 22 he asked a reconvened As-

[30] *MHJ*, 18:47–48, 126; *An Account of the Land Bank*, pp. 257–59; *New England Weekly Journal*, 16 September 1740.

sembly to ratify the proclamation. Instead, the House threatened to summon the Silver Bankers for disbanding their scheme in compliance with what the House deemed an unconstitutional proclamation. Belcher then escalated the conflict. On the morning of December 19 William Pepperrell stood at the door of the House chamber requesting that Joseph Blanchard appear before the Council to be removed as a justice of the peace. Twenty minutes later John Chandler was summoned. The attempt to coerce the province's professional politicians into observing the proclamation was not an unreasonable strategy for a man in Belcher's position. But it should have been abandoned once it became clear that, instead of deterring those professionals who supported the Land Bank, it would merely increase their intransigency. To dismiss men who were important House leaders—and to compound the insult by summoning them from the Assembly chamber—was political suicide.[31]

The Assembly's response only demonstrated the futility of further reprisals. Hale drafted and secured passage of a message charging Belcher and the Council with portraying "divers members of this House . . . as subverters of the government, and disturbers of the peace." And when Hale moved to investigate the proclamation outlawing the Bank, Belcher learned the full consequence of his policy. That the motion carried 42 to 28 was no surprise. But on the previous roll call involving the Bank, three-fourths of the leadership had sided with the governor and against the Bank. Now nearly half of the leadership voted against Belcher.[32]

Still Belcher refused to moderate his stand. While the Council was busily dismissing Land Bankers from their government posts, the House had launched its own program of harassment.

---

[31] *Publications of the Colonial Society of Mass.*, 4:7–18; *MHJ*, 18:130–34, 167.
[32] *MHJ*, 18:184–86.

During December the Assembly approved a controversial revision of the province's lawbooks, enacted a supply bill calling for the emission of £110,000 old tenor, and ordered repairs on Castle William to be supervised by the House rather than the governor. In dealing with this vote on Castle William, Belcher could choose among three alternatives.

Though dissatisfied, he could accept the vote in an attempt to reestablish a basis for negotiating with the House. Or he could veto the measure, alleging some technical deficiency in the bill. Finally he could meet the issue head on, righteously rejecting the measure as an ill-disguised and illegal attack on the governor's constitutional prerogatives. Belcher chose the last. When the House asked what had become of the measure, Belcher replied, "I cannot give my consent to the vote, because it would be to divest the king's governor of the powers and authorities granted and reserved to him by the Royal CHARTER." The House was only too happy to continue this new dispute. Within six hours the Assembly drafted and approved a message declaring:

> By what your excellency now insists upon, the people of this province are brought to this deplorable dilemma, either to part with their ancient liberty and usage in this affair, which tends so much for their security, or they must still lie in their exposed condition. This is truly shocking! [33]

Once again Belcher had widened the breach. He had transformed a legislative issue into a question of constitutional prerogative and thus increased the Assembly's intransigency.

By this time Belcher had also exhausted the patience of his few remaining supporters. The province's principal merchants had expected him to crush the Land Bank and to stabilize the government's chaotic finances. Now, with the Bank's notes in

[33] *MHJ*, 18:181, 184–85.

circulation and with the House still insisting on more government paper and no taxes, these merchants adopted a more drastic strategy. With the support of the English mercantile establishment, they petitioned Parliament to outlaw the Land Bank. To his credit, Belcher understood the danger inherent in any appeal to Parliament. In November he had warned the House that unless it endorsed his proclamation, England would impose its own solution to the monetary crisis. The following May, after the Land Bankers had swept the provincial elections and sent thirty-six freshman representatives to the Assembly, Belcher analyzed the problem for Thomas Hutchinson, who was then in London as a quasi-official agent for the governor:

> You say it would be much better if some other way than by application to Parliament could be found out to suppress . . . [the Land Bank]. I assure you the concerned openly declare they defy any act of Parliament to be able to do it. . . . What the act of Parliament will be respecting this vile, wicked projection, I can't tell, but if it be no better than the bill I have seen, it will by no means answer the end. The common people here are taught by their advisers to believe they are pretty much out of the reach of the government at home; nay, our Assembly are sometimes made to think by their leaders that they are as big as the Parliament of Great Britain, but surely as occasions require, I can't help thinking we shall always to our loss and cost find otherwise.[34]

Though Belcher perceived the dangers and could, with surprising detachment, analyze the mood of his opposition, he could not apply the same lessons to his own conduct. When the newly elected representatives assembled on May 27, they were in an ugly mood. Their target, however, was to be the former Council, which, in support of Belcher, had steadfastly obstructed every attempt to sanction the Land Bank. For speaker the House elected Samuel Watts, one of the Bank's more conciliatory di-

[34] Belcher to Hutchinson, 11 May 1741, Belcher Papers, 2:386–90.

rectors. When Belcher vetoed this election, the House exacted its revenge. When the votes for the Council had been sorted and tallied, sixteen councilors had been retired from office. Belcher then played his final scene. Dissolving the Assembly, he declared:

> The management of the elections made yesterday, discover to me so much of the inclination of your House to support the fraudulent, pernicious scheme commonly called the Land Bank, condemned at home by his majesty and both houses of Parliament of Great Britain, that I judge it derogatory to the king's honor and service, and inconsistent with the peace and welfare of this people, that you sit any longer in General Assembly.[35]

By May 1741, however, it no longer mattered what Belcher did. Newcastle had already ordered the Board of Trade to draw up the necessary commission for William Shirley. In the final analysis, Shirley became governor because he had conceived and faultlessly executed a complex campaign to deny Belcher imperial patronage. Yet Belcher had been given his opportunity. Thomas Hutchinson probably reported the most concise analysis of the contest. To the elder Benjamin Lynde, he wrote: "I suppose you will have the . . . news of Mr. Shirley's being appointed our governor. . . . Your two countrymen Waldo and Kilby claimed the merit, and say it is owing to their gratifying the Duke of Grafton by making interest for Lord Euston at Coventry, where they have spent a month first and last soliciting his election. But I had it from Lord President's own mouth that Governor Belcher's security for some time had been his steady conduct in the affair of the money." [36]

[35] *MHJ*, 19:4–9.
[36] Hutchinson to Lynde, n.d., [F. E. Oliver], ed., *The Diaries of Benjamin Lynde and of Benjamin Lynde, Jr.* (Boston, 1880), pp. 221–23. Great Britain, *Journal of the Commissioners for Trade, 1734–1741*, pp. 381–82.

What, then, might have been the results if Belcher had acted differently, if he had marshaled and preserved his resources instead of squandering them in a headlong rush to put down the opposition he saw brewing? Belcher was probably incapable of adopting any strategy but the one he chose. But the first roll call on the Land Bank on June 19, 1740, at least suggests the outline of a possible compromise. On that vote thirty-seven representatives had supported the governor. More important, Samuel Watts, a director of the Bank, had broken with his faction and supported the idea of a cooling-off period. Conceivably Belcher could have taken advantage of Watts's defection and appealed to the more moderate of the Bank's adherents. To do so he would have had to abate his opposition to a new issue of government paper, guessing that another £100,000 in bills of credit would undercut the Land Bank's strength. He would, of course, still have had to contend with London. And by bowing to the inflationists, he would have strengthened Shirley's case. But he would also have augmented his own influence within the province, and he could, with some justification, have told London that the compromise had ended a crisis London itself had created.

The province's political system was never very tidy. There were always crises. England incessantly interfered and frequently undermined the influence of her royal officials. And there were always ambitious politicians ready to take advantage of a governor's mistakes. Nonetheless, the obstacles were not insurmountable. Belcher failed, not because he lacked sufficient constitutional authority, but rather because he squandered the political resources at his disposal. His inability to preserve his importance to London was matched only by his inability to cope with a domestic crisis and to maintain the allegiance of the province's political community. His successor would demonstrate that the same opportunities and resources were sufficient to dominate a seemingly intractable province. And William Shirley would begin by resolving the monetary crisis that had destroyed Belcher.

6

William Shirley and the
Politics of Persuasion

WHEN SHIRLEY LEARNED OF HIS APPOINTMENT AS ROYAL GOV-
ernor in June 1741, the province knew him as a clever,
resourceful lawyer with powerful friends in London and
a knack for politics. His connection with London merchants like
Thomilson and his associations with the province's own trading
community might have also marked the new governor as a friend
of hard money. Yet he had studiously avoided committing himself on the Land Bank, and despite his nine years in Massachusetts, few men could say with certainty just where Shirley stood
on paper money, inflation, and government deficits. Shirley
proved in no hurry to enlighten the province. While Massachusetts celebrated the appointment of a new governor, its enthusiasm was dampened by a second dispatch from London: Parliament had applied the 1720 Bubble Act to the province in order
to outlaw the Land Bank. Some men talked of armed insur-
rection and demanded that the General Court defy the edict;
most provincials, however, simply sat and waited for their new
governor to announce his intentions.[1]

[1] John A. Schutz, *William Shirley, King's Governor of Massachusetts* (Chapel Hill: University of North Carolina Press, 1961), pp. 38, 44–49; *Publications of the Colonial Society of Massachusetts* 4 (1910): 19–21.

Not until August did Shirley break his silence. The occasion was his inaugural address, which he opened with a summation of his own hopes for the future. Being governor, he suggested, conferred both opportunities and burdens which he assumed

> the more cheerfully, when I reflect that it is the happiness of his majesty's servants, that the most effectual means they can make use of to approve themselves to their royal master is to employ that power and authority, with which he invests them, in consulting and promoting the good of his people: This, *gentlemen,* however unequal I may be to it, shall be the sincere aim of my administration.[2]

Moving to specific problems, Shirley next deplored the condition of provincial defenses and the province's past reluctance to meet the military requests England so justly made. He wanted Castle William repaired, larger appropriations for the province's frontier forts, and more provisions and troops for the king's forces fighting Spain in the Caribbean. As Shirley portrayed the issue, defense preparedness became a patriotic duty. England was engaged in a worldwide struggle with cunning and unscrupulous enemies whose defeat would bring glory not only to England herself, but to all her possessions and, more particularly, to the inhabitants of her far-flung outposts. Thus Shirley invited Massachusetts to forget internal quarrels, to focus instead on the new imperial crusade against Catholic Spain, which promised new commands, new supply contracts, and new markets for the province's agricultural surplus.

Before broaching the currency issue, Shirley introduced one more topic promising harmony. The territorial integrity of the province was a touchy subject. Already New Hampshire had won control of a dozen townships Massachusetts claimed, and now royal commissioners had ruled in favor of Rhode Island

[2] *MHJ,* 19:64.

in another dispute. Shirley had helped prepare the province's brief before he became governor, and now he suggested, "the maintenance of your ancient possessions against the demands and pretensions of our fellow-subjects and friends . . . of *Rhode Island,* may challenge your attention." For his part, he added, he would actively support any appeal the province might make.[3]

Ready to discuss the currency, Shirley began with a bow toward the deflationist minority. Commiserating with those whose fortunes had been depleted by inflation, he lamented

> that a creditor . . . having an outstanding debt . . . of *one thousand pounds* sterling . . . contracted in 1730, can recover no more . . . [than] *six hundred fifty pounds* sterling: the great injustice and oppression of which upon the creditor, and the tendency it has to introduce a general spirit of dishonesty into the community, which I mention as the very worst of the many bad consequences attending it, are too plain to need any thing further to be said upon this head.[4]

True to his word, Shirley said no more and instead turned to Parliament's own plans to reform the province's currency, suggesting that some danger lay in having a body three thousand miles away set the conditions for returning to a stable currency. "I am not ignorant," he declared, "how difficult it may be for the wisest legislature to find out an adequate remedy for every part of our misfortunes in this respect, which can't be affected without an exact knowledge of them, and of the particular circumstances of this province." Shirley's only request was that the General Court prepare a comprehensive report setting forth the unique situation Massachusetts found itself in. But by reminding the Court, and particularly the House, of the dangers inherent in any parliamentary review of provincial policies, he

---

[3] *MHJ,* 19:65.
[4] *MHJ,* 19:66.

invited the province to enact effective legislation before England imposed a solution of her own.[5]

Shirley completed his brief review of the currency problem with another appeal for unity in the face of external pressures. Again the target was Rhode Island, which, to the province's chagrin, had successfully established a stable paper currency. Somewhat irrationally, both inflationists and deflationists believed many of the province's current difficulties were attributable to the circulation of Rhode Island notes within Massachusetts. Shirley did nothing to lessen this conviction.[6]

There had been no constitutional ultimatum, no mention of his instructions, and no demand that the House observe the 1741 deadline. Shirley knew that soft words and kind phrases were not an answer to the problems facing him. At some point he would have to be explicit, clearly defining the kind of monetary solution he would accept. But in the beginning, the tone of the speech was important, not because it lulled the Assembly's contentious majority, but because it suggested that Shirley was interested in creating an atmosphere conducive to conciliation. Perceptive legislators could, if they wanted to read between the lines, view the speech as an invitation to reach a compromise meeting at least some of the demands of everyone.

The success of any bargaining, of course, depended on Shirley's relations with the province's professional politicians. He was the new governor and thus, temporarily, at least, immune to threats to replace him. Shirley, however, never pressed this advantage. He resisted the temptation to dismiss men who might harass his administration. In his first year in office he made only four new appointments, each time merely filling an office vacated by death or retirement. Later he would build his coalition, singling out

[5] Ibid.
[6] *MHJ*, 19:66–67.

some men for special posts and increased personal power. But in the beginning he threatened no one.[7]

The Land Bankers posed a special problem. Robert Hale and John Choate still controlled a united House majority bent on issuing enough government paper to compensate for the loss of Land Bank notes. Because any program of fiscal reform required the Assembly's endorsement, Shirley had to devise a formula acceptable to these two men. Hale and Choate, like Shirley, were professionals in the best sense of the word. They were interested in a rational political order in which men could reach bargains beneficial both to themselves and to the society they served. An invitation to become major leaders in the coalition Shirley was then building would have been an attractive offer. But Hale, Choate, and the other directors of the Land Bank also faced a personal dilemma which in turn gave Shirley the added maneuverability he needed.

Parliament, in ordering the Bank's suppression, had made its directors personally liable for all damages incurred by those who had accepted its notes. Originally most Bank supporters had wanted to defy the edict, but when the directors themselves counseled restraint, a curious reaction had set in. Their anger spent, holders of Bank notes began demanding reimbursement. To Shirley fell the task of enforcing Parliament's edict. If he pursued a strict policy for liquidating the Bank and suing for the immediate and full recovery of all damages, Hale, Choate, and the other Bank directors would be financially ruined.[8]

In August Shirley met separately with the leaders of both bank schemes. What transpired at the meeting between the

---

[7] William H. Whitmore, ed., *The Massachusetts Civil List for the Colonial and Provincial Periods, 1630–1774* (Albany, 1870), pp. 68ff.; Schutz, *Shirley,* pp. 70–71.

[8] George Athan Billias, "The Massachusetts Land Bankers," *University of Maine Studies,* 2d ser. no. 74 (April 1959), pp. 36–39.

governor and the directors of the Land Bank is necessarily con-
jecture, but the subsequent course of events strongly suggests
that either then, or at some later meeting, these men worked
out a compromise which satisfied their own peculiar needs while
promising an end to the immediate crisis. Apparently Shirley
agreed to the Land Bankers' demands for more paper in return
for House acceptance of monetary reforms limiting the effect
of increased inflation. The governor also assured the directors
that he would insist that the assessment of damages arising
from the liquidation of their Bank be kept to a minimum. In
return, Hale and Choate promised to support Shirley's legislative
program.[9]

With the formalities of installing a new governor completed,
the tempo of legislative activity again quickened. Shirley delivered his inaugural on Monday, August 17. On Tuesday the
speaker appointed a committee to draft a new supply bill. On
Wednesday the General Court began drafting a new bill for
regulating the collection of private debts. Thursday was spent
considering a plan to reapportion the provincial tax, and by
Friday the new supply bill was ready for debate. By August 29,
when Shirley granted a two-week recess, the House had passed
the supply bill, begun considering a currency stabilization measure, received from the Council a bill establishing local procedures
for liquidating the Land Bank, and voted Shirley £2000.[10]

When the Court reconvened in mid-September, the Council
rejected the Assembly's supply bill. Hale's committee then
readied a new measure which it reported on September 23. By
the first week in October, the House had enacted a single bill

[9] Shirley to Newcastle, 17 October 1741, Charles Henry Lincoln, ed., *The Cor-
respondence of William Shirley*, 2 vols. (New York: Macmillan, 1912), 1:76–79;
Thomas Hutchinson, *The History of the Colony and Province of Massachusetts-
Bay*, ed. Lawrence Shaw Mayo, 3 vols. (Cambridge, Mass.: Harvard University
Press, 1936), 2:305–06; Schutz, *Shirley*, pp. 44, 48.
[10] *MHJ*, 19:68–92.

both regulating the repayment of private debts and supplying the Treasury. Shirley, apparently content to let the inflationists make the first move on fiscal policies, concentrated on military affairs, reiterating his demands that the House approve more aid for an expedition to Cuba. By October 13 the governor had cajoled the House into approving bounties for local recruits and had extracted a promise that suitable vessels for transporting the men to the Caribbean would be voted. Having secured this victory, Shirley was ready to cope with the peculiar problems Hale's supply bill created.[11]

The measure provided both a massive infusion of paper notes and a mechanism for stabilizing farm prices. Henceforth, farmers were to be allowed to pay their taxes in certain commodities which were to be given an artificially high value. Moreover, the Treasury was not to dispose of these products unless the market price equaled the inflated rates set by the General Court. The supply bill ended Shirley's silence on monetary policy. Adroitly he had played his waiting game, but now, if ever, was the moment to exert his leadership and to outline clearly his own solution to the problem. Although announcing his willingness to work within the framework established by the bill, Shirley declared that significant alterations would be necessary. In an hour-long speech to a joint session, Shirley went through Hale's bill paragraph by paragraph, pointing out its weaknesses, chiding the representatives for ignoring the creditors' just claims, reminding the Court of the need to resolve the crisis instead of effecting another temporary solution, and complaining of the impracticality, if not the injustice, of using a fiscal policy to stabilize agricultural prices.[12]

For each defect Shirley suggested an appropriate remedy. To

---

[11] *MHJ*, 19:93–105.
[12] *MHJ*, 19:105–11; Shirley to Newcastle, 23 January 1741–2, Lincoln, *Correspondence of Shirley*, 1:79–82.

bolster the creditor's chances of receiving full value in a court of law, he wanted the section governing the repayment of private debts drafted into a separate bill. To insure the stability of the new notes, he proposed two alternatives: either redeem all outstanding old tenor bills or make the new notes interest-bearing. For restricting the measure's mechanism to support commodity prices, he suggested giving the treasurer discretionary power to sell farm produce he was to accept in lieu of taxes.

With his critique completed, Shirley announced he would veto the bill. By the terms of his instructions he could do nothing less, and for his predecessors this would have been sufficient explanation. But in refusing his consent, Shirley used the opportunity to remind the Court that a governor was an independent chief executive rather than a royal spokesman whose sole duty was to enforce the letter of his instructions.

> I am not ignorant, *gentlemen,* of the straits which the province is in for want of a new supply of the Treasury, its defenseless condition, the ruinous state of our fortifications, the arrears due to the . . . soldiers in our garrisons and all our public officers, and our want of warlike stores, and the scarcity of our paper medium; and it is with regret that I find myself necessitated to refuse giving my assent to a supply bill at a time when the exigencies of the province are so pressing . . . ; but I cannot in duty to his majesty, or in fidelity to the province, break through two of the royal instructions . . . to pass an act which I am fully persuaded will be extremely hurtful and destructive to the province, and therefore could not have consented to, though I had been restrained by no instructions.[13]

Shirley now proposed his compromise, one which would insure the inflationists most of what they sought while increasing his own control over the province's fiscal policy. The proposed

[13] *MHJ,* 19:109.

quid pro quo was the 1741 deadline against which Shirley offered to lobby if the House drafted a supply bill meeting his
demands.

Among some inflationists the speech apparently did not sit
well. Probably its most galling section was the governor's charge
that the House had again shortchanged the creditor. Shirley, in-
voking the rhetoric so long used by deflationists, had warned
against perpetrating another "train of dishonesty, fraud, injustice
and oppression." In a speech remarkable for its moderation, the
section dealing with debtor-creditor conflicts was, no doubt, carefully planned. There was little in what Shirley proposed that
would provide succor for the province's conservatives. Clearly
he planned to return to inflationary monetary policies, and just
as clearly he intended to meet at least halfway those men who
had founded the Land Bank. A call for greater protection for the
creditor was the least the conservatives would have expected.
Sensing that debate would destroy the spirit of amiability he
had so carefully fostered, Shirley granted a recess.[14]

The month-long cooling-off period produced the desired results. When the House reconvened in mid-November, Hale began drafting a new supply bill. A week later John Stoddard,
conservative spokesman for the Connecticut Valley, was appointed chairman of a committee drafting a separate bill to protect creditors. Shirley, again affecting the stance of a man pre-
occupied with military affairs, pressed for more aid for the
Cuban expedition and simultaneously worked to fulfill his part
of the bargain. He sent Newcastle a detailed copy of the vetoed
supply bill along with his speech and suggestions. He made no
apologies for what he had proposed. In his own mind it was the
most that a House dominated by men who had given their

[14] *MHJ*, 19:108, 113.

allegiance to the Land Bank would accept. Permission to sign a supply bill emitting more than £30,000 and yet lacking a suspending clause was needed, he suggested, to put himself

> into a capacity of being more serviceable by my influence with the people with whom it would much ingratiate me to be thought instrumental in obtaining it and beget or rather fully establish the opinion they have of my being sincerely disposed to promote the welfare of the province.

But Shirley knew that political expediency, in itself, would have little weight in London. Thus Newcastle was given an alternative reason for making this concession. If London refused to relax the instruction governing suspending clauses, there would be no appropriations and no contributions to either local or imperial military adventures. "And should a war with France break out in the spring," Shirley continued, "my refusal to give my assent to a supply bill without a suspending clause in it might be of fatal consequence to the province." [15]

On January 15 a supply bill emitting £30,000 new tenor and a separate measure regulating the payment of private debts were ready for Shirley's signature. The supply bill's most important clause dealt with the redemption of the new issue. Under Belcher the House had emitted paper and then promised to levy the necessary taxes to redeem the notes when they were scheduled to be retired. Yet both persuasion and London's edicts had failed to compel the House to honor its own commitments. Shirley would not face this problem. The £30,000 in new tenor notes were to be redeemed in 1742, 1744, 1745, and 1746; and the requisite taxes, whatever the Assembly's subsequent mood, would be levied by the provincial treasurer in compliance with the act's redemption schedule and the current tax apportionment.

[15] Shirley to Newcastle, 17 October 1741, Lincoln, *Correspondence of Shirley,* 1:77. *MHJ*, 19:114–173.

The House had also abandoned its attempt to inflate commodity prices by converting the Treasury into a depot for farm surpluses. But for the first time since 1727 farmers would be able to use farm products to pay their taxes. Finally, the separate bill regulating the payment of private debts afforded provincial creditors at least some protection against continued inflation.[16]

Shirley appeared before a joint session to announce his intentions toward the two bills. He began his address by informing the Court that England had relaxed his instructions and then warned that

> this is an alteration, which . . . has been occasioned, through my accession to the government, I mention it to you, with no small satisfaction; and I hope, *gentlemen,* that we shall not by any abuse of this indulgence . . . make it necessary . . . to renew the same instruction.

Having reminded the Court of the obvious fruits borne by conciliation and cooperation, Shirley next reviewed the major clauses of the two acts, and embarked, in typical Shirley fashion, on a detailed account of the measures' minor deficiencies, suggesting that it might "not be of disservice to point out . . . what I do not approve of in these acts." [17]

For Shirley, the acts he now signed were important victories. If the supply bill was another excursion into inflationary economics, it was, nonetheless, also an experiment which ended the government's lack of operating funds and at least promised currency stability. True, the supply bill did nothing to solve the province's basic financial dilemma. As long as Massachusetts ran a trade deficit, its currency would depreciate. But the measure did relieve most of the immediate pressures, did provide a mechanism for diffusing the political repercussions of redemption, did offer some relief to creditors, and did insure Shirley the cooperation of the province's inflationists. Six months after Parliament suppressed the Land Bank, the currency issue was all but dead. Provincial conservatives might grumble, but most of the province was undoubtedly relieved by the prospect of a continuing supply of paper money and continued deficit financing. Despite the magnitude of the crisis, Shirley had fashioned a workable political solution to an essentially economic problem. Having achieved the compromise which had so long eluded Belcher and managed a calm liquidation of the Land Bank, Shirley confidently contemplated the future and enumerated his considerable accomplishments. To Newcastle he wrote:

> A punctual obedience has been paid to the act of Parliament for suppressing the Land Bank . . . And as a very considerable part of the House of Representatives consists of persons who were concerned in that scheme . . . I have used all my influence to reclaim them to the true service of his majesty and the country, in which I have succeeded so far as to bring them . . . to join in passing these two new acts . . . which method of laying the malignant spirit, that I found in these people . . . and bringing them into the service of the public, instead of irritating them and driving them out of it by that means, I hope will not be disapproved of by his majesty.[18]

England did approve the acts, thus ending a crisis largely of her own making. Newcastle apparently accepted Shirley's contention that paper money, despite its obvious effects on the imperial economy, was acceptable as long as it encouraged Massachusetts to support a larger war effort. Shirley's success was a product of his own concept of the empire as a working system of business and political alliances dominated by London, in-

[18] Shirley to Newcastle, 23 January 1741–2, Lincoln, *Correspondence of Shirley,* 1:81.

trinsically bound up with the vicissitudes of English politics, and yet inevitably disrupted by England's attempts to govern men who counted themselves Englishmen. Shirley accepted the supremacy of British authority. But he also understood that the governor's prerogatives generated little real power. Massachusetts could be coaxed and manipulated into voluntarily complying with London's edicts. That was his responsibility, and he had no intention of being encumbered by local constitutional quarrels which divided the province and angered the Assembly. More important, perhaps, Shirley understood the central role that fiscal legislation played within the province's political system. He was not a fiscal reformer, and he was probably as bored as he was frustrated by the problems that a chaotic fiscal policy created. But he accepted the provincials' own preoccupation with economic issues and understood that successful fiscal and monetary reforms ordinarily required the support of the provincials themselves.[19] It was a lesson few other British officials ever learned.

For Shirley, politics was essentially a question of patronage. He was, of course, neither the first nor the last provincial governor who accepted this truism of eighteenth-century politics. But he was by far the most accomplished. Shirley had an uncanny ability to avoid personal animosity no matter how long he frustrated hopes for political advancement. He was cold, dignified, reserved, and in a provincial political arena often populated by impetuous men, these traits gave Shirley a special charm and attractiveness. More important, perhaps, Shirley, far better than the native Belcher, understood the men with whom

[19] See, for example, William Shirley, "Reasons against an immediate . . . suppression of Paper Bills," ibid., pp. 106–07, and Shirley to Clinton, 1 August 1749, quoted in Schutz, *Shirley*, p. 140.

circumstances forced him to deal. Provincial politicians were proud of their American heritage, which, they thought, not only differentiated them from their English cousins, but made them better men—more virtuous, less tempted by corruption, and more committed to the principles of a free government in a free society. But they were also fascinated by the sophistication and apparent worldliness of London, its subtlety, its emphasis on manners, and, above all, its politics. Whether consciously or not, Shirley capitalized on this fascination. He was an Englishman who practiced politics as though he were in London. Those who joined his coalition were treated as insiders, as men who understood politics for what it was—a not always idealistic blend of practical considerations, personal ambitions, and noble plans. If some grumbled that "Shirley never promoted any man for merit alone," most professionals readily acquiesced in his programs and accepted his leadership.[20]

In coping with the monetary crisis, Shirley had benefited from the fact that Newcastle would scarcely remove one of his own creatures without first giving him an opportunity to restore order to the province. Thus the professionals had been confronted with a governor who, for the immediate future at least, was immune to attempts to oust him. After 1742 Shirley faced the same dilemma confronting every provincial chief executive: he would have to prevent the creation of an opposition strong enough to embarrass him in London. Moreover, Shirley's own policies had created a second problem. To insure a tractable House and build a coalition which the rural majority would support, he had embarked on a program of controlled inflation. To quiet the conservatives upset by this policy, he needed an economic boom which would make them forget their animosity toward a paper currency. Finally, he had to mollify the professionals whose own

[20] JA-Diary, 1:109.

appetite for offices, militia commissions, and supply contracts was almost insatiable. In short, Shirley needed to augment the resources traditionally available to a royal governor.

Shirley was an expansionist by conviction. He believed that the destiny of the empire lay in expelling the French from North America and in making the Caribbean an English preserve. He began his administration sensing that at last England was ready to exert herself militarily in the western hemisphere. This belief in the efficacy of war had a practical as well as an ideological foundation. The potential political dividends war would bring were imposing. War always justified inflationary economic policies and, particularly when England footed part of the bill and sent her own provisioners into American ports, always meant new outlets for domestic products, a loosening of credit, and an increase in the amount of silver in circulation. The merchant would be happy. Shirley would have an ample supply of contracts and commissions with which to reward the professionals. And the back-bencher would tell his constituents that their government followed policies designed to improve local economic conditions. In June 1744, as the war in Europe broadened into a general contest among continental powers, France provided the opportunity Shirley needed. Quickly, brutally, French troops assaulted a small outpost in Nova Scotia, and by July they threatened New England's vital cod fisheries. Shirley had his war.

His response was characteristically well organized, thorough, and intense. On his own initiative he proposed that Massachusetts take the lead in capturing Louisbourg, the French fort on Cape Breton. Playing on Newcastle's desire to dispatch as few British troops as possible to North America and the province's own pride and ambition, Shirley secured approval of a massive assault on the fort. Initially the campaign yielded all that he desired. Raising and equipping a 3600-man expeditionary force provided enough patronage to satiate all but the most ambitious men. Newcastle was both impressed and gratified by Shirley's efforts, and when the fort fell with miraculously little loss of life, Shirley controlled a proud, united, and prosperous province.[21]

Ironically, the Louisbourg campaign also engendered a new crisis, which, in large measure, was again a product of England's refusal to understand the provincials' own aspirations and political sensibilities and of the opportunism of some professionals who, sensing that the governor was vulnerable, moved for his ouster. Initially, Shirley had hoped that the fall of Louisbourg would be followed by a Canadian campaign in which provincial troops and commanders would play major roles. Newcastle did approve an expedition but gave the major commands to professional British soldiers. Meanwhile London celebrated the fall of the French fort, giving major credit, not to the colonial troops who had compelled the fort's surrender, but to the English naval squadron that supported the assault. Then Newcastle ruled against further action in the American theater. The end of the war spelled an end to the province's economic boom. No longer did English specie flow into Massachusetts, and no longer could Shirley offer lucrative supply contracts to local merchants. The sudden contraction of the economy plunged Massachusetts into near-depression conditions. Specie became scarce, the value of paper currency again spiraled downward, taxes became impossible to collect, and in the House, inflationists clamored for more paper.

Shirley also faced the task of auditing the accounts of the Louisbourg campaign, which England had promised to under-

---

[21] Shirley to Newcastle, 14 January 1744–5, Lincoln, *Correspondence of Shirley,* 1:161–65; Schutz, *Shirley,* pp. 80–122, 131–45.

write. This arduous chore was made more difficult by sloppy accounting procedures and petty attempts to inflate the value of services rendered. An honest audit would not enhance Shirley's popularity within the province, and to forward inflated accounts would make him vulnerable in London. The major threat came from his old supporter and ally Samuel Waldo, who had been a brigadier in the campaign. When Shirley received the accounts, he was amazed to find that Waldo had not been content with petty larceny. Yet Shirley hesitated to accuse Waldo of fraud. The merchant and his friends had long been bulwarks of Shirley's coalition. To alienate them meant recasting his entire system of political alliances. Shirley played for time, appealing to Waldo's sense of loyalty and offering to compromise on the question of the accounts. Waldo, however, had different plans. Deciding that Shirley was now vulnerable, he moved openly into opposition. In London Christopher Kilby, the province's agent and now Waldo's ally, began undermining Shirley's English support and laying the groundwork for a campaign to topple the governor.

In London, Kilby and Shirley's son-in-law William Bollan negotiated for the promised parliamentary grant reimbursing Massachusetts for the Louisbourg campaign. But from the beginning the two men worked at cross-purposes, as Kilby assiduously and with near success lobbied to have Parliament use the promised specie grant to retire the province's paper currency. Kilby spoke for fiscal conservatives within the province and for English merchants trading with America who feared the Assembly would use the funds as a substitute for tax revenues and thus continue the cycle of inflation and deficit financing. Kilby's efforts also posed a personal threat to Shirley. If Parliament reneged on its promise and instead compelled the adoption of a specie currency, Shirley's influence within the House would have ended. Shirley, working through Bollan, averted this calamity, but only at the price of promising to secure voluntarily what Parliament proposed to accomplish by edict.[22]

As Shirley set out to redeem this promise, the home government further complicated his task. In the fall of 1748, Boston learned the details of the Treaty of Aix-la-Chapelle, which concluded the War of the Austrian Succession. Massachusetts, long disillusioned by the war, received the final blow to its pride. Restoring the status quo, England returned Louisbourg to France. Shirley had promised glory and security. The empire, as he had portrayed it, would wax strong, extending English influence and enriching all who shared and contributed to the fulfillment of that dream. But having been presented with a military victory permanently crippling France's ability to harass New England, British politicians had turned their backs on America, restoring France's military capability and belittling New England's military efforts. Daniel Fowle, who, as the editor of the *Independent Advertiser,* had opposed the war and ridiculed Shirley's dreams of military conquest, asked the obvious question: "Who can tell what will be the consequence of this peace in times to come? Perhaps this goodly land itself—even this beloved country, may share the same fate with this its conquest—may be the purchase of a future peace." [23]

Nonetheless, Shirley began the contest to impose a specie currency on a disaffected province with three important advantages. Thomas Hutchinson had won the speakership without Shirley's support, but once installed in the speaker's chair, he had become a powerful adjunct to Shirley's coalition. For a decade Hutchin-

[22] Malcolm Freiberg, "William Bollan, Agent of Massachusetts," *More Books* 23 (1948): 91–98. See also Shirley to Newcastle, 23 January 1749–50, Lincoln, *Correspondence of Shirley,* 1:493–98.
[23] *Independent Advertiser,* 14 November, 1748. See also "Report of Joint House-Council Committee," in *Documentary History of the State of Maine,* ed. James Phinney Baxter et al., 24 vols. (Portland, Me., 1869–1916), 12:236–41.

son had pleaded for the adoption of a specie currency. Having already drafted a plan of his own, his power and skill compelled the House seriously to entertain redeeming Shirley's promise. Moreover, the opposition itself was in trouble. Kilby, for his attempts to divert the grant, had been dismissed as an agent. Within the House, Waldo's supporters could make fiery speeches, but with the exception of James Allen, none could match the administration's spokesmen in legislative experience and skill. And with Allen expelled from the Assembly for personally attacking Shirley, only the entrenched bias against a specie currency swelled the opposition's ranks.

But more important, perhaps, Shirley was able to depend on the loyalty of the province's political community. The House never recorded the ayes and nays on redemption, but an embittered James Allen later published a list of forty representatives who allegedly voted to return the province to a specie currency.[24] If Allen's list was accurate—and there seems little reason to doubt its authenticity—then the contest over a specie currency illustrates Shirley's ability to maneuver within the legislative arena. Probably seventeen Assembly leaders voted on the issue of whether or not to sanction a specie currency. Twelve sided with the administration despite the leadership's normal disunity on economic issues. The two most important converts to hard money were Hale and Choate. For these traditional leaders of the Assembly's inflationist majority, the question of a specie currency posed a personal dilemma. For a decade they had served as the chief architects of the province's inflationary fiscal and monetary policies. But they were also loyal lieutenants of the administration. If the failure to redeem Shirley's promise resulted in the appointment of a new governor, their special power and influence would have ended. Whatever their reasons,

[24] [James Allen], *A Letter to the Freeholders of Boston* (Boston, 1749).

Hale and Choate voted for redemption and were apparently responsible for convincing enough back-benchers to support the measure to give the administration a three-vote victory.[25]

The establishment of a specie currency redeemed Shirley's promise. If the terms of the 1749 Currency Act were more inflationary than the program espoused by Parliament, still the new policy was voluntarily adopted and all the unpleasantness of a parliamentary edict avoided. But Shirley was aware that political pressure rather than popular sentiment had secured his victory. To the Duke of Bedford he predicted new elections would produce an Assembly much less sympathetic to administration proposals. "I could not answer for another Assembly's passing the like act," he told the Duke, "because . . . the election of members of the Assembly is annual, and it is uncertain what turn the passing of this act may give to ensuing elections." In May 1749 provincial voters verified Shirley's prediction with a vengeance. Absent from the new Assembly were at least twenty men who had yielded to administration pressure and voted for a specie currency. Hutchinson, as the acknowledged author of the act, was an expected casualty, but more disturbing was Hale's defeat.[26] Still, to Shirley the struggle was worth the price. In September, having secured his domestic victory, he departed for London to defend himself against Waldo's attacks.

The difference between Shirley's and Belcher's responses to similar crises is striking. Belcher had survived ten turbulent years as governor, a considerable feat in itself. But by 1741 he had exhausted his political capital. He had dominated provincial politics without ever really persuading the provincials he served their true interests. His attempts to manipulate the political system, while often successful, had eventually alienated the pro-

[25] See the statistical appendix.
[26] Shirley to Bedford, 31 January 1748–9, Lincoln, *Correspondence of Shirley*, 1:467. *A&R*, 3:430–41.

fessional politicians on whom every governor depended for support. In a crisis his mistakes came back to haunt and then to destroy him.

Shirley, on the other hand, surmounted his difficulties because he was always a convincing political leader. His eight years in office had increased, rather than restricted, his maneuverability. He was able to approach the Assembly as a politician rather than as a spokesman of a royal prerogative. Having neutralized the constitutional conflicts that for three generations separated governor and Assembly, Shirley was free to make his compromises, to build his coalitions, and to consider policy issues as questions of practical politics. Of equal importance, Shirley had made himself the principal politician within the province, and this enabled him to dominate, if not control, the province's political community.

While Shirley was in London, the leaders of his coalition demonstrated just how extensive the governor's influence was. During the governor's absence, Hutchinson, Choate, and Hutchinson's brother-in-law Andrew Oliver were responsible for protecting the administration's interests and dealing with Waldo's attempts to stir up local opposition. Then in January 1750 the General Court elected William Bollan permanent agent and thus assured Shirley a loyal spokesman in London as well as defeating Waldo's attempts to have one of his own allies elected to the post. Joseph Heath, writing to Waldo, described what happened:

> Our state artificers omit nothing in their power, that may tend to support Mr. Shirley's interest . . . which is very natural to such whose only aim is, to continue to ride under the chief rider and accordingly on the 19th . . . after much management was brought on the choice of an agent. The votes were divided between Doctor Avery and Mr. Bollan, the former had the majority

in the House, but 19 out of 21 at the Board being for the latter he was chosen.

Another Waldo ally put the case more succinctly: "Many are surprised that Mr. B[olla]n should be chosen. . . . [To] Mr. S[hirle]y and his prime minister T. H[utchinso]n we owe our acknowledgment for this." [27]

Though a consummate master at the game of colonial politics, Shirley was too much an Englishman not to chafe at the chaotic nature of the colonial political arena. There was always the irrational and the unpredictable to upset even the most cleverly designed legislative programs. In 1754 he asked the representatives to increase tax revenues in order to pay for improved defenses. The House responded by proposing an expanded excise on rum. The measure itself, which solved none of the problems created by increased defense expenditures, was inconsequential, and yet it embroiled the General Court in a seven-month dispute. For Shirley the excise controversy was a near disaster, straining his coalition, delaying his legislative program, and accentuating domestic divisions. To end the deadlock he tried a half-dozen expedients. During the early stages of the dispute, he remained scrupulously neutral and was probably responsible for having Hale, Choate, and four other administration spokesmen abstain from voting on the measure. When the bill passed the House and then squeaked through the Council (largely because Hutchinson was absent), Shirley attempted to sidetrack the issue by having the House send the bill to the constituencies, a gambit usually employed to kill potentially divisive measures.

[27] Heath to Waldo, 29 January 1749–50, Massachusetts Archives (State House), Boston, Mass., 53:484–85. Sparhawk to Waldo, 8 March 1749–50, ibid., pp. 494–95.

But this time the maneuver only broadened the scope of the controversy. For the next five months the excise bill tied up the General Court, and Shirley ended the crisis only at the price of finally assenting to a bill he believed was poorly conceived and knew would enrage much of the province. To the Board of Trade he justified his action:

> The supply of the Treasury, my Lords, for the current year had been now obstructed for six months after the usual time of making it; no funds raised for discharging the growing debts of the province; many of the soldiers and all the officers and servants of the government were suffering by being kept out of their pay; great sums of money were wanting to purchase fire arms and powder, which the province stood in need of, and every part of his majesty's service labored, all occasioned by the suspending of my consent to the late excise bill.[28]

The excise controversy, probably better than any other dispute during Shirley's administration, demonstrated the inherent independence of the Assembly's majority and its potential for disrupting, if not destroying, an orderly decision-making process. In the long run, of course, the uncertainty and confusion thus introduced into politics was a by-product of the Assembly's permissive procedures. But for Shirley that uncertainty was a constant irritant, not because he disliked responsive political institutions, but because his own political style assumed a rational, pragmatic, and efficient political system.

But only reforming the system itself would have made provincial politics more rational. Neither a reflective politician nor an ideologue, Shirley spent little time mentally refashioning the provincial government. He correctly sensed that the benefits gained by a reordering of local political institutions would never

[28] Shirley to the Lords of Trade, 12 January 1755, *A&R*, 3:828.

offset the turmoil and resistance that any reorganization would engender. His only suggestion for reform came in 1743 when he asked the Board of Trade to restrict the creation of new towns. The problem, he pointed out, was that an ever-expanding Assembly in which every town was entitled to at least one representative inevitably diluted the Council's influence and independence. Shirley was even more disturbed by the right of towns with more than 120 families to elect two representatives. Currently, only Boston, Ipswich, and Salem, among the scores of towns entitled to do so, regularly elected more than one representative. "But," as Shirley told the Board,

> still they have it in their power upon an extraordinary emergency to double and almost treble their numbers, which they would not fail to do, if they should be desirous of disputing any point with his majesty's governor, which they might suspect their ordinary members would not carry against his influence in the House.[29]

Then in 1749 in compliance with a request from Newcastle, Shirley drafted a plan of government for Nova Scotia. For the most part he suggested simply duplicating the Massachusetts charter complete with its liberal voting qualifications and its elected Council. Yet Shirley's proposed alterations clearly reflected his own conception of the problems he faced in Massachusetts. To decrease the independence of the civil service, he proposed giving the governor the right to remove political appointees. In Massachusetts this alteration would have quadrupled the patronage at his disposal while allowing him to enforce a rigid discipline within the political community. And to decrease the prospect of local disturbances infecting the entire province, Shirley suggested that the home government retain the right to

[29] Shirley to the Lords of Trade, 18 October 1742, *A&R*, 3:70.

review town charters. Still upset by Boston's 1747 impressment riot and the apparent inability of local authorities to control that town's "mobish factious spirit," Shirley justified giving the home government a larger voice in determining the structure of town government by citing the "bad influence" Boston's mob "had upon the other towns . . . and upon their own members which are generally leading men in the Assembly." [30]

Shirley saved his most revisionist proposals for the Assembly itself. Arguing that the House ought to contain a fixed number of representatives, he went on to suggest that each county, rather than each town, should elect a small number of representatives. In effect, Shirley's proposal would have all but eliminated the parochial back-bencher from the Assembly. Only men with substantial reputations and considerable political skill would be capable of winning election as county representatives. Thus the House would have been numerically, as well as politically, dominated by professionals who ordinarily were more sympathetic to the governor's attempts to enact comprehensive legislative programs. Finally, Shirley proposed making Assembly elections triennial. Immune to short-range fluctuations in popular sentiment and freed from the responsibility of annually seeking reelection, House members would come to share the governor's appreciation for order and stability and would be more willing to support temporarily unpopular programs promising solutions to the myriad problems plaguing the province.

> I have been induced [he concluded] to propose this alteration from the experience I have had of the inconvenience occasioned to his majesty's government in . . . Massachusetts . . . by annual

[30] William Shirley, "General Heads of a Plan of Civil Government for Nova Scotia," Lincoln, *Correspondence of Shirley,* I:474. Shirley to Willard, 18 November 1747, ibid., pp. 406–09.

elections of members to serve in the Assembly; it being a general observation that the Assembly at the latter end of the year endeavor to distinguish themselves by their opposition, and moving some popular points in order to recommend themselves to their constituents, and secure their elections for the ensuing year, which (among other inconveniences) is wholly owing to the frequency of their elections.[31]

Shirley had no desire to oppress the people. He was above all a politician who sought order and efficiency rather than arbitrary power. In his view the degree of local autonomy and responsiveness unbalanced the Massachusetts political system, and he wanted nothing more than to right that balance by increasing the government's stability. The tension between political stability and popular control has always confronted free men attempting to govern themselves. Shirley's answer to this dilemma was to reinforce the ability of a central government to make effective political decisions within a framework in which ultimate political control still belonged to the people. He wanted a rational political order in which the rules of the game were constant and public policy was the domain of professional politicians who understood and accepted the pragmatic nature of politics. This, he believed, coupled with the people's ability to check but not cripple their government, in itself guaranteed political responsibility.

Shirley's fifteen years in office testified to the inherent strength of the governor's position. Without constitutionally reforming the government, he made the politics of Massachusetts reflect his own political style. If the government had been remodeled along the lines he suggested, perhaps a less resourceful governor could

---

[31] Shirley, "Plan of Civil Government," ibid., p. 473.

have achieved the same success. But necessarily he would have to accept Shirley's basic premise: that governing a proud, potentially wealthy, and important colony was essentially a political process. A governor had an obligation to protect the larger interest of the empire and to honor the demands made by English politicians. But he would achieve these goals, not by echoing abstract defenses of prerogative authority, but rather by seeking accommodations with local political leaders and by pursuing policies designed to mollify the inherent distrust most provincials felt toward royal authority. Finally, he would have to convince London that the imperial system would work only if the province could be prevailed upon to comply voluntarily with the empire's trade and defense policies. Twice Shirley persuaded London of the wisdom of this advice: first in 1741, when the home government abandoned its attempts to reform the province's currency, and again in 1754, when Shirley convinced the Board of Trade not to disallow the rum excise. His letter to the Board spelled out the kind of local sovereignty England would have to grant if she expected a prosperous and cooperative empire:

> I am persuaded that a disallowance of this act would greatly shock the minds of the representatives and disserve his majesty's government, especially at this crisis: though they have learned to acquiesce in being restrained from passing acts . . . which intrench upon his majesty's prerogative, which . . . weaken his government, affect the foreign trade of Great Britain . . . diminish her trade to the colonies, lessen the consumption of commodities . . . ; but to restrain them . . . by disallowance of their acts . . . from laying a duty upon liquors . . . I say my Lords to restrain them from exercising such a discretionary power among themselves would, I am satisfied, grieve them very much at this time, and might tend to quench that ready spirit, which they

have hitherto exerted for promoting his majesty's service and the general welfare of his dominions upon the continent; and might also disserve his government in other respects.[32]

When England sought more than this, the provincial political system no longer provided governors with sufficient opportunities to guide their governments.

[32] Shirley to the Lords of Trade, 12 January 1755, *A&R*, 3:828–29.

7

Robert Hale and John Choate, Insiders

LTHOUGH HE MET SHIRLEY ONLY ONCE, IT WAS GEORGE
Washington who best summed up the governor's impact
on American leaders. "I have had the honor to be introduced to . . . Mr. Shirley whose character and appearance has
perfectly charmed me, as I think every word and every action
discovers the gentleman and great politician." [1] Much of Shirley's
influence depended on this capacity to inspire awe in other men,
particularly other politicians. Yet still to be contended with was
the Assembly's rank and file, that ever-changing group of local
politicians largely unaffected by contests for patronage and preferment.

Although inexperienced in the legislative arena, the back-
bencher was scarcely a political novice. In his own community
he was probably a militia officer and town official, suggesting
that it was not the extent but rather the scope of his political
experience and personal interests which separated him from the
Assembly's traditional leadership. The top rung in a local po-

[1] Washington to Fairfax, 23 April 1755, John C. Fitzpatrick, ed., *The Writings of George Washington*, 39 vols. (Washington, D.C.: Government Printing Office, 1931–1944), 1:116.

litical system with its own rewards and criteria of success, a seat in the Assembly allowed the rural back-bencher to join in the excitement which filled Boston when the General Court was sitting and gave him an opportunity to rub elbows with the province's great and near great. The House was also a place to hear of attractive ventures and to make new political friends. But these pursuits hardly occupied all or even most of the back-bencher's considerable energy. The chance to seek minor rewards was not sufficient inducement to keep a member away from farm and community for weeks on end. For the back-bencher, service in the House primarily bestowed an opportunity to work for favorable legislation, which in eighteenth-century America meant taxes other men would have to pay, fiscal policies encouraging the economic development of his own community, and defense measures which did not require the mobilization of his militia company or the drafting of his sons.

Indeed the back-bencher was essentially a localist inclined to view all political problems in terms of his own constituency. "The business of a representative," one pamphlet reminded the Assembly's rural majority, "is to consult the good of the whole body, and to take particular care that the town he represents does not pay a greater proportion of the charges of government than it ought to do; and in case the town wants any relief or assistance, in any affairs that are under the cognizance of the General Assembly, that he use his utmost endeavors to accomplish it."[2] In concrete terms this meant more paper money, larger government deficits, and, above all, lower taxes. These goals could be secured by cutting back defense expenditures, limiting the scale of governmental operations, and shifting more

[2] [William Fletcher], *The Good of the Community Impartially Considered* (Boston, 1754), p. 47.

of the tax burden to the province's mercantile communities. But most of these goals could also be attained by simply doing nothing. An Assembly that failed to enact taxes, approve military campaigns, and vote appropriations would guarantee continued inflation, deficit financing, and military passivity. With their own constituencies unharmed by legislative stalemates, most back-benchers found it easy and often profitable to obstruct legislative proceedings and thwart administration programs.

The Shirley legislative style evolved largely in response to the dilemma posed by the back-bencher's parochialism. By avoiding constitutional conflicts, he also avoided reinforcing the back-bencher's inherent hostility to executive authority. Shirley was, as he never tired of reminding the House, a reasonable man, more concerned with solving common problems than with asserting prerogatives or debating abstract concepts of power. He convinced the House, and more particularly the suspicious back-bencher, that the issues separating them were amenable to political solutions. He was able to condition the House to accept his programs as comprehensive attempts to deal with the province's problems. Successfully resolving the currency crisis at the outset of his administration, Shirley established his reputation as a resourceful problem solver. Thereafter the rank and file trusted him, relied on his ability to suggest legislative solutions, and accepted him as a legitimate political leader.

Yet primary responsibility for lining up the necessary votes within the House belonged, not to Shirley, but to his friends, to Thomas Hutchinson and James Otis, Sr., and above all to Robert Hale and John Choate. If Shirley was the professional executive, the master of patronage politics and imperial intrigue, Hale and Choate were the complete legislators, men persuaded of the necessity of compromise, adroit at understanding and diverting the Assembly's rural majority, secure and comfortable in their role as administration insiders.

Of the two, John Choate was the less complex in his devotion to the political arena. He was also something of an upstart. In the latter part of the seventeenth century, his father had cleared and then populated Hog's Island, the largest of several drumlins a glacier had thrown up along the edge of Ipswich Bay. There he raised his nine children—John being the fourth—developed his orchards, tended his cattle, and shepherded a flock of sheep whose mutton was celebrated throughout Essex County. In time, Thomas Choate became a Massachusetts rarity, a wealthy farmer entitled to the sobriquet "governor," a captaincy in the militia, and, for three undistinguished terms, Ipswich's seat in the General Court.[3]

Beyond the status and wealth of his father, we know little about John Choate's youth. Presumably he was taught to read and write at home and then later traveled the causeway to the Chebaco parish school where at best he was an indifferent student. There he probably came under the influence of John Wise, who dominated Chebaco parish for thirty years, impressing his rustic congregation as much with his physical prowess as with his ready wit, which could reduce even the most glib to mumbling silence. Eventually Choate read law, possibly with one of Ipswich's six justices on the Essex County Court of Common Pleas, and, when ready, he began to take over some of his father's local responsibilities. Then in 1731 Ipswich sent the younger Choate to the House of Representatives. Despite the parochialism of his Ipswich apprenticeship, Choate was immediately welcomed

[3] Katharine Thompson, manuscript on "John Choate" (to be published by Ipswich Historical Society), p. 4.

into the Assembly's inner circle. Then in 1735 he withdrew
from the House, choosing instead to concentrate on local affairs
and his growing family. Such tranquillity lasted less than a
year. In the spring of 1736 an epidemic of throat distemper
swept through Essex County, killing more than fourteen hundred children, including Choate's four. He now abandoned
Hog's Island and moved his wife into the center of Ipswich,
where they occupied the old Compton tavern. They converted it
into a large, rather dark, but nonetheless imposing mansion.
Two years later Miriam Choate again bore him an heir; but the
child died before his first birthday.[4]

In part the void left by his children's death was now filled by
the Land Bank. Perhaps Choate's faith in paper money was a
legacy from John Wise. Or, like many landed men, perhaps he
saw in the Bank a means of converting his idle acreage into
liquid assets. Choate returned to politics over the issue, rewin-
ning his seat in the Assembly during the 1741 election, which
turned on the question of the Bank. As a calculated insult to
Belcher, the House elected Choate speaker. Never one to ignore
a challenge, Belcher negated the election, and Choate joined
Hale and the Bank's other directors in tolling the last hours of
the Belcher administration.[5]

If Choate was something of an upstart, an uneducated but
naturally gifted politician trading on landed wealth inherited
from his father, Robert Hale was much more to the manner
born. The Hales had arrived with Winthrop and then staked
out their special claim to Beverly, a small seacoast community
nestled in the shadow of Salem. The first Hale was a blacksmith,
the second a Harvard-trained minister who lent imprimatur and

[4] Ibid., pp. 6–11.
[5] *MHJ*, 19:15.

guidance to the witchcraft prosecutions at Salem Village. Once his wife stood accused, however, Thomas Hale admitted his own doubts about the process. Later he collected his musings into a *Modest Enquiry into the Nature of Witchcraft*. The next Hale followed in his father's footsteps, returning to assist and later inherit the Beverly congregation. Robert Hale, Sr., also served as the town's physician, an occupation he in turn passed on to his son Robert, who became the third generation of Hales to trek to Cambridge for a public education.[6]

Unlike father and grandfather, Robert Hale never occupied a pulpit. His father died when Robert was still at Harvard, and when his mother married John Gilman of Exeter, New Hampshire, Hale joined them as the community's schoolmaster. After his marriage to his stepsister, Hale returned to Massachusetts. He finished his medical studies and then reclaimed his family's place in Beverly's affairs.

Besides being the community's physician, Hale was the keeper of Beverly's vital statistics, something of an architectural historian, and the town's leading intellect, a collector of books and paintings, and would-be historian of England's imperial adventures.[7] Then, in the early 1730s, Hale became Beverly's principal spokesman in the General Court. Like Choate, he quickly assumed a major role in House affairs. By 1735 Hale was an outspoken critic of Belcher and shortly thereafter became the principal architect of the legislative strategy that ended the governor's influence within the Assembly. Whether Hale's opposition to Belcher or his advocacy of soft money came first is a moot question. Unlike Choate, Hale was essentially a cerebral legislator, an inventor as well as an enactor of policies and programs. Al-

---

[6] *SHG*, 6:483–89.

[7] *The Essex Institute Historical Collections* 5 (1863): 16, 6 (1864): 46; Robert Hale, "Chronicle Relating to Some Remarkable Transactions," Curwin Papers, American Antiquarian Society, Worcester, Mass.

though fiscal orthodoxy left little room for imaginative invention, toying with a paper currency was an innovator's delight. It was probably the experimental nature of the Land Bank as much as its economic and political potential which intrigued Hale. Whatever the cause—opposition to Belcher, commitment to inflation, or fascination with the engineering of a currency— Hale joined Choate and a handful of other House leaders in organizing the enterprise in the summer of 1739.

The Bank was but the first of a long series of collaborations between the two men. The financial liability they shared after the Bank's demise encouraged their political cooperation, as did their position as administration insiders during Shirley's governorship. Then, too, the proximity of their communities and joint responsibilities in Essex County—Hale as sheriff and Choate first as a member and later as chief justice of the Court of Common Pleas—extended the value of their alliance beyond Assembly chamber and governor's parlor. By the mid 1740s, their association, probably more than any other eighteenth-century political alliance, came to depend as much upon mutual affection as political reciprocity. Thereafter the two men worked not so much together as in tandem, drawing and building on their friendship and complementing the talents each brought to their quest for influence within the political arena.

Because the House kept its doors closed, we can only speculate about which arguments convinced the back-bencher to surmount his parochialism. In a mixed chamber such as the Massachusetts House of Representatives, however, style probably played a preeminent role. The back-bencher needed to be flattered, cajoled, wheedled—all without being insulted. Thus the leader had to appear both above and yet somehow on the same plane as the back-bencher—one of the boys, so to speak, who had inside information. Apparently this was Choate's unique talent. What little remains of his correspondence reflects the same earthy wit that Wise had used with such devastating effectiveness. In an age when letters were not only formal but stilted, Choate could write to the Council's half of a joint committee of war:

> · As I am now an unworthy member (if I take it right) of what one may call the lower house of the committee of war I must (providence permitting) set out the beginning of next week . . . [and since] I propose no long stay in Boston . . . [I hope] that a little cash may be ready, a necessary article you will easily think in traveling and doing business. I hope I ask this with propriety as I am told the upper house of this constitution have the purse strings." [8]

Humor was only part of Choate's charm. By eighteenth-century standards he was painfully unlettered—not illiterate, just incapable of writing either clearly or correctly. To some, Choate's awkwardness was a source of amazement as well as chagrin. When Choate died in 1765, Nathan Bowen, one of Marblehead's more substantial merchants, noted in his diary:

> John Choate, Esq., died at Ipswich! He was Judge of Probate . . . [in] which office his ignorance was not his only foible; his pride put him upon attempts vastly beyond his power. To see the judge laboring to distribute an estate among a number of orphans by the common and ordinary rules of arithmetic would naturally put a man in mind of the fable of the monkey turned carpenter. What pity he had not died three years and one month sooner!

But to the back-bencher, Choate's fabled syntax and grammar only made him more attractive, more trustworthy. Here was the governor's confidant who spoke and wrote as they did—only with more understanding and self-confidence. Once Choate submitted a committee report to the speaker that was all but il-

[8] Choate to the Committee of War, Massachusetts Archives (State House), Boston, Mass., 55:151.

legible. When the speaker chided him for his poor penmanship, Choate replied, "Now the paper before you contains the word the—t-h-e—, which I think is spelled quite right. If you cannot read it, pass it to me, and I will read it myself." [9] The guffaws must have reverberated through the chamber.

Hale's talents lay in other areas. He was a superb tactician, a calculator of the right moment to introduce legislation or call for a vote or move for adjournment. And so thoroughly could he dominate the Assembly that, despite the general anonymity of official documents, Hale's name was blazoned across the pages of the House Journal: "a motion was made by the member from *Beverly*"; or, "Dr. Hale . . . reported according to order"; or again, the bill was "read a second time and recommitted to Dr. *Hale* to fill up the blanks." [10] Hale alone won such recognition.

At the same time he was, along with Thomas Hutchinson, the Assembly's most gifted innovator. He probably never intended to pass the supply bill he drafted in the fall of 1741. Rather it was a tactical ploy, a measure extreme enough to frighten fiscal conservatives into supporting Shirley's program of moderate inflation. Nevertheless, the bill marks one of the rare eighteenth-century attempts to restructure economic relationships by manipulating fiscal and monetary policy. Its key provision required the provincial treasurer to receive and store a long list of agricultural commodities accepted in lieu of taxes. Only when the market price of a commodity equaled the arbitrary rate established by the General Court could the treasurer sell the goods. Hale's bill was nothing less than an eighteenth-century forerunner of the New Deal's plan for an ever-normal granary. [11]

Because Shirley's political style avoided confrontation and kept

[9] *Essex Institute Historical Collections* 91 (1955): 267. Ibid., 3 (1861): 11n.
[10] *MHJ*, 18:184, 19:25, 203.
[11] *MHJ*, 19:105–11.

the legislative process within doors, Hale's and Choate's historical visibility is inversely related to their political skill. They were the men behind the scenes, and there they intended to remain. Only when accident or miscalculation embroiled the House in public controversy did their roles become clear. One such occasion was the excise controversy of 1754. In June, Shirley should have accepted the measure as an unwise but necessary sop to the Assembly's rural majority. Instead he had sent the bill to the towns for their consideration, and the colony's seaports publicly condemned the measure as both economically discriminatory and unconstitutional. More ominously, the Assembly's rural majority still insisted that Shirley accept the bill, and to drive the point home the Assembly blocked all legislation until he did so. Not until the end of November was the administration able to move. Then Shirley granted a week's recess while speaker of the House Thomas Hubbard asked Choate to draft a new excise bill. During the recess Choate, probably in conjunction with William Brattle, the Cambridge gadfly who had led the battle for the excise, worked out the elaborate charade that the administration hoped would end the deadlock. When the House reconvened on December 4, Choate introduced a bill which taxed, not the consumption, but rather the distillation of rum—an even more direct challenge to the seacoast's recreational pursuits. On cue, the province's rum industry condemned the plan, and the next morning a delegation of distillers trooped into the House personally to plead its case. Within twenty-four hours Choate's bill was dead, and Brattle, Choate, and Boston's James Bowdoin began drafting yet another version of the bill. Over the next two weeks the House enacted, the Council concurred, and Shirley signed a compromise incorporating the report initially submitted to the House on June 1. Private consumption would be taxed and every citizen would have to swear an oath as to how much rum he annually imbibed.[12]

Stunned by their defeat, the anti-excise forces rushed into print with their own account of the Assembly's perfidy. One writer, obviously privy to the Assembly's proceedings if not actually a member of the House, charged that the distillers had no sooner left the chamber than Brattle had reintroduced the original excise bill:

> The motion was very powerfully supported by many, whose names I hope will be published and remembered; particularly by Col. *Ch - - - e* of *Ip - - - - h* and Col. *H - l -* of *B - v - r - y*. These men after strenuously laboring the revival of this bill, and finding it had many votes to spare, gave their negative, when it passed to be engrossed. And now they may say with truth, that they voted for the bill, and that they voted against it; just as it happens to suit their convenience.[13]

Such was the nature of effective legislative leadership.

The controversy over the establishment of a specie currency which embroiled the House in 1748 offers a second opportunity to speculate on the kinds of resources available to men like Hale and Choate. Again the public nature of the controversy momentarily relaxed the taboo against revealing what transpired within doors. This time it was James Allen, angered as much by his expulsion from the House as by the creation of a specie currency, who violated the privacy of Assembly proceedings by naming the forty representatives who had voted for hard money. Allen's list allows us both to recreate the probable alignments

---

[12] *MHJ*, 21:38, 46, 140–41; Kenneth Colegrove, "New England Town Mandates," *Publications of the Colonial Society of Massachusetts* 21 (1919): 435; *A&R*, 3:782–90; Otis to Otis, 18 December 1754, Otis Papers, Massachusetts Historical Society, Boston, Mass.
[13] *The Review* (Boston, 1754), p. 5.

the issue created and to identify those representatives most open to the blandishments of an aggressive administration.[14]

Hale and Choate were joined by Hutchinson, then speaker of the House, in coordinating the administration's forces on this issue. Hutchinson, already the author of the bill, was probably the chief tactician. The administration entered the fray with two serious handicaps, however. Despite the length of the session, the bill was brought before a full House—at least seventy-seven representatives were present to vote on the measure. More ominous was the absence of the Hampshire County delegation, a group of men remarkable in their devotion to a specie currency. On the other hand, Hale and Choate's willingness to support the measure and Allen's expulsion from the House stripped the rural majority of effective leadership. All that remained to them were numbers. The administration's job was to further reduce even this basic resource.[15]

The administration probably began by guaranteeing the loyalty of the Assembly's leadership. Of the seventeen leaders present and voting, twelve supported a specie currency. Next to be won over were nine of the eleven back-benchers from communities whose representatives had regularly supported fiscal conservatism. James Otis was probably responsible for keeping Barnstable County in line, and this meant three more votes for passage in addition to his own. At this point the administration had twenty-four of the necessary thirty-nine votes. But now the pickings got slimmer. Out of a group of representatives with little inclina-

[14] [James Allen], *A Letter to the Freeholders of Boston* (Boston, 1749); see the statistical appendix.

[15] Shirley to Bedford, 31 January 1748–9, Charles Henry Lincoln, ed., *The Correspondence of William Shirley*, 2 vols. (New York: Macmillan, 1912), 1:467; Thomas Hutchinson, *The History of the Colony and Province of Massachusetts-Bay*, ed. Lawrence Shaw Mayo, 3 vols. (Cambridge, Mass.: Harvard University Press, 1936), 2:336–37; Hutchinson to Williams, 1 February 1748–9, Williams Papers, Massachusetts Historical Society, Boston, Mass.

tion to support a specie currency and without ties to the administration, Hutchinson, Hale, and Choate needed at least fifteen votes. Nine came from a group of representatives who were either in at least their fourth term or were justices of the peace. More experienced than most back-benchers, more independent, perhaps, of their constituencies, and more acclimated to the needs and strategies of the administration, this group, to be sure, voted against a specie currency, but not overwhelmingly. The remaining votes came from an odd assortment of men. One was a Harvard graduate and Maine land speculator. Two more came from communities with highly erratic voting records on economic issues. The remaining four, for whatever reason, gave the administration its majority.

The vote reflects the unique blending of questions of policy and matters of patronage which so often influenced political decisions. The core of the administration's majority was almost equally made up of representatives who were political professionals—and thus dependent on the administration—and men who came from constituencies which, for a variety of reasons, believed fiscal orthodoxy best served their own interests. The balance of the necessary votes depended on the leaders' ability to convince the often passive back-bencher to support the administration. Thus Otis was able to deliver the votes of his Barnstable neighbors while Hale and Choate went to work on the more experienced back-benchers—men who knew and presumably trusted their judgments.

Providing majorities for Shirley's legislative program was the prime, but not the sole, responsibility of the administration insider. Part of his task was to serve as a conduit of information from and to the governor. Men like Hale and Choate served also as official emissaries to other colonies. Because so much of

Shirley's program centered around military adventures, there was a constant need to inform and enlist Massachusetts' neighbors in the never-ending struggle against French encroachment. Early in 1755, as the American phase of the Seven Years War commenced in earnest, Shirley dispatched a series of emissaries to coordinate colonial defenses. Jack Shirley was sent to Philadelphia to meet with Robert Morris; Choate and Samuel Wells journeyed to Hartford; and Hale went to see Benning Wentworth in New Hampshire.[16]

Hale's mission was particularly delicate. Tucked in the shadow of her larger neighbor, New Hampshire saw herself as something akin to a poor cousin, more in need of protection than glory. If Massachusetts felt the call of crown and empire, so be it; New Hampshire men had more important things to do at home. From this turnip Hale was to squeeze five hundred soldiers for an expedition against Crown Point.

Because he had once lived there and continued on friendly terms with Wentworth, Hale received only a brief set of instructions from Shirley. The governor suggested that he lobby directly with the New Hampshire Assembly if possible, and he included a number of dispatches Hale could reveal if he thought they would prove helpful.[17] Beyond this he was on his own. Hale arrived on March 12, delivered his dispatches to Wentworth, and then watched the governor address his wary Assembly. Informing the representatives of the planned attack against Crown Point and New Hampshire's predestined role in this holy war against Catholic France, Wentworth sounded the trumpet of imperial glory.

[16] John A. Schutz, *William Shirley, King's Governor of Massachusetts* (Chapel Hill: University of North Carolina Press, 1961), pp. 191–93.
[17] Shirley to Hale, 22 February, 4 and 16 March 1755, Curwin Papers, American Antiquarian Society, Worcester, Mass.; "Journal of a Voyage to Nova Scotia Made by Robert Hale," *Essex Institute Collections* 42 (1906): 219.

Let it not hereafter be told in Gath, or ever published in the streets of Askelon, that so many populous colonies of Protestants should tamely submit to entail irretrievable misery and bondage on the generations yet to be born (a burden which our fathers could not bear), without making our strongest efforts to repel the threatening danger. . . . Nothing therefore remains to be done on our part, but to make use of the means which I hope to find fully advised to in the report of your committee.[18]

Duly impressed, the committee recommended a force of six hundred men provided with sufficient stores to see them to their rendezvous with the rest of the expedition. The House, however, cut this figure to four hundred men and delayed their departure until sufficient outside funds could be found to underwrite the entire effort. At this juncture, Hale asked permission to address the Assembly. The arguments he encountered were later summed up by Theodore Atkinson, the colony's secretary. Hale had brought with him "the quota each government was to bear from his own Court ready assigned: thus, 600 men from New Hampshire, 1200 from Boston, 500 Rhode Island, 1000 Connecticut, 800 New York. We could not compare our quota with any other governments . . . so well as the Massachusetts with whom we never bore more than 1 to 10, and we have been often concerned in expeditions together." Hale replied that Massachusetts' quota was in addition to the separate regiments raised by Shirley and William Pepperrell; to which the New Hampshire men replied, "in *those four* regiments there were more than a double proportion of New Hampshire men, and though they might have the credit of raising those regiments they had not a proportion of Massachusetts men in them, which was really the case." And so it went: Hale cajoling and the New Hampshire Assembly re-

---

[18] "Journal of the House," New Hampshire, *Provincial Papers, Documents and Records relating to . . . New Hampshire from 1749 to 1763*, ed. Nathaniel Bouton, 7 vols. (Nashua, N.H., 1867–73), 6 (1872): 357.

calling sacrifices already made. Eventually Hale played his trump card. Without really saying so, he left the impression that New Hampshire's troops would be supplied and perhaps paid by those southern colonies not contributing directly to the expedition. If New Hampshire would get the men to Albany, they would be taken care of. Beguiled, the Assembly reversed itself and authorized the targeted six hundred men and in due course dispatched them to Albany.[19] Shirley had asked nothing more.

Men with this kind of talent are always rare. In part, Hale remained loyal to Shirley because he enjoyed exercising the kind of power available to the governor's friends. Yet he, along with Choate, expected more tangible rewards as well. As he promised, Shirley protected both men from the Land Bank's creditors; and both received more than their share of patronage. In 1745, as the Louisbourg campaign generated the expected political largess, Hale and Choate stood first in line, each receiving a regiment, the scarlet tunic of a colonel, and the recruiting bonuses which accompanied the responsibilities of command.[20]

Unfortunately Hale was no soldier; more than that, he carried the instincts of the politician with him onto the battlefield, and that proved disastrous. Assigned to Samuel Waldo's artillery brigade, Hale demonstrated a marked aversion to committing his troops to battle. They were, after all, his neighbors, and more than that, his constituents. Against all precedent he kept two companies as a personal guard and thus kept them out of harm's way. Consistently he refused or sidestepped requests to supply details for particularly hazardous assignments. When one of his

[19] Atkinson to Thomlinson, 9 December 1755, ibid., pp. 439–40. "Journal of the House," ibid., pp. 362–63; Phips to Wentworth, 10 April 1755, ibid., pp. 377–78.
[20] Thompson, "Choate," p. 33; SHG, 6:486.

companies was put ashore against his wishes, Hale suggested that since plenty of volunteers could be found (presumably from someone else's regiment), his company might be put to better use elsewhere. "I refer it to your honor's judgment," he wrote Pepperrell, "whether it might not be best for orders to go to every colonel to draw out of his regiment such as are willing to stay instead of those desirous to go. For those unwilling to work will do but little work, though very well there."[21]

More revealing was his letter to Pepperrell requesting leave for Josiah Pratt, now a lieutenant in Hale's regiment and formerly a member of the Assembly.

> Captain Pratt . . . represents to me the peculiar situation of his circumstances, which seem to require his being at home for a short space, and has therefore urged me to give your honor this trouble, and I wish it were in my power to gratify him and everyone else; your honor will please to consider whether, as he has the credit in his town to have been last year one of the House and more troops are sent for, he may not be very serviceable in spiriting up the people in that part of the country where he lives to enlist themselves, especially as they have hitherto sent perhaps a much less proportion than the towns eastward. One person of intelligence and command from the army is worth a hundred hearsays and will beget more confidence. Another argument in his favor may be that although he has been a captain in his town, yet here is but a lieutenant to Major Hodges, which he is uneasy at and would therefore do his utmost to raise a company in order to have the command of them. I beg your honor to forgive my importunity and doubt not of your determining what will in this affair be most for the general good and that will be perfectly satisfactory to all.[22]

[21] Hale to Pepperrell, 14 April 1745, Pepperrell Papers, Massachusetts Historical Society, Boston, Mass. See also Pepperrell to Cushing, 9 August 1745, *Collections of the Massachusetts Historical Society*, 6th ser. 10 (1899): 354.
[22] Hale to Pepperrell, n.d., Pepperrell Papers.

Pratt, as a client instead of a subordinate, was to be carefully wooed, not simply ordered about.

Even before Louisbourg fell, Pepperrell, Waldo, and the chaotic nature of the expedition had exhausted Hale's meager patience. Once from Canso and again from the siege camp outside Louisbourg, Hale appealed directly to Shirley. The pretext for his letters was his belief that Pepperrell had prevented the regimental surgeon from ministering to Hale's men. But clearly what was at stake was Hale's own pride and self-importance. Shirley did not respond until after Pepperrell's army occupied the fortress, and by then Shirley had no intention of taking Hale's side in what was at best a petty quarrel. Pepperrell was now the savior of North America and a logical candidate to lead further expeditions against the French. Not wishing to antagonize his commander, Shirley instead chose to mollify his friend. He dispatched a second surgeon to minister specifically to Hale's regiment and tried to calm its commander by reporting Choate's imminent departure for Louisbourg. Still the governor could not avoid a mild reproach. "I gave you a regiment purely out of the regard I had for you and should have been glad if the command might have been of service to your interests. . . . In the meantime . . . perfect harmony between the field officers [should] now be a more certain method of establishing the character of every gentleman there." [23]

Hale should have taken Shirley's advice. But as the summer wore on and conditions within the captured fort deteriorated, Hale returned to the attack, this time lodging his complaints with Thomas Hubbard, then speaker of the House. It was a rather obvious strategy. All of New England had rejoiced at Louisbourg's fall; by July, however, ominous news was coming

[23] Shirley to Hale, 23 June 1745, Gilman Papers, Massachusetts Historical Society, Boston, Mass. See also Hale to Shirley, 19 May and 18 June 1745, Pepperrell Papers.

from the north. Probably less than two hundred men died during the siege—a fact more attributable to French incompetence than Pepperrell's tactical brilliance: the French had built their impregnable fortress in a valley and then failed to secure the high ground that commanded its western approaches. But once inside, New Englanders began dying like flies. A month after the fort's surrender, Boston was rife with reports of disease, desertion, and mutiny. With the troops wanting to go home and the General Court inclined to let them, Hale renewed his charge that Pepperrell had mistreated his men. And still he got nowhere. The speaker never presented his letter to the House. Then Pepperrell sent Hubbard a letter of his own, suggesting that if Hale had obeyed orders and kept his men in their assigned stations they would not have lacked medical attention. Indeed only Hale's ill health "has freed him from my manifest resentment for his disobedience." [24] But Hubbard, no doubt in conjunction with Shirley, had already decided to suppress the quarrel, as much for Hale's own protection as for the sake of the administration's attempts to stabilize conditions at Louisbourg. Pepperrell's letter, with its damaging charge of insubordination, was similarly denied a public airing.

In September, Hale returned to Boston and again took his place on the floor of the House. Perhaps chastised and clearly delighted to return to his old haunts, he now abandoned direct attacks on Pepperrell. But for the first time in his career Hale became an expert on questions of military preparedness. He chaired the committee reviewing Massachusetts' frontier forces and was probably responsible for establishing troop levels substantially below Shirley's expectations. Predictably Hale took an equal interest in the conditions at Louisbourg. In November

---

[24] Pepperrell to Cushing, 9 August 1745, *Collections of the Massachusetts Historical Society*, 6th ser. 10 (1899): 354. Robert Emmet Wall, Jr., "Louisbourg, 1745," *New England Quarterly* 37 (1964): 65–83.

Pepperrell's son-in-law would write from Boston, "I am every day expecting to go to the General Court where I understand Colonel Hale determines to be very troublesome." [25] Hale was unlikely to forget that he had been abused.

Nor did Shirley forget. If Pepperrell was too important to threaten with Hale's petty complaint, the good doctor could not be left to sulk. In 1746 Shirley appointed Hale sheriff of Essex County. The office assuaged Hale's pride and added measurably to his affluence. He now built a handsome addition to the family mansion in Beverly; and lest anyone doubt the source of his new prosperity, his enlarged front hall prominently displayed the spontoon emblematic of the office of sheriff.[26]

Of the two men's careers, however, Choate's was the fuller, more robust one. Hale was too much the House man, the legislative tactician and administration insider, to survive Shirley's departure in 1756. He suffered a significant loss of influence when the new governor sought other alliances and different friends. Even Hale's major contributions—the Land Bank and Shirley's espousal of inflationary economics—reflected the ephemeral nature of his career. Choate, on the other hand, successfully transferred his loyalty and thus maintained his influence, capping his career with a seat on the Council. And in the end it was Choate, rather than Hale or Otis or even Hutchinson, who left the most visible monument to his political prowess.

For years Ipswich had lamented that its old wooden bridge tarnished the town's reputation as a thriving seaport. Then in 1764 the selectmen asked Choate to propose a new crossing more in keeping with the town's increased trade and prosperity. Choate reported a new bridge was well within the town's grasp,

[25] Sparhawk to Pepperrell [November 1745], *Collections of the Massachusetts Historical Society*, 6th ser. 10 (1899): 389. *MHJ*, 22:103.
[26] Thompson, "Choate," p. 47.

provided the County Court of General Sessions would underwrite half of the cost. Choate presided over that court.[27]

Having secured financing for his bridge, Choate next supervised its design and construction. He was now in his sixty-
seventh year, without new honors to win or alliances to forge or
friends to make. Having done it all, he now set about building
his own monument. Most eighteenth-century bridges were comparatively simple structures: two stone abutments and pillars
spanned by timbers and rails. Choate built a better bridge, an
all-stone structure of archways patterned, probably unconsciously,
after those of ancient Rome. The bridge, probably the first in
America to incorporate the stone arch, still stands today.

There is a significant postscript to this story, one perhaps
more revealing of what motivated the colonial politician than
even Choate's desire to leave an indelible mark upon his community. Not until 1792 did Ipswich properly name the crossing
"Choate's Bridge." By then most of the principals were dead,
and those remaining had forgotten the curious imbroglio that
signaled the bridge's completion. The town had no sooner celebrated its new marvel—a rebuke to those who had named the
pile of rocks "Choate's Folly"—than the good judge presented
his bill for services rendered. The town was aghast: Choate expected to be paid for the privilege of altering Ipswich's landscape.
And when the town refused to allow this "extraordinary charge
for care and trouble," Choate indignantly protested. There was,
after all, a principle at issue, a question of proper status and
deference to be settled. Only after the town reversed itself,
granting to Choate what was rightfully his, did he donate his
fee to the town treasury.[28] It was the last act of one of the eighteenth-century's more gifted professionals.

[27] Ibid., pp. 1–3.
[28] Thomas Franklin Waters, *Ipswich in the Massachusetts Bay Colony*, 2 vols.
(Ipswich, Mass.: The Ipswich Historical Society, 1905), 1:445.

8

Thomas Hancock, Merchant

"SEABOARD MASSACHUSETTS," SAMUEL ELIOT MORISON OBSERVED in 1921, "has never known such a thing as a social democracy; and in seaboard Massachusetts, as elsewhere, inequalities of wealth have made political democracy a sham. Few town meetings have been held near tidewater where the voice of shipowner, merchant, or master mariner did not carry more weight, than that of fisherman, counting-room clerk, or common seaman. . . . The 'quality' dressed differently from the poor and middle classes, lived in finer houses, expected and received deference, and 'ran' their communities because they controlled the working capital of ships and goods." [1] The appeal of Morison's brief assertion lies in its eminent reasonableness, although more concrete proof of the merchants' ability to dominate political men and institutions is easily supplied. Of Massachusett's four native-born royal governors, for example, two, Jonathan Belcher and Thomas Hutchinson, were merchants with imposing fortunes. Then, too, Council lists were literally a Who's Who of the trading community. All the great

[1] Samuel Eliot Morison, *The Maritime History of Massachusetts, 1783–1860* (Boston: Houghton Mifflin, 1921), p. 23.

men of commerce served there: the Hutchinsons, Bowdoins, Apthorps, Ervings, Hancocks, Allens, and Belchers. Even in the House their weight was felt. Few merchants elected as representatives failed to become leaders; and speakers of the House, more often than not, were Boston men of commerce, men like the three Thomases—Hutchinson, Hubbard, and Cushing.

Morison's observation of the political importance of the New England trader in the eighteenth century comes at the beginning of a work dealing with Massachusetts' commercial expansion after the Revolution. Most descriptions of the merchant's political prowess have been just that, introductory remarks in which the author merely summed up what everyone already knew before embarking on more interesting—and presumably controversial —themes. Arthur Meier Schlesinger's *The Colonial Merchant and the American Revolution* remains the only major study of the merchants' role in the struggle for independence; and Schlesinger, like Morison, simply assumed that merchants exerted an inordinate influence on public affairs prior to 1763.

But is the assumption warranted? Could merchants, as Schlesinger maintains, "be expected to carry things their own way"? For Schlesinger, the classic exercise of this pervasive influence came when "the merchants of Boston contributed powerfully toward defeating the Land Bank . . . which was being pushed by the farmers and debtor class generally in the province." Unfortunately, Schlesinger based this conclusion on the work of Andrew McFarland Davis; and Davis, in turn, was so alarmed by the great banking and monetary debates of the 1890s, that he portrayed the Land Bank as a revolutionary scheme which sound-thinking, sound-money merchants defeated in the nick of time.[2] Actually the Land Bank crisis did pit the bulk of the

[2] Arthur Meier Schlesinger, *The Colonial Merchants and the American Revolution* (New York: Columbia University Press, 1917), p. 29. See particularly

province's merchants against a majority of their neighbors. But from the merchants' perspective, the results of this confrontation were hardly gratifying. They had sought not so much to suppress the Bank as to stabilize the province's chaotic finances, ending, once and for all, Massachusetts' experiments with an inflationary paper currency. Instead, the General Court, with Shirley's cooperation, had initiated yet another inflationary spiral. Such was the merchants' influence in 1741.

The Land Bank crisis can be explained by only two hypotheses, neither of which supports the traditional image of an all-powerful mercantile establishment. Either these merchants could not force the province to adopt monetary policies favorable to their interests; or these merchants used whatever influence they possessed to achieve goals not associated with questions of monetary policy—or, for that matter, with public policy in general.

To choose, in any definitive sense, between these alternative explanations is not possible, largely because we have no way of measuring the merchants' actual influence within the political system. For example, the absence of organized trading associations or spokesmen makes it impossible even to define a merchant position on most issues. Then, too, the historically visible merchants are, with one exception, those who became professional politicians. And whether someone like Thomas Hutchinson enjoyed political power because he was a merchant or because he was a professional politician is a moot question. The one exception is Thomas Hancock; there exists a remarkably rich collection of his letters covering nearly three decades of intense business and political activity. Although we cannot measure the merchants' aggregate influence within the political system, we can ask—and tentatively answer—two questions: What did Hancock

Andrew McFarland Davis, *Currency and Banking in the Province of the Massachusetts-Bay*, 2 vols. (New York: Macmillan, 1900, 1901).

want that only effective political action could supply? And, did he possess sufficient resources to achieve his political goals?

Even in an age crowded with Horatio Alger heroes, Thomas Hancock's emergence as a commercial magnate and entrepreneur is one of the great success stories of the eighteenth century. The second son of a country parson, Hancock grew up in Lexington, then little more than a frontier village of cantankerous farmers, crude buildings, and an impoverished minister. Because his father could afford to send only his eldest son John to Harvard, Thomas was apprenticed to a Boston bookmaker. By 1724 Hancock had completed his apprenticeship and opened a small shop of his own under the sign of the Bible and three crowns. There he observed the central axiom of eighteenth-century economic life: one succeeds only if one has important friends. Of the Bostonians Hancock met, and whom he obviously impressed, by far the most helpful was Daniel Henchman, a middling merchant with valuable connections and a marriageable daughter. By 1730 Henchman was Hancock's occasional partner, and father-in-law.[3]

Indeed it was the Henchman alliance that allowed Hancock to abandon the status of petty retailer. He continued to deal in books, but he did so now as a wholesaler and agent for British publishing firms. He also invested in a paper factory and bought shares in ships bound for Atlantic ports of call. By the middle of the decade he was heavily involved in the export of New England whale oil, and by 1740, still three years shy of his fortieth birthday, Hancock was a wealthy man, a Boston selectman, and a merchant with a network of friends and contacts spread throughout the Atlantic empire. By every standard of eighteenth-

[3] W. T. Baxter, *The House of Hancock* (Cambridge, Mass.: Harvard University Press, 1945), pp. 3–10. Unless otherwise noted all biographical information has been drawn from this source.

century society, Hancock had arrived. He dressed opulently, built a mansion on Beacon Hill, rode through the town in an ornate coach, and was welcomed in Boston's best homes, including the governor's house on Marlborough Street.

By 1740 Hancock had also acquired an impressive number of political resources, not the least of which were the obvious advantages great wealth conferred. In the seventeenth century, merchants, having grown rich providing the essentials on which survival depended, had been suspect members of a community which considered itself knit together by bonds of Christian charity. Robert Keayne, the most successful of New England's first-generation merchants, summed up the inevitable conflict between religious and economic goals when he asked, "If I value my estate to be worth 4000^{lb} or thereabouts, how could I get such an estate with a good conscience or without oppression in my calling?" Keayne had good reason to be concerned. Twice he had felt the wrath of a Puritan community of which he considered himself an integral part. The most serious clash had come when the merchant stood accused of exorbitant profiteering because he sold six-penny nails for 10d. Fined £200 and publicly rebuked by no less a personage than John Cotton, Keayne's final mortification was to be censured by his own congregation, at which time the merchant "did, with tears, acknowledge and bewail his covetous and corrupt heart." The experience rankled. For fifteen years Keayne brooded, finally venting his frustration in a will and apologia which, in some one hundred fifty-eight folio pages, rehearsed the story of the nails in agonizing detail. Not satisfied with protesting his innocence and virtue, Keayne directed that his public bequest be used to build a Town House that would serve as a merchant exchange as well as the seat of government. At least symbolically, Keayne reminded Massachusetts that her future depended as much on the cleverness of her merchants as on the wisdom of her rulers.[4]

By the middle of the eighteenth century, Massachusetts had more than absorbed this lesson. Great wealth still bred envy, and some provincials continued to excoriate the merchant for corrupting the morals of a struggling people and impoverishing an essentially agrarian economy. But such rhetoric had lost its sting. Great wealth—and in the eighteenth century, trading was the only way New Englanders could establish fortunes—had become a symbol of success, a testament to a man's industry and frugality. Not only were men of wealth looked up to, they became pillars of society entitled to the deference due such lofty status.

But wealth also brought more tangible political rewards. If overt bribery seldom figured in provincial politics, the English officials responsible for dispensing favors important to the colonists exhibited a more cosmopolitan attitude towards the giving of gifts. Both Jonathan Belcher and William Shirley benefited from timely investments of cash, and Hancock thought nothing of instructing his London agent, "The Board [of Ordnance] will . . . want agents at Cape Briton. . . . If a few guineas be necessary to expend in the affair, let it be done, and anything else you . . . think proper." Cash, of course, was not the only form a gift could take. A man of wealth, particularly a trader, could repay a friendly official in a variety of ways. Sometimes Hancock extended credit to temporarily embarrassed officials. Frequently he provided hospitality, allowing visiting dignitaries to consider his home their Boston headquarters. Or, as was most often the case,

[4] Boston, Mass., *Report of the Record Commissioners of the City of Boston,* 39 vols. (Boston, 1881–1909), 10:47. James Savage, ed., *The History of New England by John Winthrop,* 2 vols. (Boston, 1925), 1:316. See also Bernard Bailyn, "The *Apologia* of Robert Keayne," *William and Mary Quarterly,* 3d ser. 7 (1950): 568–77; Perry Miller, *The New England Mind: From Colony to Province* (Cambridge, Mass.: Harvard University Press, 1953), pp. 40–52.

the merchant demonstrated his appreciation by filling the official's cupboard with well-cured beef or oysters or a cask of expensive Madeira or some item the official particularly fancied. Just after the fall of Louisbourg, Hancock wrote a brief though awkward note to Charles Knowles, the new governor of Nova Scotia. Hancock wanted the contract to supply the garrison at Louisbourg, and since he had never met Knowles, Hancock could only cite his obvious credentials and close by adding, "in anything I may be serviceable to your excellency . . . I beg sir you will command." Hancock sent the letter via John Bastide, another English official already friendly to the merchant's interests. Bastide, however, held the letter, suggesting that an alternative approach to Knowles might be more strategic: "I did not think it seasonable to deliver your letter to Mr. Knowles, but as he luckily asked me to get some friend of mine to procure him some pigeons for breed I pitched on you which will give you an opening for a correspondence." Hancock needed little urging. Two weeks later he replied, "Am very glad, you have put it in my power to oblige Mr. Knowles with the pigeons, which please to tell him I am providing, and they shall be sent by first good opportunity." [5]

Whether or not Hancock bestowed such favors on local politicians is not known. He did extend credit to Shirley and was, at one time, an agent for Thomas Pownall, Shirley's successor.[6] There is, moreover, no reason to believe that he was not of equal service to the province's other leaders, particularly those who were friends as well as political allies.

Finally, wealth conferred one not-so-obvious advantage. Eight-

[5] Hancock to Bernard, 29 July 1745, Thomas Hancock Letter Book, Massachusetts Historical Society, Boston, Mass. (hereafter cited as THLB-MHS). Hancock to Knowles, 8 July 1746, vol. 11, fol. 1, Hancock Papers, Baker Library, Harvard University, Cambridge, Mass. (hereafter cited as HP-BL). Bastide to Hancock, 2 August 1746, ibid. Hancock to Bastide, 15 August 1746, ibid.
[6] Hancock to Kilby, 23 June 1753, and Hancock to Pownall, 14 July and 24 September 1760, Hancock Letter Book (TH4), Baker Library, Harvard University, Cambridge, Mass. (hereafter cited as TH4-BL).

eenth-century Boston was, as Hancock told his young ward, "an expensive town," where only a man of means could expect to move in the best circles. Life among the city's principal merchants was not unlike that among their English counterparts. The Hancock mansion on Beacon Hill boasted luxuriant gardens, a well-stocked library, the latest in London furnishings, and a liveried slave doubling as butler and majordomo. In such surroundings cavorted a provincial upper-class which, among other notables, always included the province's royal governor. Men like William Shirley were undoubtedly good company. They often knew London well and gave a cosmopolitan air to any gathering they attended. But the dinner party was also an important political arena, an opportunity to consume good food and engage the province's chief executive in frank conversation. To move in the same social circle as the governor conferred its own kind of influence, an influence Hancock regularly used to good advantage. Once he assured the lieutenant governor of Louisbourg that he could be of material assistance by simply reporting, "Governor Shirley with a number of gentlemen dine with me today when I will have the pleasure of drinking you[r] good health." Or, Bastide, anxious to become a captain in a regiment commanded by Shirley, entreated, "I hope you always take the necessary caution in my behalf to cultivate a good understanding between Governor Shirley and I." Hancock could reply, "I dined with Governor Shirley this day . . . when I took the opportunity of making your compliments to him. I told him you were informed he had come to fill up the vacancy in his regiment, etc., to which he said he had no advises nor orders, and I am certain there is nothing in the report. The vacancy I hope you'll get." [7]

Although the third largest city in America, Hancock's Boston

[7] Hancock to Kilby, 18 February 1758, ibid. Hancock to Hopson, 11 September 1747, HP-BL, vol. 10, fol. 4. Bastide to Hancock, 3 August 1746, ibid., fol. 3. Hancock to Bastide, 15 August 1746, ibid., vol. 11, fol. 1.

was still very much a small town. One could still walk from one end of it to the other in less than an hour, and if Boston no longer exhibited that celebrated cohesion of the New England village, little that happened ever escaped the notice of the city's always curious inhabitants. The commercial district was even more compact, occupying a mile of frontage stretching from Clark's shipyard in the North End to the South Battery opposite the Long Wharf. More important, this central district was the hub not only of the city, but of the province as well. And here, from his headquarters on Ann Street, Hancock ran his growing empire. Next door was Faneuil Hall, home of the Boston town meeting; the Court House was less than five blocks away; and the governor's mansion only another minute beyond the square. When men gathered to make decisions they gathered here, at the Court House or in the governor's parlor or in one of the dozen taverns supplying the rum New Englanders thought essential for good company.[8]

Political influence is often a function of distance, and in a province where travel was difficult and written communications rare, the problem of distance was particularly important. It explains why, for example, Connecticut Valley river gods played such ambivalent roles within the provincial political arena and why, particularly in times of crisis, there was always somebody demanding that the Court abandon Boston for more tranquil surroundings like those provided by rural Watertown. Yet in itself Hancock's proximity to the seat of power was only part of the special advantage he, and merchants like him, enjoyed. To men attuned to the modern business world, commercial practices in eighteenth-century Boston often appear desultory. Bookkeeping was at best sloppy and organized inventories unheard of. Men

[8] Walter Muir Whitehill, *Boston: A Topographical History* (Cambridge, Mass.: Harvard University Press, 1959), pp. 22–46.

formed complex partnerships without ever committing their agreements to writing, and a man's word was his bond. And then there was the custom of closing down the business district daily between one and four in the afternoon so the merchants could "go on 'change" by congregating at the Court House. These meetings largely compensated for the absence of a more formalized organization. There men sorted out their complex ventures, exchanged business gossip, and launched new enterprises calculated to increase Massachusetts' overseas trade. But whether by design or accident, these gatherings also served a second function. For when the merchant went "on 'change" he mingled as easily with the politicians who occupied the upper floors of the Court House as with the men of commerce who crowded into the building's lobby.[9]

In any enumeration of Hancock's political resources, the importance of these daily sessions should not be underestimated. Simply put, he enjoyed an opportunity denied all but a handful of his countrymen who either lived outside of Boston or were engaged in occupations requiring their constant attendance. In either case, their opportunity to influence public officials was clearly impaired.

No less important was the merchant's familiarity with the political arena—a familiarity which began with a proper appreciation of the province's chief executive. "Depend my friend," Hancock told Christopher Kilby in the spring of 1740, "few of Belcher's enemies will like a change for S[hirle]y." Like that of many Boston merchants, Hancock's skepticism continued well into the second year of Shirley's governorship. Shirley's courting of the Land Bankers and his willingness to experiment with new emissions of paper notes scarcely pleased men of Hancock's persuasion. More critical was Shirley's energetic prosecution of local

[9] *MHJ*, 16:248, 31:162–63; *Boston Evening Post*, 29 January 1738–9; Baxter, *Hancock*, pp. 184–208; *Proceedings of the Massachusetts Historical Society*, 1st ser. 16 (1879): 69.

smugglers—a policy which both enriched the governor and infuri-
ated the merchants. Not until 1743 did Shirley relax his vigilance.
About the same time, he forged an effective though uneasy alliance with Hancock. It assured Shirley of the merchant's support
and strengthened Kilby's hold on the provincial agency.[10]

Shirley's ability to dominate provincial politics both intrigued
and alarmed Hancock. During the winter of 1749, when many
suspected Shirley of wanting his son-in-law William Bollan to
be the agent, Hancock warned Kilby, "The governor's interest
only made you standing agent, and keeps you in, which he did
with great difficulty." Indeed, "should the governor but hold up
his finger, he'd have every vote of both houses" for Bollan. When
Bollan, after replacing Kilby in 1750, resigned from the agency
in 1755, Hancock again pushed Kilby's candidacy and was again
thwarted by Shirley. For Hancock the experience was particularly galling, partly because he had carefully enlisted the aid of
John Erving, a principal Shirley lieutenant in the Council, and
partly because of Shirley's choice of tactics. Though he could
have simply vetoed Kilby's election, Shirley chose instead to deny
him the support of the Assembly's leadership. "I have been deeply
concerned for your election [as] agent," Hancock told Kilby,
"but we lost it, the governor strongly opposing you. . . . He was
hard pressed but to no effect, the most leading members of the
House I got absolutely to promise it should be done in case I
would say the governor would accept . . . you." Hancock's only
recommendation was to "make up the breach between him and
you." Then too, as the estrangement increased, Hancock's own
influence with the governor declined. When Kilby asked about
Shirley's plans for the 1756 campaign against the French, Han-

---

[10] Hancock to Kilby, 17 May 1740, Thomas Hancock Letter Book (TH3), Baker
Library, Harvard University, Cambridge, Mass. (hereafter cited as TH3-BL).
John A. Schutz, *William Shirley, King's Governor of Massachusetts* (Chapel
Hill, University of North Carolina Press, 1961), pp. 64–79.

cock replied, "I know nothing of his matters, he having not been in my house these sixteen months nor I scarcely in his." [11]

Hancock's estimation of the province's other leaders was equally perceptive. He had guessed right in enlisting Erving in Kilby's behalf, for if anyone could put pressure on Shirley it was Erving, a wealthy merchant whose son had recently married the governor's daughter. Hancock also understood the importance of men like Cushing and Hutchinson, both powerful speakers of the House, who could smooth the way for favored enterprises as well as thwart most projects to which they objected. As long as Kilby enjoyed Shirley's patronage, Hutchinson was an invaluable ally. When the Council sent an anti-Kilby resolution to the House, "Mr. Hutchinson [the] speaker was so good as to put it in his pocket, [and] went to the governor and let him see it— (well done this)." Shirley rushed to the Council Chamber where he "was very warm upon it, would not leave the chair . . . till they had recalled that vote and passed your grant." Once Kilby no longer enjoyed the governor's support, Hutchinson became, as Hancock told his friend, "your greatest enemy." Hancock hardly needed to dwell on the consequences of Hutchinson's enmity— there is, he reported simply, "no talk of any grant to pay you." [12]

A second index of Hancock's political knowledge is his comments about lesser-known figures. When John Choate embarked for Louisbourg, Hancock cautioned Bastide, "Take some notice of him; he is a leading man in government here. And at times a necessary one." [13] Hancock also knew which of the Assembly's minor leaders he could enlist in his friend's behalf. One was Roland Cotton, the contentious clerk of the House whom Hancock persuaded to steer Bastide's accounts through the Assembly's

[11] Hancock to Kilby, 10 February 1746–7, THLB-MHS. Hancock to Kilby, 26 June 1755, TH4 BL. Hancock to Kilby, 6 April 1755, ibid.
[12] Hancock to Kilby, 23 January 1746–7, THLB-MHS. Hancock to Kilby, January 17, 1748–9, ibid. See also Schutz, *Shirley*, p. 174.
[13] Hancock to Bastide, 26 April 1746, HP-BL, vol. 10, fol. 1.

balky committee system. Hancock's note to Bastide covering this transaction did not mention the need to repay the clerk, and Cotton was probably enough of a parvenu to be satisfied with a few kind words and a pat on the back.[14] Otis Little, on the other hand, was a much more professional politician, and consequently his relationship with Hancock more clearly involved an exchange of mutual favors. Little's importance, Hancock told Kilby, was his "good interest with the country gentlemen," the Assembly's back-benchers who cast a jaundiced eye on provincial agents who expected salary for occupying a position so beneficial to their own interests. What exactly Little did is not clear, but Kilby did receive his salary and Hancock felt obliged to be of some assistance. Little was interested in Nova Scotian land speculation. Hancock probably refused to invest his own money in Little's enterprise, but when the obliging representative sailed for London to interest English officials in his schemes, Hancock wrote Kilby, "This comes by Major Little to whom I beg your usual civilities, he's your friend and always been so at Court." Still, Little was not of the first importance, and Hancock closed by warning, "As to Mr. Little's circumstances they are unknown to me, be cautious not to go too far." [15]

Hancock's comments about politics reveal a remarkable understanding of the nuances of political manipulation. To be sure, most provincials recognized the inherent importance of the governor's office. They probably also possessed a crude understanding of the mechanics of political action. But precise information about the mechanics of influencing public institutions was simply not part of their political repertoire, partly as a result of their own lack of interest and partly because they were physically distant from the center of power. In sharp contrast, Hancock's knowledge

[14] Hancock to Bastide, 13 May 1745, ibid., fol. 4.
[15] Hancock to Kilby, 14 February 1745–6, THLB-MHS. See also Hancock to Kilby, 23 January and 10 February, 1746–7, ibid.

of the political system was not only firsthand, it was precise. If he appreciated Shirley's strengths, he similarly recognized the governor's weaknesses, particularly his vulnerability to attacks in London. Hancock could also gauge the importance of men like Hutchinson and Choate as well as anticipate what kinds of favors would enlist the services of men like Cotton and Little. Moreover, the merchant knew that speakers of the House could put votes in their pockets and that successful legislative activity often depended upon enlisting the aid of key leaders in order to circumvent the Assembly's committee system. In short, Hancock's understanding of political men and means suggests a familiarity more characteristic of the professional politician than of the political outsider.

Such familiarity raises an obvious question. If wealth, proximity to power, and an accurate understanding of political men and means constituted Hancock's principal resources, what distinguished the merchant from professional politicians like Hutchinson and Cushing, who clearly enjoyed the same basic advantages? The answer lies in the particular use Hancock made of his resources.

New England traders inevitably encountered a variety of obstacles. Not only did they frequently lack suitable exports, but English Navigation Acts denied them some natural markets. Atlantic storms were hazardous, and their cargoes often came under the guns of French privateers and English customs agents. Yet the most vexing obstacle—the one that consumed most of the merchants' time and talent—was a historical accident: England had come to possess a commercial empire before she had established a central banking system capable of standardizing currency exchanges and providing sufficient monetary units to finance commercial expansion. England might have compensated for this deficiency by allowing gold to leave as well as enter the country. But this she was unprepared to do. Consequently she doomed her overseas merchants to a frantic scramble for what the eighteenth century called bills of exchange, what we consider bank checks drawn on business accounts.

Unfortunately, bills of exchange not only came in all shapes and sizes, they were also of questionable value. Least reliable were notes issued by a colonial merchant on his London account. Ordinarily the merchant was sufficiently in debt to his agent that this official consumed most of the sterling credits his clients earned. Only slightly more reliable were notes issued by obscure English firms or merchants located outside of London or Bristol. Next on the scale were bills issued by the English government itself, usually to buy American naval stores or to pay for military operations on the American continent. Theoretically these notes should have been as good as gold, except for the bureaucrats' unfortunate habit of issuing notes before Parliament appropriated the necessary funds. Even when Parliament's generosity matched the bureaucrats' expectations, the Treasury insisted on auditing every account before issuing sterling certificates—a process which could, as in the case of the Louisbourg campaign, take years to complete. In the meantime the merchant held a bill of unknown value redeemable at some future but unspecified date. If he enjoyed sufficient reserves he could hold the note; otherwise he had to sell it at a discounted rate to someone rich enough to engage in currency speculation. The last category of bills of exchange, and by far the most reliable, were notes bearing the imprint of a well-established London or Bristol firm. Because America habitually imported more than she exported, however, these bills were always at a premium and frequently unavailable.[16]

These persistent trade imbalances, rather than the medium of

[16] Baxter, *Hancock*, pp. 11–38, 120–21.

exchange, were the real villains. And it would be an oversimplification of the colonies' economic problems to attribute their trade deficits entirely to the merchants' reliance on bills of exchange. England's restrictive navigation policy along with preferential tax rebates encouraging exports to the colonies clearly played a role, as did the colonists' insatiable appetite for English luxuries and New England's corresponding lack of marketable products. In addition, English habits and customs encouraged speculative enterprises and the extending of credit on the flimsiest kinds of security. For the most part, however, these consequences would have been moderated, if not corrected, had the monetary system itself checked the overly ambitious. Specie transactions, for example, would have forced the merchant to balance his accounts, to import only what his exports justified. Bills of exchange might have fulfilled a similar function, but they didn't and for several obvious reasons. The merchant who accepted a bill of exchange automatically became something of a speculator. Bills of exchange circulating in Boston were at least eight weeks away from the accounts on which they were drawn. To issue notes on the prospect of future earnings was a temptation few colonial merchants resisted. In effect, the merchant relied on the uncertainty of the money market to finance his own enterprises, gambling that his cargoes would reach London ahead of his outstanding notes. When they did not, or when his cargoes earned less than anticipated—a frequent occurrence—the merchant again found himself overextended or, as was more often the case, further in debt to his London agent. A second factor was the role local currencies played in imperial trade. Whenever he could, the merchant paid for domestic products in local notes, which were always worth something less than their face value. The pegging of these exchange rates obviously increased the opportunity for speculation, which once again allowed the merchant to overestimate his actual sterling resources.

In effect, this reliance on bills of exchange created an enormous speculative bubble. But then this was the eighteenth century, and the English were a people who made the lottery a national mania and considered the South Sea bubble great fun while it lasted. Moreover, colonial trade was something more than pure speculation. English manufacturers did find a ready market for their goods, and the colonial merchant, if clever and lucky enough, could grow rich despite a chronic shortage of capital.

Nevertheless, even Englishmen placed some limits on their willingness to gamble. A merchant who never paid his bills eventually stopped getting his supplies, just as merchants possessing valid bills of exchange enjoyed an advantage in terms of both credit and access to English suppliers. The problem, simply put, was to acquire valid bills of exchange. In the long run, those merchants who survived were those whose ingenuity, courage, and skill opened up fresh sources of English sterling credits.[17]

In the early 1730s this was the dilemma facing Hancock. If he intended to compete for either the domestic or West Indian carrying trade, he would have to discover a stable source of bills of exchange. An attempt to become a prime agent of an English publishing firm proved a disaster, as did an attempted paper factory. But either through foresight or luck, Hancock made one wise choice: he became interested in the New England whale. The 1730s marked the first real boom in New England's whaling industry. Not only did the oil sell at a profit, but the trade allowed New Englanders to export directly to the mother country rather than participating in the risky carrying-trade with the West Indies. Hancock, in partnership with William Tyler, was one of

[17] See, for example, Hancock to Kilby, 14 June 1746, Hancock to Bourryau and Schafer, 15 July 1745, THLB-MHS; Hancock to Kilby, 2 July 1750 and 1 May 1754, Hancock to Kilby and Barnard, 30 November 1752, TH4-BL.

the first to establish a network of agents for buying, loading, and shipping the oil to London. He also had the good sense to engage Francis Wilks as his agent. By 1735 Wilks, who then doubled as provincial agent, was so successful at finding buyers for Hancock's oil, that the whale was supplying more than half of Hancock's burgeoning sterling requirements.

Then in 1739 Hancock abruptly abandoned the export of whale oil. With a war against France looming, the merchant saw little future in a trade so obviously liable to French harassment. Nothing so dampened Hancock's normally ebullient spirit. Well into 1740, he was still writing Kilby, "We are in great doubt as to peace or war; if the latter with France the Lord have mercy on us here, for we are in a naked exposed country." But when war came, Hancock proved more optimistic, a reflection, no doubt, of France's initial decision not to become involved in England's war against Spain. And then, wars had their own advantages. "The government," Hancock wrote Kilby, "is now buying provisions and taking up transports, I sold them this day 75 lb pork and beef. Pork @ £8.10s which is cheap." Far more important, however, were new opportunities for currency speculation. "Governor Belcher has received . . . £1300 Sterling in bills of exchange drawn by Blakney on Mr. Pelham. . . . I have the offer of taking what sum I please." What worried Hancock, however, was the bills' true value. "I . . . am a little afraid what fate they may have at home. . . . I told the committee of Council I thought they were not so good as private gentlemen bills, therefore [they] should be sold at a lower advance, and I believe they will be fixed at 400%, which is at least 50% under the now current exchange." Hancock closed by asking Kilby's opinion "whether or no I may be safe in purchasing such bills" since "another opportunity may again happen in the run of the year." [18]

[18] Hancock to Kilby, 23 March 1739–40, TH3-BL. Hancock to Kilby, 2 August 1740, ibid.

Hancock's letter uniquely reflects the intricate mingling of economic and political considerations involved in the merchant's search for valid bills of exchange. Governor Belcher dispensed the notes; the Council determined whether Hancock purchased them at 5:1 or 5½:1, and Kilby, from his London vantage point, discovered whether or not the Treasury would honor Henry Pelham's notes. Hancock need only pay the same attention to politics and politicians that he once paid whales and the English oil market.

He did just that. By 1745 Hancock was a major commercial figure and an accomplished political entrepreneur—he was the governor's crony, a close friend of the province's agent, and, along with Charles Apthorp, the principal contractor for Massachusetts' assault on Louisbourg. But while he celebrated Shirley's great triumph—"this noble expedition for a young country . . . will in all ages make a figure in history"—Hancock also knew that a period of adjustment was at hand. England, slow to take interest in Massachusetts' military problems, but quick to claim the fruits of victory, sent her own agents to dispense contracts for supplying the newly conquered territory. Boston abounded with rumors of a new Canadian expedition commanded by British officers and financed by the English Treasury. These would be exciting times, but only for those with the proper contacts. "I suppose," Hancock told Kilby in the heady aftermath of the fall of Louisbourg, "there will be work for the Board of Ordnance at Cape Briton. . . . I beg you will remember me at the Board, let nothing slip worth taking." [19] Thus began Hancock's campaign to become a prime contractor to the English government.

At times he was almost despondent about his chances for success, though in reality only two competitors seriously threatened him. The first and by far the most resourceful was Charles

[19] Hancock to Kilby, 15 July 1745, THLB-MHS.

Apthorp, reputedly the richest man in Massachusetts. Ordinarily Hancock could have counted on Shirley's support, but not in competition with Apthorp. Shirley, though only tangentially involved with English supply problems, could be of considerable assistance. A few contracts actually passed through his hands and these he could award directly to his friends. More often, however, it was simply the governor's recommendation which London sought and frequently heeded. So crucial, in fact, were Shirley's good offices, that by November Hancock despaired of receiving anything approaching a fair share of the supply business, "Mr. Apthorp [being] . . . in expectation of all advantages, by the interest of Governor Shirley." [20]

Curiously enough, Hancock's other major competitor was James Allen, whose commercial ventures were frequently as turbulent as his political enterprises. Not particularly influential in London, Allen had hit upon a novel scheme for securing exchange contracts; he would simply bid higher than anyone else. Hancock was incensed. How much preferable it would be, he told Kilby, to have the contract "fixed on us, and pray if possible to let the exchange [rate] be fixed by the Board." For Allen to try to bid the price up "is mean and ungentlemanlike in my opinion." But ungentlemanly or not, Hancock would play the game. If a few guineas placed in the right hands failed to solve the problem, "give 10% more than . . . [Allen] offers, let it be what it will." Nor was Hancock above forging a temporary alliance with Apthorp and his London agent, John Thomilson, who, Hancock told Kilby, will "join with you against the attempt Allen may make against us at the Board." Allen was offered the contract, but at a rate not only higher than Hancock's bid, but considerably above Allen's own competitive offer. When Allen refused the contract on those terms, Bastide, as the Board's agent, awarded

[20] Hancock to Kilby, 30 November 1745, ibid.

it jointly to Hancock and Apthorp at a figure substantially lower than was offered Allen. It was hardly necessary for Hancock to add, Bastide's "behavior in this I quite like." [21]

Not so pleasant was the prospect of sharing this or any contract with Apthorp. But there was little Hancock could do. When he learned that Peter Warren as well as Shirley had recommended Apthorp for the Louisbourg contract, Hancock told Kilby, "I trust you have been early enough in favor of me. . . . I should be exceeding desirous to supply the honorable Board of Ordnance for that place separate, but I think I am entitled to the half at least with Mr. Apthorp, and I rely wholly on your good offices herein, having asked no favor of the governor, nor anybody else." [22] While Kilby was rarely able to secure Hancock the whole loaf, the merchant received half shares enough to supply most of his wants.

That at the same time Apthorp was also denied the whole loaf was a testament both to Hancock's own success as a political entrepreneur and the effectiveness of his friends, particularly Kilby and Bastide. Christopher Kilby was one of a handful of New England traders whose travels made them men of two cultures, equally at home amongst their Boston neighbors and the great merchant princes of eighteenth-century London. Bred to commercial pursuits, by his twenty-first birthday Kilby had become a partner of William Clark, a wealthy Boston merchant with an imposing mansion and a minor penchant for politics. As was so often the case, the partnership was cemented by Kilby's marriage to Clark's eldest daughter, Sarah, and while Clark managed the firm's Boston headquarters, young Kilby roamed the Atlantic in search of better markets and more advantageous contacts. Three times Kilby found himself in London, and he came

---

[21] Hancock to Kilby, 22 July 1745, ibid. Hancock to Kilby, 1 August 1745, ibid.
[22] Hancock to Kilby, 30 October 1745, ibid.

to prefer its cosmopolitanism to the more domesticated pursuits of a provincial capital. Elected to the House of Representatives from Boston in 1739, he served but half a term before again embarking for England, this time as the agent of an Assembly bent on reversing Belcher's instructions governing bills of credit. Kilby, however, spent his time assisting Shirley's campaign for the governorship, and was amply rewarded for his efforts by being elected provincial agent in 1741. For all but seven of the next thirty years he lived in London, where he became a principal partner in one of the leading firms supplying the American trade.[23]

Kilby's usefulness to someone like Hancock was immeasurable. He had probably met Newcastle through Shirley; and he used his position as provincial agent to cultivate the Duke of Bedford's friendship. In 1741 the Bostonian had helped the Duke of Grafton arrange a parliamentary election, and some men believed that this, as much as anything, had made Shirley governor.[24] Wealthy, resourceful, well-placed Kilby knew them all, and they in turn introduced him to anyone else worth knowing. When a British expeditionary force was about to embark for Boston, Kilby wrote Hancock:

> I have mentioned you to most of the staff officers on this expedition. Mr. Abercrombie, who is Muster Master General, having directions to you in his pocket-book, and if it should be necessary will introduce you to the general, to whom indeed you'll not need it, but apply to him as early as possible with the use of my name, and I hope he will receive you as my best friend. We have been often together since his return to town, and I believe he has a good opinion of my services in recovering the expedition after it was laid aside.
>
> Pray do him all the service you can, and if you find it not in-

---

[23] Charles Wesley Tuttle, *Capt. Francis Champernowne, The Dutch Conquest of Acadie, and Other Historical Papers* (Boston, 1886), pp. 225–38.

[24] Hutchinson to Lynde, n.d., [F. E. Oliver], ed., *The Diaries of Benjamin Lynde and of Benjamin Lynde, Jr.* (Boston, 1880), pp. 221–23.

convenient offer him a lodging in your house for a night or two, till he can be otherwise accommodated. His power is great and may be useful to you; he is honest, open, and undissembling; you'll like him very well on increasing your acquaintance.[25]

Yet this was only a small reflection of Kilby's importance. In part, he fulfilled the traditional role of a London agent, advising Hancock of current business trends in London, the nature of the sterling market, and, that all important matter, just which bills of exchange were worth accepting and which presented opportunities for profiable speculation. To this Kilby could add information garnered while making his rounds at Whitehall. Provincial agents were not necessarily the first to know what England planned for her American possessions, but ordinarily they were informed long before the ministry publicly announced its intentions. Far more important, however, was Kilby's status as a political insider. Some favors Hancock sought were rather routine, involving little more than a minor position for some friend or ally. Sometimes, however, Hancock went after bigger game. When he learned a new governor for Louisbourg was about to be named, he suggested Samuel Waldo, adding, "I know your interest with the Duke [of Bedford] can do the thing, pray think of it." And because that interest had already contributed to the undoing of one governor and the making of another, Kilby represented an implicit check against any attempt Shirley might make to thwart Hancock's own ambitions. But it was, to use Hancock's phrase, Kilby's "friendship and assistance for the Board of Ordnance" which mattered most and for which Hancock was most indebted to Kilby.[26]

Because few of Kilby's letters to Hancock survive, the exact

---

[25] Kilby to Hancock, 18 July 1746, Tuttle, *Francis Chamerowne,* p. 236.
[26] Hancock to Kilby, 15 December 1746, THLB-MHS. Hancock to Kilby, 14 June 1746, ibid. See also Hancock to Kilby, 30 November 1745 and 17 January 1745–6, ibid.

means the agent used to influence the Board remain a matter of speculation. One apparent ploy, however, was for Kilby to put Hancock in touch with the Board's American representative. In 1745 this was John Henry Bastide, a British army engineer dispatched to Louisbourg to supervise the provisioning of British forces. On a smaller scale, Bastide fulfilled many of the same functions as Kilby did. From his vantage point at Louisbourg, the engineer provided both information and contacts which Hancock used to their best advantage. And, as an official agent allowed considerable latitude over the awarding of contracts, Bastide was in a position to be of direct assistance. Some of his efforts were quite open, like awarding temporary contracts to Hancock pending official confirmation. Other services involved what we—but not necessarily the eighteenth century—would consider questionable practices.[27] Typical of such arrangements was Kilby's 1746 plan to secure Hancock a contract for exchanging government bills for local currency. The problem, Kilby informed Hancock, was that the Board had instructed Bastide to accept the highest bid. To guarantee both victory and profit, Kilby continued, Hancock must discover what his rivals had bid and then act accordingly. "Therefore," Kilby concluded,

> you must fix upon some means of having an offer in Mr. Bastide's hands . . . that may be at least equal if not something exceeding theirs. Can't this be done by a very short proposal on a separate paper and a blank left to be filled up in figures by Mr. Bastide which may make 560 if the others offer at 550, or can't you come at Mr. Bastide in such a way as to put 2 or 3 different proposals into his hands for that to be made use of that he finds necessary. Or (better than either of these ways) for you know he is extremely cautious and scrupulous, can't you employ some very clever fellow at Louisbourg to find out from Captain Bastide at what rate they

---

[27] See particularly HP-BL, vol. 10, fols. 3, 4, and vol. 11, fols. 1, 2; Baxter, *Hancock*, pp. 98, 100–03.

offer, and let him deliver into Captain Bastide's hands your proposals.[28]

Small wonder Hancock thought Bastide's friendship worth cultivating.

To preserve the alliance with Kilby and cultivate the friendship of men like Bastide required a resourcefulness no less impressive. Part of what Hancock supplied the engineer has already been noted: hospitality, credit, a constant supply of luxuries, making life at Louisbourg at least bearable for a man of Bastide's tastes and temperament. But Bastide, no less than Hancock, had his own ambitions, and these, as was so often the case in the eighteenth century, depended heavily on fortuitous political connections. What the engineer wanted in 1745 was a captaincy in a regular British regiment. The obvious spot for Bastide was the regiment given Shirley as a partial reward for the victory at Louisbourg. Although the engineer volunteered to bear the expense of securing a commission, Hancock had a better plan. Shirley apparently agreed to accept Bastide if Kilby could arrange matters in London. Importuned by Hancock, the obliging Kilby "got . . . [Bastide's] commission without a bribe as well as put him first on the list." [29]

Hancock's relationship with Kilby was more complex, in part because genuine bonds of friendship united the two men, in part because Kilby's services carried a higher price tag. Kilby, of course, benefited directly from Hancock's increased trading opportunities. The more Hancock bought, the larger Kilby's commissions. Then, too, whenever Hancock could satisfy his sterling requirements, the

---

[28] Kilby to Hancock, 18 February 1745–6, HP-BL, vol. 7, fol. 1.
[29] Hancock to [Kilby?], n.d., quoted in Baxter, *Hancock,* p. 101. See also Hancock to Bastide, 19 January 1745–6, HP-BL, vol. 10, fol. 4; 14 August 1746, ibid., vol. 11, fol. 1; and Bastide to Hancock, 3 August 1746, ibid., vol. 10, fol. 3.

agent's commissions were that much more valuable. Hancock also made Kilby his prime creditor, entitled to satisfy his own accounts before distributing the remaining bills of exchange to the merchant's other creditors. Even more important, however, were those services Hancock could render in Boston. Kilby's departure for London in 1739 had closely followed the death of his first wife. Apparently anticipating a long sojourn abroad, he had named Hancock guardian of his two daughters. When the girls' maternal grandfather died intestate, Hancock secured the bulk of the estate for his two wards. Thereafter he superintended most of the girls' affairs, including the marriage of Kilby's younger daughter to a Cambridge gentleman of means. Hancock was also Kilby's personal agent in Massachusetts. Like most eighteenth-century merchants, Kilby was both creditor and debtor, and to Hancock fell the responsibility for clearing most of his friend's accounts. Kilby had also left behind a rather nasty lawsuit with Peter Luce. When Luce unexpectedly won the case, Hancock reported, "I went to Governor Shirley directly for advice, and he said by all means appeal. . . . He is very angry at the thing and judges." Hancock then closed in what he hoped was a reassuring tone. "I am extremely angry. . . . Had the governor been in town [earlier], I'd got him to wrote the judges to put it off, and doubt not but it would have been done." [30]

Aside from discharging these financial and personal responsibilities, what Hancock could do best was exert political influence on his friend's behalf. In no small measure, Kilby's influence in London derived from the contacts he made as provincial agent. Hancock was merely repeating what both men already knew when he told Kilby, "The continuance of the agency for the prov-

[30] Hancock to Kilby, 27 August 1746, THLB-MHS. See also Hancock to Kilby, 24 May 1745, ibid.; Hancock to Kilby, 18 February and 1 May 1754, TH4-BL; Tuttle, *Francis Chamerowne*, p. 233.

ince . . . [is] necessary for you to keep footing with the ministry and Duke of Newcastle, etc. . . . Be on your guard, I fear . . . my country may lose your interest on which I greatly depend." [31] A large part of this responsibility, of course, lay with Kilby. As provincial agent he was expected to produce results. In particular, the Assembly's back-benchers expected him to reduce imperial interference in local affairs. And as agent, Kilby was expected to remain loyal to Shirley. Having once benefited from Kilby's influence, Shirley had no intention of letting that power weaken his own position in London. Moreover, Kilby was expected to further Shirley's private ambitions and to protect the governor from political attacks in Whitehall.

This much Kilby could do in London. The remaining responsibility for preserving the agent's political base fell to Hancock. First there was Shirley to contend with. While he might recommend Apthorp for supply contracts, Shirley had no intention of alienating Hancock. One obvious way to mollify the merchant was to continue the alliance with Kilby and thus discourage both merchants from joining the opposition. Shirley played this game with remarkable adroitness. Despite Hancock's repeated lament that Shirley favored Apthorp's interests, Hancock's correspondence revealed no trace of bitterness. Indeed he was more than satisfied with Shirley's performance, a satisfaction no doubt encouraged by the governor's efforts on Kilby's behalf. As long as Kilby's own ambitions did not threaten the stability of Shirley's administration, the informal alliance Hancock had helped forge satisfied everyone. Shirley reaped the benefit of Hancock's support; Kilby remained the province's agent; and Hancock was thus guaranteed "that interest on which I greatly depend." [32]

[31] Hancock to Kilby, 10 February 1746–7, THLB-MHS.
[32] Ibid.

Although Shirley was of substantial assistance in protecting Kilby from attacks in the General Court, primary responsibility for coordinating legislative strategy again fell to Hancock. Most of the merchant's activities in this connection have already been noted: he enlisted the aid of men like Otis Little to mollify the Assembly's potentially hostile back-benchers; he relied on his friendship with Speaker of the House Thomas Cushing to secure the appointment of committees friendly to Kilby; and he made certain that the Assembly honored the agent's accounts and voted him an adequate salary. When Hancock told Kilby, "Yesterday we had voted you £4000 old tenor," the "we" was no more gratuitous than Hancock's promise to "lay in with the governor for the first bills that are drawn by the government." [33]

Hancock's alliance with Kilby—and, to a lesser extent, his affiliation with Bastide—suggests one principal use to which the merchant turned his political resources. Hancock converted these resources into influence, this influence into favors, these favors into a new set of resources with which to purchase political influence in London. Unable to bring pressure on English officials directly, Hancock could, by using his influence within Massachusetts, materially assist men like Kilby and Bastide, who in turn secured what Hancock wanted: government bills of exchange.

To the question, "What did Hancock want that only effective political action could supply?" we now have one answer: he wanted government contracts yielding valid bills of exchange. Was he, then, also interested in influencing public policy?

Unfortunately, Hancock's letter-book for 1740–1745 has not survived, making it impossible to discover his role in the Land Bank crisis. We know only that he was one of 137 merchants who

[33] Hancock to Kilby, 14 February 1745–6, ibid. See also Hancock to Kilby, 27 July 1754, ibid.

publicly refused to accept the Bank's notes and that he was not a subscriber to the Silver Bank.[34] His activities during the 1748–1749 struggle for currency reform, however, are less of a mystery and reveal a curiously ambivalent attitude. "I am," he told Kilby, "in none of the money schemes, hope the best use will be made of [the Parliamentary grant] . . . for the country's good, to which shall be glad to lend a helping hand." Although he offered to help and though his commitment was orthodox enough —"I . . . hope all the paper may some way or other be called in, and paid off, and make a silver currency"—Hancock wrote none of his English friends to persuade Parliament to put restrictions on Massachusetts' use of the Louisbourg reimbursement. And obliquely, at least, he warned Kilby not to become embroiled in any attempt to do so. One can sympathize with Hancock's dilemma. Currency reform was clearly important, but at what price? By December Kilby's own currency schemes had cost him the agency and Hancock a valuable political asset. Then too, to reform only the Massachusetts currency involved as many dangers as advantages. Even after Shirley and Hutchinson had rammed through their redemption program, Hancock complained, "Without an act of Parliament to fix the currency for all the colonies, I think [the present plan] . . . won't serve this province. . . . [I] hope," he concluded, "none of the grant will be paid." But again he did nothing. In his next letter to Kilby, Hancock simply indulged in a little self-pity. "It's time the bills should be sunk in some shape; I pay as tax for 1748 of £1700 old tenor. Cruel it is but two in all the colony pay a higher tax than I do viz. Apthorp and Erving."[35]

[34] *New England Weekly Journal,* 16 September 1740; *Publications of the Colonial Society of Massachusetts* 4 (1910): 199–200.

[35] Hancock to Kilby, 11 March 1747–8, THLB-MHS. Hancock to Kilby, 17 January 1748–9, ibid. Hancock to Kilby, 17 January 1748–9, post script, ibid. See also Hancock to Kilby, 31 December 1748, 13 February 1749–50, ibid., and 19 July 1751, TH4-BL.

Hancock's refusal to become involved in the currency issue is all the more revealing in light of what he could do when properly aroused. In 1750 the General Court placed a new duty on imported coffee, tea, and china. Boston, having waged a long and futile campaign against the excise, next sought to have the bill disallowed.[36] Responsibility for waging this battle before the Privy Council fell jointly to Kilby, retained by the town to coordinate strategy in London, and Boston's principal merchants, who, Hancock reported, "have now [been] desired . . . to write their friends in England . . . and earnestly beg they would unite their interest that the act . . . might not pass." Hancock quickly obliged. To Zachary Bourryau, then a principal Hancock supplier, the Bostonian addressed a long, earnest plea rehearsing those arguments which mattered most to Englishmen trading with America: the act would result in a trade depression; smuggling of Dutch tea would increase; and the East Indian trade would suffer. In a separate letter to Kilby, Hancock repeated the same arguments, adding, "I earnestly beg your instant attention at the Board of Trade and [Privy] Council office, where I doubt not but your interest may be sufficient to put a stop to [the act's] . . . being passed."[37] Nearly two years later, the Privy Council disallowed the tax.

In 1754 Boston again felt itself victimized by a special excise and again hired Kilby to plead its case. This time, however, Hancock was simply an interested bystander. He hoped that Kilby was successful, but only for an obviously personal reason. Hancock had not given up hope of restoring his friend to the agency, and now that Bollan had resigned, the merchant's advice was succinct and to the point. To Kilby's London partner John Barnard, Hancock wrote: "Have him push it with great

[36] *A&R,* 3:495–98, 508–09.
[37] Hancock to Bourryau and Co., 14 July 1750, TH4-BL. Hancock to Kilby, 7 July 1750, ibid.

vigor to show the province his power and interest at the Boards, this may have a good effect upon them and open their eyes."[38]

Only two other questions of public policy elicited a written response from Hancock. In 1747 he warned Kilby to pay closer attention to routine agency business, because "the gentlemen of the Council and House of Representatives are extremely uneasy at you . . . in particular in regard to a paper missing through your neglect . . . [and] to the Rhode Island [boundary] line which lost Bristol, etc." The remaining reference was a brief report on military plans being discussed in the Assembly. The principal topic of the letter, however, was a discussion of future contracts. Presumably, Hancock's interest in the debate was more pecuniary than political.[39]

Hancock's lack of political involvement is similarly reflected in those events of a nonpolitical nature that he reported to Kilby: the burning of the Court House in 1747; William Douglass' denunciation of Charles Knowles that same year; the 1752 outbreak of smallpox; and the 1755 earthquake. Hancock gossiped, but not about politics.[40]

Unfortunately, the merchant's letters to local politicians have not survived. His foreign correspondence, however, particularly his frequent letters to Kilby, provides an approximate guide to Hancock's political preferences. Presumably what he asked Kilby to do reflected Hancock's own priorities in terms of English political rewards. And because the Privy Council reviewed every decision taken by the General Court—and in the process regularly sought the opinion of the English merchant community—Kilby, along with Hancock's English allies, enjoyed a special op-

[38] Hancock to Kilby and Barnard, 16 June 1755, ibid.
[39] Hancock to Kilby, 10 February 1746–7, THLB-MHS. Hancock to Kilby, 16 February 1756, TH4-BL.
[40] Hancock to Hopson, 7 December 1747, HP-BL, vol. 10, fol. 4; Hancock to Kilby, 18 December 1747, THLB-MHS; Hancock to Kilby and Barnard, 30 November 1752, 24 November 1755, TH4-BL.

portunity to lobby for or against Massachusetts' public acts. Because Hancock seldom availed himself of this opportunity to influence public policy, we can say he was rarely interested in more than just government contracts.

Hancock's references to questions of political preferment—ten in all during an eleven-year period—conform to the same basic pattern. One dealt with the current status of the governor; four requested jobs for Hancock's friends; three concerned Kilby's own ambitions; one discussed Bollan's success as an agent; and one is an interesting comment on Hancock's influence. In May 1746 he told Kilby, "Tomorrow is our election of councilors, and all I desire and push is to keep Allen out. We got the better of him at the election of representatives, and doubt not, but always to do it." This came on the heels of Hancock's successful, but unpleasant, campaign to deny Allen the patronage of the Board of Ordnance. And the merchant neither underestimated his political strength—Allen never again sat in the Council—nor was he far from the truth when he told Kilby, this is "all I desire and push." [41]

In recent years social psychologists have become increasingly interested in why men become involved in politics. Robert Lane, for example, has proposed six basic needs—what he calls a "grammar of political motives"—served by political activity:

1. Men seek to advance their economic or material well-being, their income, their property, their economic security through political means.
2. Men seek to satisfy their needs for friendship, affection, and easy social relations through political means.

[41] Hancock to Kilby, 27 May 1746, TH1B-MHS. See also Hancock to Kilby, 30 November 1745, 17 January 1745-6, 15 December 1746, 10 February 1746-7, 18 December 1747, 17 January 1748-9, ibid., and 29 July, 14 December 1756, TH4-BL.

3. Men seek to understand the world, and the causes of the events which affect them, through observing and discussing politics.
4. Men seek to relieve intra-psychic tensions, chiefly those arising from aggressive and sexual impulses, through political expression.
5. Men seek power over others (to satisfy doubts about themselves) through political channels.
6. Men generally seek to defend and improve their self-esteem through political activity.[42]

Of Lane's six needs, only the first—the need to advance economic well-being—clearly applies to Hancock. Probably the crucial difference between Hancock's response to the 1750 tea excise and the 1754 rum excise was that while Hancock was a major importer of tea, he was only tangentially involved in supplying Massachusetts' rum drinkers. Indeed the merchant's interest in having the 1754 excise repealed centered almost exclusively on the political rewards that victory might bring to Kilby —rewards, Hancock believed, which could return Kilby to the agency and thus increase the merchant's opportunities to garner English contracts.

Perhaps political action similarly enhanced Hancock's self-esteem. His boast to James Wibault that "our governor is so much my friend" as to exempt his sailors from impressment, certainly reflects a pride that came from knowing that, as good friends, governors were prepared to protect his interests.[43] But the remaining four categories seemingly apply more to his business than to his political activities. Hancock's friends were drawn from the world of commerce rather than politics, except where the two overlapped. He evidenced little curiosity about political events except when they directly affected his business interests.

---

[42] Robert E. Lane, *Political Life* (New York: Free Press, 1959), pp. 101–02.
[43] Hancock to Wibault, 19 April 1745, THLB-MHS.

Whatever intrapsychic tensions plagued him—and the absence of an heir and his relationship with his nephew John suggest there were many—were relieved by intense business rather than political activity. Finally, there is simply no evidence that Hancock sought political power over others or that, thus motivated, he was willing to expend political resources to accomplish this end.

Hancock was not politically motivated, in the sense that political action satisfied few of his needs, excepting always his need for economic well-being. Three additional indices of Hancock's political personality buttress this conclusion.

The first involves the almost single-minded devotion to commercial pursuits revealed in his correspondence. With few exceptions, every event mentioned led, at least indirectly, to a discussion of business conditions and Hancock's own commercial enterprises. Typical was Hancock's lament over the death of Cushing, a long-time friend and political ally. To Kilby he wrote: "I am sorry to tell you of the death of our friend Cushing, a great loss it is to town and country." But then, without pausing, Hancock continued, "He was the Thompsons' agent here . . . I wish they may fall into good hands. I suppose you may know the gentlemen, and if you think fit to recommend me, I will accept it provided they will pay me full commissions." [44]

A second index involves a comparison of the location of Hancock's and Hutchinson's surviving correspondence. Although I have seen a large proportion of the manuscript collections pertaining to Massachusetts politics in the eighteenth century, in only two collections did I find letters either to or from Hancock. In sharp contrast, Hutchinson's letters abound. He wrote every-

---

[44] Hancock to Kilby, 5 May 1746, ibid.

body, but most of all he wrote other politicians.[45] If time expended is in fact a valid index of political interests, then the conclusion that Hutchinson cared a great deal more about politics than Hancock does seem inescapable.

A third index is a more general comparison between Hutchinson and Hancock. When Hutchinson became speaker of the House, he was thirty-five years old and as successful in his merchant endeavors as in his politics. Then he could still have chosen the course taken by his father and by some men of similar station: a dual career in both politics and business, ending in an augmented fortune, a seat on the Council, and a reputation as a distinguished provincial leader. But the acquisition of formal political power propelled Hutchinson on a different track. While he continued to be interested in mercantile affairs, he quickened the tempo of his political activity. He enjoyed the power, he savored the responsibility, and he reveled in the opportunity to imprint his own stamp on all that came within his purview. Hutchinson was essentially an activist who believed in the efficacy of his own endeavors. The speakership allowed him to give full vent to his desire to lead, to dominate, to control; and his tenure in office heightened, rather than satisfied, his appetite for more power and for a wider platform from which to organize and administer the processes of government.[46]

Professional politicians expected a variety of rewards for their services. Hutchinson sought little besides personal power. When he learned that Francis Bernard, a career British civil servant,

[45] Probably the most revealing set of letters are those from Hutchinson to the Earl of Loudoun, Loudoun Papers, Henry E. Huntington Library, San Marino, Calif.

[46] Malcolm Freiberg, "Thomas Hutchinson: The First Fifty Years (1711–1761)," *William and Mary Quarterly,* 3d ser. 15 (1958): 35–55; Edmund S. and Helen M. Morgan, *The Stamp Act Crisis* (New York: Collier Books, 1963), particularly pp. 256–79.

was to be the province's new governor, Hutchinson wrote Israel Williams, "people that know Mr. Bernard say he is not a man of intrigue, that he loves to be quiet himself and is willing other people should lead too." [47] And Hutchinson considered himself just the man to do the leading. He was no megalomaniac, and he did not lust for power in order to enrich his friends or oppress Massachusetts. But he did want things done his way, no doubt because in his view of the world he was usually right and other people so often wrong. He wanted his niche in history; but he also wanted a reputation which reflected greatness as well as ambition. He had grand plans which he believed (and most of the time rightly) would benefit Massachusetts far more than they would enhance the standing of Thomas Hutchinson. In the final analysis this was the genius of his success and the tactical weakness that produced his eventual downfall.

Hancock, on the other hand, made money. His monument was his commercial reputation, his bulging warehouses, and the impressive dock at the foot of Fleet Street. Moreover, he avoided formal power almost as assiduously as Hutchinson sought it. Although Hancock did serve as a Boston selectman, he never sat in the Assembly and did not enter the Council until 1758. By then he was fifty-five, already crippled by gout, and increasingly inclined to let John Hancock manage the firm.

Hancock was one merchant who, unlike Hutchinson, used few of his resources to achieve political goals. Hancock and Hutchinson probably represent two poles on either end of a scale measuring the merchants' political attitudes. Hutchinson typifies the trader who, faced with a choice, concentrated his considerable

[47] Hutchinson to Williams, 4 March 1760, Williams Papers, Massachusetts Historical Society, Boston, Mass.

talents and energy in the pursuit of formal power. Hancock evidenced an equally single-minded devotion, but to quite different ends.

It is possible, however, that in a government so top-heavy with merchants it was unnecessary for Hancock, and others like him, to lobby for specific policies. Put simply, those merchants in government naturally protected the interests of the entire trading community. To this proposition there are at least two objections. First is the question of whether someone like Hutchinson—or Oliver or Bowdoin or even Belcher—was a merchant or a professional politician with special political values and attitudes. The exercise of power required a special orientation that put primary emphasis on group loyalties. To be a professional was, by definition, to be different and thus not representative of one's class or occupation.

The second objection lies in the conceptual problem of defining the merchants' interest. In a political system which, for a variety of reasons, prevented public institutions from ordering either social or economic relationships, what could the merchants have sought? Probably only three issues concerned the province's traders: contracts, currency, and taxes. In the first instance, the merchants' interest in contracts happily coincided with the interest of the professional politician. Both benefited from increased government expenditures and both faced the hostility of the Assembly's back-benchers, who did not. The currency, of course, is the classic issue. But the merchants, as an organized interest group, were singularly unsuccessful in persuading the province either to balance its books or to levy taxes sufficient to retire overdue paper bills. The redemption act of 1750 was an exception. Shirley's victory depended on his own political resources rather than on the merchants' desire for a specie currency. In the question of taxation, the merchant fared no better. Both the

1750 tea excise and 1754 rum excise demonstrated the back-benchers' ability to levy taxes detrimental to the interests of the merchant community. And, as we shall presently see, these two acts were simply part of a larger pattern of tax discrimination. The merchant did in fact enjoy a special influence over the course of events, but only when (or because?) he sought rewards of little value to most of his neighbors.

9

A Conservative Balance

WHEN HE SET FOR HIMSELF THE TASK OF DEFINING THE SCOPE and power of conservatism in eighteenth-century America, Leonard Labaree began with the colonial council that, in every royal colony, served as the governor's executive cabinet as well as the upper house of the legislature. In part, Labaree began here because council rolls provide a natural compendium of what he considered the eighteenth century's "ruling families"—in Virginia the Pages, Byrds, Carters, and Lees; in New York the De Lanceys, Livingstons, Schuylers, and Smiths; and in Massachusetts the Cushings, Hutchinsons, Bowdoins, and Olivers. But Labaree also began with the council because from his perspective no other institution so dramatically testified to the vitality of political conservatism in colonial America. Thus in every colony the "men of wealth and position" who joined the colonial government as distinguished and respected councilors brought to bear their considerable talents and immense prestige in defense of an economic and political status quo which guaranteed them and their children a preeminent place in colonial society and provided "that coin of advantage" from which they "manipulated affairs of state in the interests of their own aristocratic class."[1]

Labaree was primarily concerned with the social backgrounds of those who became councilors, and from this perspective the upper chamber appears to have been the natural preserve of a small, remarkably close-knit colonial aristocracy. In Massachusetts, for example, the Council that Thomas Hancock joined in 1758 included the province's only baronet as well as eight of Massachusetts' richest merchants. Nearly a third of Hancock's colleagues had attended Harvard, where they all had ranked either near or at the top of their classes. Eleven councilors occupied places once held by their fathers or grandfathers; only Hancock and Samuel Watts did not enjoy inherited wealth.[2]

Yet the 1758 Council can also be described in quite different terms. Again with the exception of Hancock, all had commenced their political careers as justices of the peace. All but seven had served in the House, and of these only one—Richard Cutt, who probably did not bother to attend House sessions— had not belonged to the Assembly's leadership. The Council similarly included ten members of the county judiciary and two of the four members of the Superior Court. Even among the seven who had not served in the House, none could be counted a political novice. Stephen Sewall was the province's chief justice; Hancock, John Erving, Jacob Wendall, Benjamin Pick-

---

[1] Leonard Woods Labaree, *Conservatism in Early American History* (Ithaca: Cornell University Press, 1948), pp. 1–31; the quotation is from p. 31.

[2] Biographical information for the 1758 Council has been drawn principally from the following: *SHG;* John A. Schutz, *William Shirley, King's Governor of Massachusetts* (Chapel Hill: University of North Carolina Press, 1961); John A. Schutz, *Thomas Pownall* (Glendale, Calif.: A. H. Clark, Co., 1951); W. T. Baxter, *House of Hancock* (Cambridge, Mass.: Harvard University Press, 1945); Bryon Fairchild, *Messrs. William Pepperrell* (Ithaca: Cornell University Press, 1954); Ralph Davol, *Two Men of Taunton* (Taunton, Mass., 1912); William H. Whitmore, ed., *The Massachusetts Civil List for the Colonial and Provincial Periods, 1630–1774* (Albany, 1870).

man, and John Osborne were prominent merchants while John Hill was a Maine timber baron.

Apparently service on a Council primarily responsible for superintending the distribution of provincial patronage held little attraction except for those who counted themselves political professionals. One way to test this proposition is to focus on Council attendance as at least one measure of interest in political affairs. The 1758 Council met as a legislative chamber ninety-eight times. Eight councilors appeared at ninety or more sessions, and taken together they make an interesting group. The most faithful was Andrew Oliver, who first won election to the Council in 1746 after having lost the Assembly's speakership by a single vote. Next followed James Bowdoin, William Brattle, Osborne, Watts, Erving, Wendall, and Thomas Hutchinson. Of these men, only Erving and Wendall, both Boston merchants, had not served in the Assembly. Hutchinson, of course, had served three years as the speaker of the House; Watts and Brattle had both provided effective leadership to the Assembly's agrarian majority; Osborne, another Boston merchant, was in his twenty-sixth term on the Council; and Bowdoin had become a major House leader while still in his twenties. Eight councilors attended less than fifty-four sessions, two—Silvanus Bourn and James Minot—because of illness. Sir William Pepperrell, having achieved the title so many Americans sought and so few attained, was already in semiretirement. Benjamin Lynde was probably distracted by the work of the Superior Court, an institution which had absorbed the energies of the Lynde family for nearly half a century. Samuel Waldo, though he avidly sought political power, never gave much time to the offices he won. As partial reward for his efforts in Shirley's behalf, Waldo first won election to the Council in 1742, but he was either defeated or, as was more likely, declined to run again four years later. Boston sent him to the House in 1749, but he resigned midterm to embark for London, where a new campaign to topple a provincial governor was being waged. In 1758 he emerged from retirement and again sought and won a seat on the Council. George Leonard and John Hill probably owed their places as much to the requirement that at least four councilors reside in Plymouth County and three in Maine as they did to their own political skill and interest. Benjamin Pickman's disinterest was probably generic. Though a leader when he sat in the Assembly, his performance in that chamber had been equally as erratic as his performance in the Council.

The Council's official minutes, besides providing detailed attendance records, also list the number of times each member was appointed to a joint legislative committee. Again, men with prior service in the House were the most active: Brattle, Watts, Osborne, Hutchinson, John Cushing, Bowdoin, as well as Erving —who for the last five years of Shirley's governorship had served as a principal administration spokesman—and Stephen Sewall.

These two records—of attendance and committee service— suggest a great deal about his majesty's councilors.[3] Clearly, power within the Council—as measured by committee service— was distributed in proportion to a member's willingness to attend Council sessions. And again, those most willing to assume responsibility for managing the Council's legislative calendar were men who had previously made a career of providing that same expertise in the larger, less disciplined Assembly. Equally suggestive are the two groups which prove exceptions to the rule that a councilor's attendance record is an adequate predictor of his service on joint committees. Four councilors received far fewer assignments than they were entitled to. Ezekial Cheever and Isaac Royal were both senior councilors who had graduated from House to Council. Yet despite their seniority neither had ever

[3] See the statistical appendix.

achieved political prominence. Royal, during his first try for the Council, was guilty of such blatant electioneering that Spencer Phips, presiding over the colony in Shirley's absence, vetoed Royal's election, charging that his "conduct in that affair . . . may (if countenanced) be of evil influence and example in future elections."[4] Chastised, Royal conducted a much more professional campaign the next year and was allowed to take his seat. Hancock, of course, was a legislative neophyte, skilled in the art of political manipulation and yet still unfamiliar with the technical details of the legislative process. Though he faithfully attended all but a dozen of the Council's sessions, it was not until the waning moments of the term that he was entrusted with the delicate task of compromising House-Council differences over a major piece of legislation. The fourth member of this group, Jacob Wendall, was probably a genuine exception, having in previous years played a major role in Council affairs; what caused a decline in his power despite his continued attendance is simply not known.

Three councilors served on more committees than their colleagues with similar attendance records. John Cushing was in the last years of a distinguished political career. Whatever the cause of his frequent absences, when he did attend, the Council drew heavily on his experience and skill. Stephen Sewall and Benjamin Lynde were both members of the Superior Court, which probably explains their attendance records and the frequency with which the Council drew on their skill and specialized knowledge when drafting legislation.

Provincial councilors were drawn from the ranks of the gentry; but it was, above all, a selective process, in which councilors, like their counterparts in the House, were recruited from among the ranks of the province's professional politicians. Those whose

[4] *MHJ*, 28:7.

attitudes were most professionalized—men like Hutchinson, Watts, and Erving—or those who could provide specialized knowledge—like Sewall and Lynde—naturally enjoyed both power and prestige. Those who had still to learn the mechanics of the legislative process—Hancock, for example—or who were less interested in the exercise of power—Pepperrell, Waldo, and Pickman—or who simply were not politically effective—Cheever and Royal—enjoyed only the prestige attached to their position and the satisfaction of knowing they belonged to the province's most exclusive club.

Councilors were also legislators intent on having public policy reflect their own preferences and biases. Equally important, most councilors were in fact conservatives firmly committed to a fiscal orthodoxy which preached balanced budgets and a specie currency and naturally inclined to support a provincial chief executive as the political symbol of an expanding, mutually beneficent empire. Moreover, the legislative process itself afforded these men a remarkably active role in the setting of public policy. Nearly a fourth of the bills annually brought before the General Court were initiated by the Council, and another fourth were first considered by joint House-Council committees. Indeed, one way or another, most major legislation—including tax and supply bills—was at some point considered by a joint committee that traditionally was chaired by a member of the Council.[5]

And yet, as the province's constant experiments with a paper currency suggest, the Council's ability to check the Assembly's inflationist majority was clearly limited.

Francis Bernard, a perceptive analyst if seldom a successful

[5] William Douglass, *A Summary, Historical and Political of the . . . Present State of British Settlement in North America*, 2 vols. (London, 1760), 1:495; see also Choate to the Committee of War, 21 March 1756, Massachusetts Archives (State House), Boston, Mass., 55:151.

politician, had been in America less than three years and governor of Massachusetts less than sixteen months when he decided, "If . . . there should be a new establishment of the governments in N. America upon a true English-constitutional bottom, it must be upon a new plan." Then in the spring of 1764, while London was preparing a stamp act for the colonies, Bernard spelled out exactly what the new plan should be. If the goal was to make America constitutionally resemble England, he reasoned, then the king had to create in America the same conditions which prevailed at home. Specifically he had to create an American nobility capable of countering the passions of the people and their representatives. "A *Nobility* appointed by the *King* for life, and made independent," Bernard argued, "would probably give strength and stability to the *American* governments, as effectually as an hereditary *Nobility* does to that of *Great Britain*." [6] An upper house of life peers would, in other words, assure the king of the service of a distinguished group of colonials freed of any need to curry the people's favor. And the governor would be guaranteed the support of a powerful and resourceful ally in his never-ending struggle to convince unruly colonials that the best of all constitutions required the subordination of their own province to the welfare of the empire as a whole.

Bernard's ideas, had they become known in Massachusetts, would have been about as welcome as a smallpox epidemic or a decision by Parliament to tax Americans. Yet there were men within the province who similarly deplored the people's power to disrupt the orderly and prudent processes of government. At least two, William Douglass and Thomas Hutchinson, both

---

[6] Bernard to Barrington, 15 December 1761, Edward Channing and Archibald Cary Coolidge, eds., *The Barrington-Bernard Correspondence* (Cambridge, Mass.: Harvard University Press, 1912), p. 44. Francis Bernard, *Select Letters on the Trade and Government of America* (London, 1774), p. 83. See also Edmund S. and Helen M. Morgan, *The Stamp Act Crisis* (New York: Collier Books, 1963), pp. 19–35.

dismayed by the province's chaotic finances and its paper money, similarly diagnosed the government's weakness in terms of the Council's inability to check the Assembly's apparent irresponsibility. To these fiscal conservatives, the source of the trouble was obvious: it was not that councilors lacked character or integrity, but that the peculiar manner in which they were chosen made them too often subservient to the whims of the House.

The 1691 charter ordered the General Court annually to elect a new Council on the first day of a new House term, and, after some confusion, the province determined that the members of the previous year's Council, along with the newly elected representatives, were entitled to cast ballots. The process began with each elector casting eighteen separate votes for councilors to represent the counties originally encompassed by the Massachusetts Bay Company. In succession the General Court then elected four councilors from the old Plymouth colony, three for Maine, one for Sagadahock and Nova Scotia, and two councilors at large. The Court then submitted the twenty-eight names to the governor for his approval.[7]

Douglass was convinced that the 1691 charter, in giving the governor a veto and the House the bulk of the votes, had made certain that councilors would never be "FREE agents." Councilors, he argued, were torn between two often conflicting forces. On the one hand they might "be INTIMIDATED by the . . . governor, as he has a power of negativing any councilor's election, without alleging reasons." On the other hand they stood "in AWE of the members of the . . . House of Representatives." To protect their own interests councilors were often "arbitrarily led, or rather drove by the governor, to prevent future negatives." More ominously, councilors, "as their election . . . [was] annual . . . [could] be biased by the humor of the majority of the representa-

[7] *A&R*, 1:12; *MHJ*, 25:5–8.

tives (this I have particularly observed in the cases of multiplied emissions of paper currency) lest they should be dropped next . . . election." [8] Douglass readily acknowledged that most councilors were reelected as a matter of course. But like all fiscal conservatives, he remembered with horror the year the House had purged sixteen councilors for opposing the Land Bank.

In his history of the province, Hutchinson documented Douglass' complaint. As a friend and admirer of John Stoddard, Hutchinson lamented the punishment a shortsighted House had meted out to this conservative spokesman for the Connecticut Valley. Stoddard, as Hutchinson told the story, "had been several years [a] member of the Council, but being in favor of the prerogative, generally met with great opposition, and having been divers times left out he at length declined being any longer the subject of contention, and chose a seat in the House, his town thinking it a favor that he would represent them." Ironically, Stoddard had also indirectly contributed to the downfall of another venerable member of the upper house. In 1741 he had secured passage of a plan to let the senior councilor from each county determine just how much the paper currency had depreciated. "This [was] at best," suggested Hutchinson, "a very partial cure . . . [since] the councilors appointed to estimate the depreciation never had firmness enough . . . to make the full allowance. . . . The popular cry was against it, and one year when Nathaniel Hubbard, . . . a gentleman of amiable character . . . who filled the several posts he sustained with applause, endeavored to approach nearer to a just allowance . . . he felt the resentment of the House who left him out of the Council the next election." [9] For Douglass and Hutchinson, then, the Council's apparent impotence nicely ex-

[8] Douglass, *Historical Summary*, 1:376–77n, 486–87.

[9] Thomas Hutchinson, *History of the Colony and Province of Massachusetts-Bay*, ed. Lawrence Shaw Mayo, 3 vols. (Cambridge, Mass.: Harvard University Press, 1936), 2:329n, 307. See also ibid., p. 272.

plained the abandon with which the General Court printed money
and debased the economy.

Hutchinson and Douglass notwithstanding, the Council did in
fact enjoy a measured independence, in part at least because political orthodoxy in Massachusetts still defined the good ruler as
a man apart, wiser, more virtuous, and more independent than
the people he governed. The definition derived from the Puritan's
contention that civil magistrates, though elected by the people,
were called by God and remained accountable to him alone. To
this belief eighteenth-century New Englanders had grafted a
social ethic which held that men of wealth, talent, and stature
should naturally monopolize places of power and honor. Thus
councilors were to be

> men of capacity, wise and understanding, i.e., who know the
> world, men and things; the constitution, the civil and religious
> interests of their country; of a genius for government, of real
> exemplary virtue and religion; of inflexible integrity, who dare to
> be honest in all times. . . . In a word, men who are to be such,
> tried men, and generally approved of.

Samuel Fisk put the case more succinctly: councilors were to
come from "families of distinction, education and subtance." [10]

Yet the concept that good rulers ought to be recruited from
among the ranks of the talented and successful only partially
explained the representatives' proclivity for electing men like
Hutchinson, who regularly and publicly dissented from the views
held by most provincial voters. For, ironically, while the election
itself allowed the House to dictate the composition of the Council,
the balloting procedure mitigated against major political purges.
Without nominations or floor discussions to guide him, each elector wrote the names of the twenty-eight men he wanted elected

[10] William Welsteed, *The Dignity of the Civil Magistrate* (Boston, 1751), p. 48.
Samuel Fisk, *The Character of the Candidate for Civil Government* (Boston,
1731), p. 40.

to the Council. This procedure gave an obvious advantage to candidates with established reputations and reduced the effectiveness of any cabal attempting to control the Council. It took, of course, little coordinated effort to unseat especially unpopular councilors like John Stoddard or Nathaniel Hubbard; but ordinarily they were merely replaced by men whose political views were remarkably similar.

The most complete descriptions of Council elections come from the diaries of the two Benjamin Lyndes, father and son, who together served a total of fifty-one years in the upper house. Ordinarily Council elections attracted between 120 and 130 electors. In good years a Lynde could count on being named on nearly all the ballots. With obvious pride the younger Lynde laconically recorded election results: 1738, "I was again chosen a councilor of the Massachusetts, and had the highest vote, 121"; 1739, "I was chose a councilor for the Massachusetts Colony, and had 118 votes, the highest number"; 1740, "I was again chose a councilor in the first 18, and my cousin William Browne chose a councilor at large." The Lyndes did not always have such an easy time. In 1736 Elisha Cooke and Thomas Cushing devised a clever plan to unseat the elder Lynde. By suggesting that Benjamin, Jr., might also make a good councilor, Cooke and Cushing hoped that in the ensuing confusion neither Lynde would receive enough votes. The plan nearly worked. The younger Lynde, apparently unaware that his votes had come at his father's expense, was impressed that "at this election I had 34 votes from the House for a councilor of the province, without my knowledge of such a design." Safely installed for another term, the father described what had happened.

Election. Mr. Holioak—excellent performance. I had but 89 votes from the 124 voters, upon a design of Thomas Cushing, Cooke, etc., to bring in my son, by leaving me out, which when proposed to me, I said, they might vote as they pleased for me and my son, whom if they brought in, I could as well dismiss myself. Mr. Dudley, whom there [was] great talk of leaving out, had 117 votes.[11]

Then in 1741, after the elder Lynde had retired, Benjamin, Jr., lost his bid for reelection. His diary's entry for May 27 told the story:

> Election, where most of the number were Land Bankers. . . . Very great alteration in the Council and but two of the 18 Massachusetts last year's councilors chose. All of us councilors for Essex left out, and 16 new councilors chose. Governor Belcher negatived 13 of the councilors . . . [and] the next day he dissolves the General Assembly.[12]

It was, of course, this election which haunted men like Douglass and Hutchinson. Yet in 1741 the debate and turmoil surrounding the Land Bank had divided public opinion. Those for the Bank combined with and voted for men who shared their convictions, so that from February through August, Massachusetts had, in effect, two well-defined political parties. When the representatives convened in Boston, they were already committed to a specific program and were more than prepared to band together in the sort of cohesive faction a purge of the Council required.

In the 1760s the same pattern was repeated when Hutchinson and the Otis family publicly dueled for control of the province. Then Britain's attempts to tax America gave the Otises an ideological issue with which to unite their supporters. Massachusetts was again dominated by party politics, and the composition of

---

[11] [F. E. Oliver], ed., *The Diaries of Benjamin Lynde and of Benjamin Lynde, Jr.* (Boston, 1880), pp. 72–73, 154, 156, 161.
[12] Ibid., p. 162.

the Council again became a party issue. By 1769 Bernard, no longer dwelling on the grander aspects of imperial reorganization, was pleading with Britain to put an end to an elected Council.

> For these 4 years past so uniform a system of bringing all power into the hands of the people has been prosecuted . . . with such success, that all that fear, reverence, respect and awe which before formed a tolerable balance against the real power of the people, are annihilated and the artificial weights being removed, the royal scale mounts up and kicks the beam. . . . [And if his majesty] cannot secure to himself the appointment of the Council, it is not worthwhile to keep that of the governor.[13]

The struggles of the 1760s emasculated the Council, ending its power as an independent check on the Assembly. But in its own way, the Land Bank crisis had already restricted the Council's autonomy. After 1741 councilors knew that the Assembly's power was not illusory, that in fact, once sufficiently angered, the representatives were more than capable of political mayhem. This knowledge circumscribed the Council's power by curbing its appetite for protracted legislative deadlocks. The Council could harass, admonish, and advise, but once delay and persuasion failed to wean a majority of representatives away from a measure, the Council had no intelligent choice but to swallow its pride and acquiesce in the Assembly's demands.

Eighteenth-century Americans made much of the fact that theirs was a balanced form of government—an eminently reasonable amalgam of royal prerogative, popular expression, and conservative control. It was this last element which the provincial Council contributed to the political system. While the Assembly's inherent power restricted the Council's independence, the deference paid to councilors as men of high status similarly limited the

---

[13] Bernard to Barrington, 18 March 1769, Channing and Coolidge, *Barrington-Bernard Correspondence*, p. 198.

Assembly's own intransigence. Thus, provincial conservatism was a force to be reckoned with, not because it sought to preserve an oppressive or even restrictive social system, but rather because those men who counted themselves conservatives—men like Hutchinson and Erving—were effective political leaders who understood the nature of power and authority in the eighteenth century.

10

A Question
of Accountability

Among the conditions often thought essential to political democracy, only two are fundamental: the opportunity to participate in political decisions must be widely shared among all adult citizens; and, because political power is always exercised by what, for lack of a better term, can be called governmental elites, those men accorded power must consciously hold themselves accountable to the people they govern. Until recently, provincial Massachusetts was thought to have satisfied neither of these conditions. It was simply assumed that in the eighteenth century restrictive property qualifications disfranchised most citizens, and, given a society in which less than a fourth of the adult males could vote, public officials were accountable at best to this small but wealthy elite. In 1952 Robert Brown substantially revised this image of the political system by proving that not only could most men vote, but the distribution of Assembly seats and the requirement forcing assemblymen to reside in the communities they represented meant that the General Court was numerically dominated by men of middling status.[1] Besides choosing among rival

[1] Robert E. Brown, "Democracy in Colonial Massachusetts," *New England Quarterly* 25 (1952): 291–313.

candidates for the Assembly, could the provincial voter also influence his representative's legislative behavior? In short, was the provincial legislator accountable to the citizens who placed him in office?

To answer such a question has proved an all but impossible task, in part because we lack sufficient information, but equally because of an ingrained belief that legislative accountability basically depends upon a citizen's ability to instruct his representative. Most of us, in fact, bring to any study of representation a belief that public officials ought to represent the will of their constituents. And to the extent that colonial representatives actually did so, we will gladly consider eighteenth-century America to have been democratic. In this light a town's right to issue what Edmund Burke called *"authoritative* instructions . . . which the member is bound . . . to obey, to vote, and to argue for" has traditionally served as an index of accountability, for seemingly it measures the ability of the ordinary citizen to initiate public policy.[2]

Yet in fact only rarely do public officials, even in the most democratic political systems, respond to the actions of interested citizens, largely because interested citizens are extraordinarily rare. Thus usually it is the politician who initiates the actions to which his constituents respond. Moreover, even in democratic systems, the citizenry responds to only a small portion of the politician's acts. To this basic phenomenon we must add a second generalized attribute of political behavior: even a legislator who believes in the existence of political mandates never represents his constituents' views; rather, he represents his own image of those views.[3]

[2] *The Writings and Speeches of Edmund Burke,* 12 vols. (Boston, 1901), 2:95–96. See also Kenneth Colegrove, "New England Town Mandates," *Publications of the Colonial Society of Massachusetts* 21 (1919): 411–49.
[3] See particularly Lewis Anthony Dexter, "The Representative and his District," reprinted in Robert L. Peabody and Nelson W. Polsby, eds., *New Perspectives*

One way out of our conceptual dilemma is to transform these insights into a somewhat broader and more elastic definition of legislative accountability. Specifically, we should expect democratic systems of representation to fulfill three basic conditions. First, most legislators must accurately perceive their constituents' sensibilities. Second, the votes of most legislators must mirror such perceptions. Third, when casting their ballots for representatives, most citizens must in some measure base their choice on the candidates' legislative performance, either actual or promised. Thus, in a system of legislative accountability, the primary path of influence begins with the constituency's views, includes the representative's perceptions of those views, and ends with the representative's roll call behavior. In such a system, a representative's own attitudes would have little or no effect on his voting or behind-the-scenes behavior except where such attitudes agreed with those of the constituency.[4]

To apply these standards, scholars interested in contemporary America interview both citizen and representative, asking the same questions of both and then comparing their answers. Obviously this is beyond the reach of the historian of colonial America. Hence we must, because we lack an independent measure of local attitudes, approach the question of accountability in a more roundabout way—must, as it turns out, focus on the election process rather than on the more direct and continuous relationships which link citizen and representative. But rather than simply discovering who could and could not vote, we must ultimately decide whether eighteenth-century elections were capable of producing legislators who believed themselves accountable to their constituents. While no criteria will satisfy

---

on the House of Representatives (Chicago: Rand McNally & Co., 1963), pp. 3–29.

[4] Warren E. Miller and Donald E. Stokes, "Constituency Influence in Congress," American Political Science Review 57 (1963): 45–57.

every image of a democratic election process, the following eight conditions appear to be fundamental.

1. Every adult citizen must be granted the right to vote.
2. Each vote must be of equal weight.
3. Every citizen entitled to vote must also be entitled to run for office.
4. No candidate can be prevented from expressing his views and soliciting votes.
5. No citizen should have to forgo another right or privilege in order to vote for the candidate of his choice (this condition rules out all forms of coercion).
6. The winner must be that candidate receiving the greatest number of (legal) votes.
7. The citizen must have access to accurate knowledge of the candidates' stands on major political issues. This is particularly important whenever the citizen must decide whether or not to vote for an incumbent legislator.
8. To a significant degree, at least, the citizen must base his choice on the candidates' stands on public issues.[5]

I propose to measure eighteenth-century elections against this standard. An additional word of caution is in order, however. For the most part, this model has been developed to aid in understanding modern data and experiences. To apply the same standard to eighteenth-century Massachusetts involves a basic assumption that certain conditions have not changed much over the last two hundred years. Specifically, it is necessary to assume that colonial Americans believed the question of who exercised legislative power was indeed important and that the social relationship between a representative and his constituents was roughly the

[5] In developing these criteria I relied heavily on Robert A. Dahl, *A Preface to Democratic Theory* (Chicago: University of Chicago Press, 1956), particularly pp. 63–85.

same then and now. To some extent, neither assumption is wholly justified.

To most provincials the central government mattered little because the central government did little. This lack of an activist government had several consequences. Probably the most significant was the willingness of a large number of communities to forgo the right to a representative in the Assembly. Most of these towns were small and located in the center of the colony. Isolated socially and economically as well as politically, they were not part of the central political system and hence were excluded from this analysis.

Even to the communities that regularly sent a representative to Boston, the central government remained distant and not very important, with one important exception. The twin issues of how large the tax bill should be and whether or not the central government should issue more paper money could and often did provoke prolonged political controversy. On these two issues, then, we can discuss legislative accountability—at least in terms of the communities regularly represented in the Assembly.

At this point we encounter a second difficulty. The model presupposes that candidates and voters are essentially strangers to one another. Congressional districts today, for example, number over 100,000 voters, and state legislative districts occasionally contain over 50,000 voters. In the eighteenth century, towns numbered their voters not in the thousands but the hundreds; and representatives, in the social sense, were not strangers, but neighbors. The larger the town—and quite a few had more than a thousand inhabitants—the more likely the model's applicability. But we will always have something less than full compliance with the assumption that *only* political constraints bound citizen and representative.

Nevertheless, it still seems profitable to ask, "How well did colonial Massachusetts fulfill our eight conditions for a democratic election process?"

The Right to Vote. To vote for a representative in eighteenth-century Massachusetts, a citizen had to be a male, at least twenty-one years of age, and a bona fide resident of the town, and either had to own land yielding forty shillings in rent a year or own property (personal, real, or both) worth at least £40 sterling. If we forgive the eighteenth century its anti-feminist bias, then the province came close to satisfying the voting condition. Although the data is fragmentary and some of his inferences tortured, Brown has proved that at least 80 percent and probably 90 percent of the province's adult males owned sufficient property to qualify as voters.[6]

Votes of Equal Weight. Unlike Virginia, Massachusetts did not allow multiple voting. All a man's holdings, whether located within his town or not, counted toward meeting the property qualification, but he could vote only in the community in which he actually resided. If we stretch the condition requiring equally weighted votes to include the current one-man, one-vote definition of equal apportionment, then Massachusetts did bestow a special advantage on citizens living in small farming communities of between forty and eighty families, an advantage of little consequence, however, in a political system in which few constituencies availed themselves of their full quota of representation in the General Court.

The Right to Seek Office. Provincial law stipulated only that "[no] town in this province shall choose any representative unless such be a freeholder and resident in that town or towns such are chosen to represent."[7] Legally, then, Massachusetts satisfied the condition that every citizen entitled to vote could also run for

[6] Brown, "Democracy in Colonial Massachusetts," pp. 291–313.
[7] *A&R*, 1:147; see also Robert E. Brown, *Middle-Class Democracy and the Revolution in Massachusetts* (Ithaca: Cornell University Press, 1955), pp. 39, 48.

office. In practice, however, at least some restrictions existed. If the same social values that helped distribute political deference within the Assembly also helped determine who became a representative, then men of small estate entered the political arena at a disadvantage. They could vote, they could campaign for their favorite candidate, but seldom could they expect to win important office for themselves. This implied restriction was reinforced by two less subtle circumstances. The first was the prodigious amount of time that service as a representative consumed. While occasionally an Assembly could complete its annual deliberations in less than seventy days, on the average a conscientious legislator could expect to be away from home at least twenty-one weeks in a given year. Only men with established businesses, rented holdings, or able-bodied sons living at home could afford the luxury of being a representative. The second circumstance discouraging a man of meager means from seeking office was the custom of representatives serving without pay. Though required by law to supply per diem expenses, many towns expected their representatives to return the money. Boston, in fact, went so far as to incorporate this expectation in an annual resolve.[8]

How serious a threat these attitudes and practices posed to democratic election procedures is not known. My own suspicion is that modern practices and values put far greater obstacles in the path of the would-be politician than did a society in which the gap between rich and poor was considerably narrower than it is today. More serious, however, was the frequent absence of political competition in the eighteenth century. Closely contested elections existed, but often, particularly in the smaller farming communities, the office went almost by default to the town's

[8] MHJ, 28:vii. SHG, 7:511, 9:474; Boston, Mass., Report of the Record Commissioners of the City of Boston, 39 vols. (Boston, 1881–1909), 14:176.

leading citizen. Perhaps the frequent absence of competition simply reflected the relative unanimity a small, cohesive community could achieve. More likely, uncontested elections reflected how unimportant the central government was to many provincials.

Freedom to Campaign. We are probably safe in assuming that few restrictions were placed upon electioneering—at least I found none. A letter from Andrew Belcher concerning practices in Milton suggests that candidates were expected to rely principally upon their friends rather than upon making personal appeals to the voters. On the other hand, John Adams' descriptions of Braintree elections include plenty of campaigning as well as considerable quantities of free rum being consumed by doubtful voters.[9]

The Absence of Coercion. Given the fact that most male provincials could vote, did they encounter opposition in either exercising this right or choosing between rival candidates? Presumably such coercion would have taken one of two forms. The community's economic elite could have threatened the citizen of meager means with economic ruin unless he supported its candidate for representative. This would certainly explain why most representatives were themselves men of means. Or, a local elite could have persuaded the poorer citizen simply to stay at home on election day, thus leaving political affairs in the hands of those best acquainted with the true interests of the community.

To disprove that such coercion actually played a role in provincial elections is an impossible task. To point out that no evidence exists to substantiate such a hypothesis merely invites the reply that the coercion was, by its very nature, so subtle as to leave no trace. In fact, no one need have actually threatened

[9] Belcher to Quincy, 6 May 1762, *Microfilms of the Adams Papers*, reel 343. *JA-Diary*, 1:191.

the poorer citizen. He could have simply understood what would happen to him if he became too uppity. Nonetheless, while disputed elections did occasionally involve charges of bribery, no one—to my knowledge, at least—ever claimed he was threatened with financial (or any other kind of) ruin for voting for the candidate of his choice. In fact, economic relationships in the eighteenth century were simply not conducive to such threats. No large laboring class existed to be intimidated, and land was still abundant enough and labor scarce enough to prevent a landlord from threatening a politically independent tenant with expulsion. Moreover, there were enough closely contested elections with large turnouts to suggest that lack of interest rather than economic intimidation accounted for the provincials' political apathy. Finally, even in Boston, where political divisions occasionally reflected economic antagonisms, the less affluent were more than capable of thwarting the ambitions of the town's merchant princes. In 1749, after advocacy of a specie currency had cost him a seat in the Assembly, Thomas Hutchinson wrote Israel Williams, "You have heard my fate. I could make but about 200 votes in near 700. They were the principal inhabitants but you know we are governed not by weight but by numbers." [10]

An Honest Count. Disputed elections involved a variety of voting irregularities. Sometimes ineligible citizens were allowed to vote, or fully qualified freeholders were suddenly ruled ineligible. Sometimes—as outraged losers were wont to charge—the use of paper ballots camouflaged the fact that some men cast more than one ballot. And on at least one occasion, a town's selectmen, doubling as a committee on elections, refused to declare as the winner a candidate receiving a majority of the ballots cast. Still, disputed elections were not only comparatively rare,

---

[10] Hutchinson to Williams, 19 May 1749, Williams Papers, Massachusetts Historical Society, Boston, Mass.

they always brought a full investigation by the Assembly. If the evidence was sufficiently confusing, the House ordinarily resolved the issue by ordering a new election.[11]

With the exception of a disfranchised female population, election procedures in Massachusetts were sufficiently democratic to make legislative accountability at least a possibility. What remains, then, is to determine whether the political system similarly satisfied our two remaining conditions.

Availability of Political Information. In provincial Massachusetts there were four basic sources of public information that did not come directly from the representative himself: gossip, Boston's half-dozen newspapers, political pamphlets, and the published House journals—the only comprehensive compendium of government decisions and political opinion. The House first published its journal in 1715 when a rancorous dispute with the governor convinced enough representatives of the prudence of documenting their resistance to the administration. Originally, the *Journal* was published at the end of every term and then distributed to each constituency. After 1717 the *Journal* was published twice weekly, thus doubling as a daily legislative reference for the members and an official account of Assembly proceedings.[12] From the beginning, however, the *Journal* was less than an ideal index of a representative's legislative behavior, largely because most eighteenth-century politicians preferred the anonymity provided by secret debates and closed proceedings. In 1719 the Council, in asking the House to suppress the inclusion of a particularly bitter resolve, typified the legislators' traditional reluctance to make the Court's proceedings public:

[11] Massachusetts Archives (State House), Boston, Mass., 49:361–62, 380–84, 392, 17:291–315; *MHJ*, 34:8, 24, 85, 115–16, 128, 140, 151, 176.
[12] *MHJ*, 1:vi–vii.

Mr. Speaker, his majesty's Council . . . understanding that this honorable House . . . passed a . . . resolve which if it appears in print, may oblige them in their own vindication to reply unto, but being desirous that the different opinions which happened at this Court relating to our impost bill, may not be again revived, having already been made too public . . . the board . . . think it convenient, to recommend it to the consideration of the House, whether it may not be better wholly to suppress the publishing any thing which may carry, or bear a reflection on any part of the Court, and be improved by those who are not our friends to our disadvantage.[13]

The House unanimously rejected the Council's plea. Good to its word, the upper chamber then issued its own bitter reply which was duly included in the *Journal*.

Thereafter, the *Journal* became not so much a catalogue of legislative opinion and activity as a compendium of formal statements in which House, Council, and governor each laid claim to constitutional legitimacy. Page after page was devoted to charge and countercharge, as first one and then another of the great protagonists debated the proper nature of authority, the limits of the royal prerogative, and the due obedience a dependent people owed to a beneficent empire.

Nevertheless, a careful and patient voter could come to some understanding of the basic issues which agitated the Assembly. Because the governor's speeches were often included, the voter could learn what the administration had proposed and from the list of motions passed and defeated could tell what stand House and Council had taken on the currency, defense measures, government salaries, and taxes. But without a record of the actual debates, no voter could learn what mattered most: just where his representative stood on these key issues.

There was, of course, one vital exception. Whenever the House

---

[13] *MHJ*, 2:166. See also *MHJ*, 2:169, 4:10–11.

resolved an issue by yeas and nays, every provincial could gauge the extent to which his own and the views of his representative were identical. If the representatives had regularly employed the roll call to decide issues, the Assembly's preference for secret debates would have had less consequence. Unfortunately, the House was almost as suspicious of the roll call as it was of making its proceedings public. Between 1739 and 1756 the Assembly published only seventeen roll calls. And in nine of those sixteen years no roll calls were published at all.

The printing of the *Journal* actually circumscribed rather than increased the available fund of political information. Any commentator who revealed more about House proceedings than was contained in the *Journal* could be fined for divulging the Assembly's secrets and compromising the dignity of that august body. As a consequence, newspapers as well as political pamphlets ordinarily confined their coverage of political events to paraphrasing what was already available in the *Journal*. The interested citizen could faithfully read all that emanated from Boston's busy presses and still know no more than he had already garnered from the *Journal*.[14]

There were, of course, a few important exceptions. In 1749 James Allen published the names of those representatives who had voted to expel him from the House, as well as a list of representatives who had voted for currency redemption. Several pamphlets dealing with the Land Bank crisis also revealed more than was contained in the public record, and in 1754 one pamphlet gave a detailed account of the maneuvering which accompanied the passage of the rum excise.[15] Indeed there is an intriguing

[14] *MHJ*, 4:11; see also *Independent Advertiser,* January 1748, passim.
[15] [James Allen], *A Letter to the Freeholders of Boston* (Boston, 1749); *A Letter to the Merchant to Whom Is Directed a Printed Letter Relating to the Manufactory Undertaking* (Boston, 1741); *The Review* (Boston, 1754). See also *The Monster of Monsters* (Boston, 1754); Daniel Fowle, *A Total Eclipse of Liberty* (Boston, 1755), and *An Appendix to the Late Total Eclipse of Liberty* (Boston, 1756).

pattern to these exceptions, one remarkably similar to the distribution of published roll calls. Of the seventeen published votes, three involved the Land Bank, three more dealt with the aftermath of currency redemption, and three involved the rum excise and its repercussions.[16] The apparent consequence of these parallel patterns is that in times of genuine crisis enough information was available to allow the average voter to assess the performance of his elected representative. During periods of relative calm the voter relied on political gossip which, I suspect, seldom chronicled the activities of the central government.

Political Saliency. Given the probability that some of the time the voter was sufficiently informed to base his choice for representative on the candidates' stands on public issues, did he in fact do so? Here the evidence is not only fragmentary, but frankly contradictory.

Today most voters allow party labels and the candidates' personal attractiveness to determine how they cast their ballots. One recent study of voter attitudes reported: "Of detailed information about [the candidates'] policy stands not more than a chemical trace was found." [17] We cannot, of course, be sure that a similar situation prevailed in the eighteenth century. But there are a number of intriguing clues that point in this direction. One is a letter from Andrew Belcher to his friend Edmund Quincy discussing a forthcoming election in Milton. "I . . . return you many thanks for your obliging concern about my political interests; upon a more deliberate consideration thereof, I much approve your method of accidently (*on purpose*) speaking to the good Miltonics as they come within your reach, which I am now convinced would have a better effect than a labored, designed application to them at their houses." Having thus set the tone of his campaign, Belcher concluded, "Since my return I find that

---

[16] For list of roll calls see the statistical appendix.
[17] Miller and Stokes, "Constituency Influence in Congress," p. 54.

the number of candidates daily decreases, my long absence and confinement induced many persons to imagine an indifference, but being otherwise informed by some of my friends, the scene is changed, and they are of opinion that the choice will be the same as last year." [18] Perhaps Belcher's friends did dwell on their candidate's public record, but both the tone and thrust of the letter suggest that personal rectitude and influence were Belcher's strongest suits.

More revealing was the advice reputedly extended to James Otis, Jr., on the eve of his first campaign for the Assembly. The dean of the Boston delegation asked Otis:

> "What meeting do you go to?"—"Dr. Sewall's."—"Very well, you must stand up in sermon time, you must look devout and deeply attentive: Do you have family prayer?"—"No."—"It were well if you did: what does your family consist of?"—"Why only four or five commonly, but at this time, I have in addition one of Dr. Sewall's saints, who is a nurse of my wife."—"Ah! that is the very thing: you must talk religion with her in a serious manner, you must have family prayers at least once while she is in your house: that woman can do you more harm or more good than any other person; she will spread your fame throughout the congregation. I can also tell you, by way of example, some of the steps I take: two or three weeks before an election comes on, I send to the cooper and get all my casks put in order: I say nothing about the number of hoops. I send to the mason and have some job done to the hearths or the chimneys: I have the carpenter to make some repairs in the roof or the wood house: I often go down to the ship yards about eleven o'clock, when they break off to take their drink, and enter into conversation with them. They all vote for me." [19]

In many American communities this advice is as sound today as it was two centuries ago.

---

[18] Belcher to Quincy, 6 May 1762, *Microfilms of the Adams Papers,* reel 343.
[19] William Tudor, *The Life of James Otis* (Boston, 1823), pp. 91–92.

Even when provincial elections were close and attracted a large turnout, the result apparently depended more on local animosities than questions of public policy. In 1757 Watertown was wracked by a rancorous election battle between the incumbent John Hunt and his challenger Daniel Whitney. The first election attracted 103 qualified voters, 53 of whom voted for Hunt. Outraged, Whitney's supporters cried fraud. In a long, laborious petition to the House, they detailed the election's irregularities: two Whitney supporters were not informed of the election—"there is reason to apprehend the omission was from design"; several of Hunt's votes came from men not qualified to vote; two Whitney partisans were illegally prevented from casting ballots; and the town's selectmen, blatant Huntites that they were, probably let some of their friends vote more than once. Sufficiently impressed by this evidence, the House ordered a new election. Unfortunately the results were as questionable as before. While the 131 ballots cast gave Whitney a majority of one, the selectmen later declared Hunt the winner.[20]

The cause of such antagonisms was perfectly understood by the participants. To the charge that they not only allowed ineligible citizens to cast ballots but also tolerated bribery in Hunt's behalf, the town's selectmen replied:

> Although we have no reason to think that any such measures were ever taken by Mr. Hunt or Mr. Whitney themselves, yet as the town is and for some years past has been divided into parties nearly equal in number and as these contentions have been so sharp, we have no reason to think but that some of each party have done every thing in their power to procure one of their own party to represent the town.[21]

Apparently, the cause of this division of the town into two nearly equal parties dated back to 1754 when the town's meeting-

[20] Massachusetts Archives, 117:191, 292–315.
[21] Ibid., pp. 296–97.

house burned. Some of the community, presumably those closest to the old site, wanted the building repaired rather than a new one constructed at some other location. However, a number of inhabitants were unhappy over the remoteness of the old meeting-house and had recently split off from Watertown. The Hunt faction, probably citing this fact, triumphed, and a new building at some distance from the old site was erected. Then two years later Hunt committed a grievous tactical error: he became a collector of the new excise on rum, a position scarcely calculated to endear him to his constituents. Thus the furor of 1757 was, in all probability, a result of a geographical split in the town exacerbated by Hunt's unfortunate choice of a part-time job.[22]

John Adams' descriptions of Braintree politics tell much the same story. One faction, under the leadership of Ebenezer Thayer and concentrated in the north end of town, regularly did battle with those loyal to Adams' father and to Samuel Niles, Braintree's representative to the General Court. When Thayer defeated Niles for representative, Adams' post-election analysis was short and to the point: "Nightingale, Hayden, Saunders, J. Spear, N. Spear, Benoni Spear would vote for any man for a little phlip, or a dram. N. Belcher, John Spear, O. Gay, James Brackett, John Mills, Wm. Veasey, etc. voted for T[hayer] for other reasons." What those other reasons were are suggested in Adams' account of his own election as a selectman in 1766. The young lawyer did not attribute his triumph to his heroic efforts during the Stamp Act crisis; rather it was the quiet campaign launched the previous spring, combined with the sudden absence of the north-end faction, which produced the winning margin.

> I thought [Adams wrote after the hectic town meeting] the project was so new and sudden that the people had not digested it, and would generally suppose, the town would not like it, and so

[22] *MHJ*, 32:219, 33:53, 452; Massachusetts Archives, 117:91–100.

would not vote for it. But my brother's answer was, that it had been talked of, last year, and some years before, and that the thought was familiar to the people in general, and was more agreeable than any thing of the kind, that could be proposed to many. And for these reasons his hopes were strong. . . . But . . . the triumph was not complete. Cornet Bass had the most votes the first time, and would have come in [first] the second, but the north end people, his friends, after putting in their votes the first time, withdrew for refreshment, by which accident he lost it, to their great regret.[23]

Nonetheless, it is equally possible to marshal a case supporting the notion that provincial voters paid attention to how their representatives behaved in Boston. There is, for example, some testimonial evidence buttressing this conclusion. A year after coming into office, William Shirley justified his decision to accept an annual rather than a permanent salary by explaining that twenty years of legislative dispute had "made . . . [the salary issue] so unpopular a point among the representatives, who by being annually elected are rendered extremely dependent upon the humor of their constituents, that even those members, who are well disposed to vote for the settlement of the salary, dare not try their strength or interest in the Assembly upon it." [24] Seven years later, Shirley correctly predicted that passage of Hutchinson's currency redemption bill would result in a wholesale change of personnel in the next General Court. On occasion, even the Assembly could be remarkably frank about the importance attached to a constituent's sensitivities. In 1721, having rejected a supply bill amended by the Council, the House suggested that if the representatives had accepted the measure, "our principles that

[23] *JA-Diary*, 1:130, 302–03.
[24] Shirley to the Lords of Trade, 23 June 1742, Charles Henry Lincoln, ed., *The Correspondence of William Shirley*, 2 vols. (New York: Macmillan, 1912), 1:88–89.

sent us here, would tell us, that though the sessions came to a speedy conclusion, yet not a happy or safe one." [25]

A second indication of the importance provincial voters attached to their representatives' public records is the crisis which embroiled Woburn in 1740. With most of the province demanding still more paper money, lower taxes, and increased deficit financing, the House, by a three-to-one margin, voted to finance current operations by printing more money. Roland Cotton, the Assembly's clerk and Woburn's representative, had called the roll, skipping, as tradition demanded, himself and the speaker. But in preparing the journal for publication, Cotton inserted his name as one of the lopsided majority favoring continued inflation. The clerk's slight legerdemain might have gone unnoticed had he not also incurred the enmity of James Allen, who wrote Woburn pointing out that Cotton had, in fact, not cast his vote with the inflationist majority. The town's first selectman, after taking depositions in Boston, called a town meeting to assess Allen's charges. Cotton averted political disaster only by swearing that he did favor inflation and that his actions had not violated House procedures. [26]

While local disputes frequently lay behind increased turnout, as in the case in Watertown, genuine political crises had the same effect. This was certainly true of Lynn in 1741, and was probably true of most communities in which Land Bankers could muster a majority. [27] Further, there is at least some evidence suggesting that how a representative stood on the banking question deeply affected his political future. Of the fourteen representatives who consistently opposed the Bank, only five (36 percent) won re-

[25] *MHJ*, 31:151.

[26] [James Allen], *A Letter to a Friend in the Country* (Boston, 1740).

[27] [F. E. Oliver], ed., *The Diaries of Benjamin Lynde and of Benjamin Lynde, Jr.* (Boston, 1880), p. 162. See also *New England Weekly Journal*, 19 May 1741.

election to the House in 1741; conversely, of the thirty-one representatives who consistently supported the Bank, twenty (61 percent) won seats in the same election.[28]

The importance of the Land Bank, in fact, suggests a way out of the dilemma of conflicting evidence. In all probability, a candidate's stand on public issues mattered only in times of heated political controversy. When not stimulated by the existence of a key political issue, most voters either stayed away from the polls or based their choices on factors other than a candidate's public stance.

Thus in eighteenth-century Massachusetts a genuinely democratic political system was at least possible. Yet there is ample reason for suspecting that many, if not most, representatives seldom allowed their constituency's preferences to influence their legislative behavior. In political systems which substantially fulfill our eight conditions, legislative accountability finally depends upon the fact that most legislators *want* to remain in office. In provincial Massachusetts, however, this was simply not the case. Whether or not they secured reelection apparently mattered little. For most representatives, serving more than a couple of terms in the Assembly involved considerable personal sacrifice, and as long as maintaining one's independence meant nothing more than retiring a year earlier than expected, most representatives were immune to threats of reprisals at the polls.

The Assembly leader must be excluded from this generalization. For him, maintaining his seat in the House was important —probably important enough to make him peculiarly sensitive to the demands of his constituents. There is, of course, a special irony in all of this. For years we have suspected that the colonial leader was an elitist, a member of a restrictive upper class bent

[28] *MHJ*, 18:304, 19:3-4, 47-48, 186.

on preserving the privileges and immunities of great wealth and prestige. Yet these same politicians belonged to the one group capable of being pressured into supporting programs favored by a majority of their constituents.

There is a second reason for believing that the Assembly's upper-class leaders were uniquely sensitive to popular opinion within their constituencies. In attempting to understand the modern legislator, political scientists have noted that while most voters remain blissfully unaware of their representative's legislative record, these same representatives continue to believe that public stands on crucial issues do sway the electorate. One answer to this paradox is that a representative can suddenly become visible, and thus the prudent course of action is to do nothing which might occasion the voters' displeasure. A supplementary hypothesis—and, I think, a more satisfactory one—has been suggested by Robert Dahl, whose study of a modern city convinced him that in general "members of the political stratum [that is, a society's professional politicians] are more familiar with the 'democratic' norms, more consistent, more ideological, more detailed and explicit in their political attitudes, and more completely in agreement on the norms. They are more in agreement not only on what norms are implied by the abstract democratic creed but also in supporting the norms currently operating." [29] We might generalize these findings to suggest that in most societies it is the member of the governmental elite who best understands and most consistently bases his actions on the generally accepted doctrines of his particular society.

In the eighteenth century, political theory taught that the function of a representative form of government was to balance a ruler's desire for self-aggrandizement against the people's dis-

---

[29] Robert A. Dahl, *Who Governs?* (New Haven: Yale University Press, 1961), p. 319.

trust of an ordered society. One corollary of this doctrine held that a representative, as a free agent, was to restrain his constituents in their attempts to evade authority and thus subvert the true purpose of government. In part, this emphasis on a representative's political independence underlay the Assembly's official reasons for keeping its proceedings secret. In 1724 the House appointed a special committee to prepare "some proper vote, the better to support the honor and dignity of the House; and to prevent the disclosing or discovering abroad of any debate that may arise and happen in the House." Two days later the committee reported and the House adopted the following resolve:

> That if any member of this House shall disclose, divulge, or make public the debates or secrets of the House, which tends very much to the obstruction of that freedom and liberty of speech so necessary for the good and welfare of the province, he shall be liable to such censure as the House shall think proper.[30]

A 1760 election pamphlet, in attempting to salvage the careers of two unpopular representatives, suggests another application of this doctrine. While the author conceded that his candidates had defied the town's known wishes, the matter involved "mere judgment and opinion," not "liberty and privilege." [31]

This distinguishing between mere judgment and matters of liberty and privileges similarly illustrates the second principle defining a representative's obligations. A system of representation in which a constituent was to defer to the judgment of a representative who did not share a corresponding sense of obligation was, by provincial standards, as deficient as a system in which a legislator was the mere tool of those who put him in office. To ward off this evil of self-serving rulers it was necessary to unite citizen and legislator in an organic relationship of interest. In

[30] *MHJ*, 6:135–37.
[31] *To the Freeholders of the Town of Boston* (Boston, 1760), p. 2.

fact, insofar as possible, the representative was to share the same circumstances, and hence the same interests, as the voters who delegated him authority. Two conditions were to encourage such a system of mutual dependency. First, constituencies were to be purposely kept small, thus increasing the likelihood that legislator and citizen would in fact share the same interests. Second, regular elections would reinforce such bonds. The people were free to choose a representative whose virtues and abilities were known and whose interests paralleled their own. Thereafter the representative's oath of office became a solemn pledge that he would support no policy which oppressed the people. Whenever a representative violated this oath, he was to be turned out of office, that is, he was to be forced to pay the same penalties he had formerly inflicted upon his neighbors.[32]

If, as seems likely, the professional politician was not only familiar with this doctrine, but also believed that it correctly described the good ruler, then provincial leaders had a second reason for heeding public opinion. While the necessity of remaining in office obviously prevented the professional from fulfilling the role of a quasi magistrate—a situation which again suggests a conflict between internalized norms and actual experience—no comparable situation existed to lessen his sense of obligation to his constituency, that is, to reduce the importance he attached to a maxim warning against oppressing the people he governed.

Finally, eighteenth-century ideas about responsive institutions also contain a plausible explanation of the link between the non-professional representative and his constituency. Most back-benchers came from small and remarkably homogeneous communities in which an organic relationship of interest united citi-

[32] Richard Buel, Jr., "Democracy and the American Revolution," *William and Mary Quarterly,* 3d ser. 31 (1964): 165–90.

zen and legislator. To the extent that the back-bencher did not believe himself accountable to the people he governed, the provincial political system was not democratic. But then it hardly mattered. Most men could vote; elections were annual and constituencies small; and a legislator ordinarily voiced his community's aspirations and grievances because he shared its prejudices. But we must also understand that this responsiveness did not transcend the eighteenth century, did not in fact prevail once America was no longer a society of near equals in which most men expected little of their government.

11

Court and Constituency

IN 1754 WILLIAM FLETCHER ROSE IN THE HOUSE AND ATTEMPTED
to define the merchant's place in a predominantly agricultural society. He began by depicting what to him appeared
the merchant's true interest. "The business of a merchant, AS A
MERCHANT, is to . . . [earn] the greatest profit; . . . it never
enters . . . his mind *when two legal branches of trade* lie open
before him, which of them is for the greatest good of the country
—no—he pursues that (and with all the reason and justice in the
world) which yields him the most profit." And yet the merchant
remained an integral, indeed essential, part of the provincial
economy. "Those common received distinctions," Fletcher lamented, "that trading interest and landed interest are in two
different boxes, are the most idle and ridiculous that ever entered
into the mind of man." What would happen if Newbury harbor
suddenly became impassable? Would the·merchant suffer? Not
really, because he could easily move to Boston or Salem or
another of the province's half-dozen seaports. But with the merchant gone and Newbury again a sleepy village, the markets
which consumed the farmer's produce and insured his prosperity

would evaporate, leaving him with little more than enough to eat.[1]

Fletcher then turned to an impost bill before the House which, among other duties, levied an increased tax on imported wines. The vagaries of mercantilism had created a special dilemma for Massachusetts. Although Europe offered a ready market for the province's fish, it paid for this staple not in specie or marketable commodities, but in wine. Against this trade Fletcher wanted to raise a prohibitive tariff. It was true, he conceded, that the trade seemed legitimate enough. Indeed if the wine had then been resold outside the province, the trade would have been truly advantageous. But the wine was consumed in Massachusetts, thus ruining the economy and debasing public morality.

> We had as good consume our own produce at first, as send it abroad, and bring in other commodities, and consume them, the exchange of them only serves to pamper our luxurious inclinations: And I look upon it when a merchant sends abroad £2000 value of his country-produce, and brings back again only a parcel of wines to be consumed, which he sells to his country for £4000, yet though the merchant himself is a gainer by it, he does not enrich his country so much as the merchant who carries out £2000, and brings home only £1000 in cash.

And if wine was all that fish could buy, then the province had best leave the cod in the sea.[2]

Fletcher's speech was one of the more reasoned statements of what troubled rural Massachusetts. More shrilly, more malevolently, other rural controversialists cursed the merchant for all the province's ills. He imported luxuries to seduce the people. He hoarded specie, driving commodity prices down and interest rates up. And while the farmer made little headway in his own

---

[1] *Boston Weekly News-Letter,* 20 June 1754.
[2] Ibid. See also *MHJ,* 31:48.

quest for abundance, the merchant waxed strong, his warehouses full, his coffers bulging, and his family enjoying all the fruits of plentiful prosperity.[3]

When they tired of castigating the merchant, spokesmen for rural Massachusetts turned to the seaport itself, the entire maritime community, including shopkeepers, artisans, and mechanics as well as the merchants who dominated the city's economy. Massachusetts boasted a half-dozen communities which qualified as embryo cities. Salem, Newbury, and Marblehead each had more than four thousand inhabitants, and although smaller, Ipswich, Gloucester, and Plymouth similarly claimed thriving merchant communities and economies no longer predominantly agricultural. Having assumed many of the characteristics of urban societies, these population centers contrasted sharply with the settled rural areas of the countryside. But in rural propaganda, the "city" meant Boston with its fifteen thousand inhabitants, majestic long wharf, teeming streets, crowded shops, and obvious prosperity.

Merchant propagandists rarely replied to the country's charges. Either unwilling to antagonize a potential market or sensing that polemics would have little impact on a contentious rural majority, the merchant contented himself with extolling the virtues of honest husbandry and counseling frugality and industry as the only cure for the farmer's problems. But other spokesmen for the city fully intended to reply with grievances of their own. The crux of the issue was economic: the country fed the city, and Boston and her sister seaports provided the flow of cash and goods on which the hinterland's prosperity depended.

In the summer of 1749 a drought scorched Massachusetts, withering crops and inflating commodity prices. For Boston the

---

[3] See particularly, *A Letter to the Merchant in London to Whom Is Directed a Printed Letter Relating to the Manufactory Undertaking* (Boston, 1741).

shortage and exorbitant cost of fresh produce made the summer heat and the city's already depressed trade unbearable. Then in July a correspondent to the *Boston Evening Post* reminded his suffering neighbors of the good old days when men had observed the law of social righteousness and practiced Christian charity. In times of crisis the strong had aided the weak and the healthy had assisted the afflicted. But now, "DISHONESTY" had become the *"reigning vice of New England."* Farmers sold what produce remained to the highest bidder, extracting the last drop of profit from a beleaguered city. Damaged barley commanded seventy pounds a load, where before, perfect grain had brought barely twenty. The price of hay had trebled, and farmers sold "butter and milk, and other things for the support of life, without any regard to *mercy,* so little has *justice* been in their thoughts." The correspondent closed with a thinly veiled threat that if farmers persisted in profiteering, the city's authorities would take remedial action. The letter was published a week after drenching rains had quenched the land. In a gratuitous note, Thomas Fleet editorially marked the impact the rains had on the province's farmers:

> The country people have abated *something* of their former extravagant demands; yet it is evident enough, that the *evil spirit* of EXTORTION is not gone out of them. . . . It is the opinion of many judicious persons, that people in the towns near *Boston,* have made a greater profit of the fruits they brought to sell, than if the earth had yielded a full increase: So that it is no breach of charity to suppose, that while many of them *fasted and prayed for rain, their hearts were going after their covetousness.* It is certain, that the drought, which was a sore judgment of heaven on the land, they made an *excuse* and *cloak,* to cover their abominable extortion.[4]

Three weeks later Rusticus replied in behalf of the much-

[4] *Boston Evening Post,* 24 July 1749.

abused farmer. It was not extortion but the simple economics of
a free market that established commodity prices. *"Extortion* can
have no place in a fair and open market, where the seller tells you
fairly his price . . . and leaves you at your liberty to take or
leave it." Boston's problem was not greedy farmers but too many
people—too many idle shopkeepers, too many unemployed work-
ers, too "many indolent . . . men, women, and children":

> I am surprised (when I am in *Boston*) to see such a number of
> healthy able-bodied men in all parts of the town, sitting idle be-
> hind their counters, or lolling over their shop-windows, and have
> been told, that some *scores,* if not *hundreds* of them were formerly
> good and useful tradesmen, who while they followed their callings,
> not only maintained their families well, but many of them got
> handsome estates, and were useful members of the commonwealth:
> Whereas *now,* they seem to be a dead weight upon the public, and
> perhaps a greater charge than if they were supported in some of
> the houses provided for the reception of poor, idle, sickly or aged
> persons; (though there they might not *fare so sumptuously every
> day*) for whatever such useless persons consume, it comes out of
> some body's pocket, and the public loses the benefit of their labor
> besides.[5]

The next issue of the *Evening Post* contained yet another rejoinder. It was true, the author argued, that dishonesty reigned
in Massachusetts. But its victims were "those who depend upon
Boston for any of the necessary supports or comforts of humane
life." Extortion? Who had less mercy than the merchant and
shopkeeper who charged a man seven years' wages for a decent
suit of clothes? And who was to deny "that the country people
are at least as honest in general, and as merciful as the *Bostonians"*?

Let the authorit[ies] take these things into consideration, and all
our towns will shout for joy, and be exceedingly glad, if we find

[5] Ibid., 14 August 1749.

they are men who will in fact judge righteously between a man and his neighbor. If you, *sir,* are a man of such integrity . . . it is my hearty wish, that you had power to put an end to all the great and little frauds and oppressions that are indeed but too prevalent throughout the land.[6]

Overcharged in the marketplace, the Bostonian also pictured himself the victim of a rural-dominated Assembly bent on forcing the metropolis to subsidize the central government. Despite the affluent image most outsiders had of the capital, Bostonians frequently lapsed into a deep melancholia when they assessed their own sagging fortunes. The city, they testified, was constantly afflicted by depression and despair. English merchants flooded the market with worthless luxuries instead of good money. The 1733 Molasses Act, imposed by an unsympathetic Parliament, had halved the city's distilling industry. The French had preempted the cod market, throwing hundreds of able-bodied men out of work. Although unable to support its own citizens, Boston had become a haven for the poor and the lame, draining the town's treasury and further depressing its economy. And the General Court, wrongly convinced of the city's wealth, had imposed an intolerable tax burden on a struggling citizenry.[7]

In 1761 the Assembly, in answer to Boston's repeated pleas for tax relief, ordered a new provincial property evaluation. Like all economic censuses, the new evaluation required every property holder to determine his net worth and then swear to its accuracy. While the evaluation was in progress, the Old South Church in Boston celebrated the installation of a new assistant pastor with a banquet that could only reinforce the farmer's image of the city as a fount of luxury, idleness, and unbounded wealth. Predictably the feast touched off a new round of anti-Boston

[6] Ibid., 21 August 1749.
[7] Boston, Mass., *Report of the Record Commissioners of the City of Boston,* 39 vols. (Boston, 1881–1909), 12:119–24, 14:180–81.

propaganda, contrasting the wealth of the city with the austerity of the countryside. "Upon each table," one writer reported, was "a . . . plum pudding, a dish of boiled pork . . . fowls . . . a corned leg of pork . . . a leg of bacon, a piece of alamode beef, a . . . roast . . . of veal, a . . . turkey, a venison pastee, besides chess cakes and tarts, cheese and butter. Half a dozen cooks were employed . . . [and] upwards of twenty tenders to wait upon the tables; they had the best of old cider, one barrel of Lisbon wine, punch . . . before and after dinner, made of old Barbados spirits. The cost of this moderate dinner was upwards of fifty pounds lawful money." [8]

In Braintree, John Adams, pondering the effect of the new tax evaluation and the richness of the banquet, prepared his own contribution to the growing debate. Adopting the guise of an aggrieved Bostonian, Adams contrasted life in the great metropolis with the lot of the poor but hardworking farmer.

The affair of taxes has been a common . . . complaint against the country . . . in this metropolis for many years. Our gentry has given frequent invitations . . . to . . . country gentlemen . . . [at which] the furniture of our houses and tables were proportionably rich and gay. Our persons were clothed in silks and laces and velvet, and our daughters especially blazed in the rich vestments of princesses. At the same time the poor gentlemen were scarcely able to walk the streets, for the multitude of chariots, or to hear themselves speak for the rapid rattling of hoofs and wheels. . . . These appearances . . . gave the country an opinion, either that Boston was vastly rich or vastly extravagant, and they dared not . . . suppose the latter lest they should give offense to us, who had treated them even with assiduous complaisance and hospitality.

Meanwhile farmers wore their tattered homespun, ate salt pork, drank cider and beer, and cheerfully saved "every penny to pay

[8] *Boston Gazette*, 11 May 1761. See also *A&R*, 4:422–23.

their taxes." But "we in Boston never would pay ours, without grumbling, and cursing country folks, and country representatives." Nor had the country's willingness to take a new evaluation extinguished Boston's complaints. "What we cry? . . . Must not we drink Madeira, eat in silver and china? Ride in our chariots? . . . Let our sons and daughters spend a few guineas a week at cards without telling the assessors, and having it recorded that we are in debt for all this, and £10,000 worse than nothing! Oh these vile shoe string country representatives." [9]

Stripped of its invective, this urban-rural debate suggested that where a man lived and how he and his neighbors earned a livelihood were more important politically than economic or class distinctions within a community. Eighteenth-century Massachusetts fell into five geographic regions.[10] Nearly a third of the province's quarter-million inhabitants lived along the eastern shore, a narrow strip of seaports and farming communities running from Newbury in the north to Barnstable in the south. The business of the East, of course, was business itself. One out of every two of the region's seventy-five thousand inhabitants dwelt and worked in a maritime community. From Boston, Salem, Ipswich, and Newbury sailed ships carrying the produce of the province, and into these ports flowed the manufactures and luxuries which, besides enriching English merchants, made life in the wilderness more comfortable. Gloucester, Marblehead, Plymouth, and a score of smaller villages harbored the fleets that fished the cod banks off Nova Scotia, supplying Spain and Portugal with salted fish in exchange for Madeira and port. Even the agriculture of the region enjoyed a commercial cast,

[9] *JA-Diary,* 1:213–14.
[10] For a list of sources detailing the economic geography of Massachusetts, see the bibliographic note.

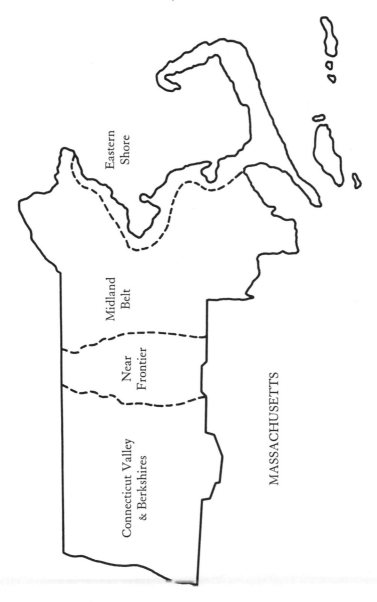

Eastern
Shore

Midland
Belt

Near
Frontier

Connecticut Valley
& Berkshires

MASSACHUSETTS

since the seaport served as both a market for fresh produce and a ready source of money and credit.

The bulk of the province's rural population, however, worked the small, seemingly prosperous farms of the midland belt, an expanse of natural pasturage and cleared forest land stretching westward from the seacoast and including the eastern edge of Worcester County. Growing his own food and satisfying most of his own needs, the midland farmer lived an arduous, ordinarily austere existence. Poor soil and an impossible climate made cultivation difficult and bountiful harvests rare. If they were often unaffected by trade depressions in the East, midland farmers also frequently failed to share in the economic booms which enriched the seacoast. The lack of a commercial crop and accessible markets meant that cash and credit were always in short supply. And while this absence of a circulating medium of exchange seldom reduced anyone to poverty, it did make most manufactured goods and luxuries virtually unattainable.

The least integrated, both economically and politically, of the province's five regions was the Connecticut Valley. First occupied in the 1630s, Hampshire County was still the province's western frontier. Along the Connecticut River lay a half-dozen old towns like Northampton, Springfield, and Hadley, which, as frontier trading centers, serviced the small communities nestling under the Berkshire Hills. Besides dictating the geography of settlement, the river had also oriented the economy of the region southward toward Connecticut rather than eastward toward Boston. Down the river floated the valley's exports, principally flax and lumber, while Hartford, Providence, and Newport supplied the few imports the valley required. Physically isolated from the rest of the province and practically autonomous, the far frontier expected Yale rather than Harvard to educate her leaders and staff her pulpits and depended on the central government only for military forces and defense appropriations.

Between Hampshire County and the midland belt lay the near frontier of Worcester County. Almost forgotten by the rest of Massachusetts, the near frontier was the least populated, the least important, and probably the poorest of the province's five regions. Dominated by pine barrens and marshland, the landscape was broken only by small farms, new villages, an occasional hamlet, and a handful of established towns. Virtually inaccessible, the region imported little and exported less.

To the north and east and detached from the rest of Massachusetts lay the farming settlements, lumber camps, and aspiring trading centers of Maine, the province's third frontier and fifth region. Like that of Worcester County, the region's economy largely reflected the settler's attempts to populate and farm a wilderness. Maine, however, enjoyed at least three special advantages. Falmouth, already a major fishing port, was rapidly becoming a commercial center servicing the growing trade with Nova Scotia. A dozen other natural harbors sheltered small fishing and trading fleets which increased the farmer's access to outside markets and products. More important, perhaps, the region's great timber stands and booming lumber camps offered profitable employment for any farmer tired of tilling his poor land or interested in supplementing his cash income.

One way to measure the impact these geographic and economic differences had on eighteenth-century politics is to focus on provincial tax policies. Four-fifths of the province's revenues came from a combined poll and property tax levied against each town. In 1756 this tax amounted to £53,000. If apportioned equally, the average assessment in each town would have been about 18 shillings per ratable poll. Yet seven out of every ten communities enjoyed a substantially lower average assessment. Three dozen communities, while paying more than the provincial average, still paid less than 26 shillings per ratable poll. And only one town—Boston—paid an average rate of more than 30 shillings. Indeed, Boston, with less than 6 percent of the province's taxable population, paid 17 percent of the province tax, or 61 shillings per ratable poll. And yet the 1756 tax apportionment simply reaffirmed longstanding anti-Boston prejudices. Despite the city's own static size and the rapid population growth of the rest of the province, Boston's share of the provincial tax remained constant.[11]

The remaining 20 percent of the province's revenues came from tariffs and excises on imported wines, rum, tobacco, East Indian china, tea, coffee, coaches, and European goods. Officially customs duties and excises were levied against all provincials. Everyone who bought European goods and spirits paid his share of the tariff. And annually the General Court went through the ritual of electing excise collectors for each of the province's eleven counties. Yet in fact tariffs and excises taxed chiefly the maritime towns, and more particularly Boston. City dwellers, not farmers, sipped their tea from china cups, wore French lace, and drank expensive wines and rum instead of beer and cider. A farmer may have longed for these amenities, but his purchases had to be more practical—an occasional suit of clothes, a few dresses for his wife, shoes cordwained in Boston, and plowshares, pots, and other ironware crafted in Massachusetts.[12]

The systematic and persistent nature of this tax discrimination suggests that on this issue politicians representing the province's farmers belonged to a remarkably effective coalition. Whether or not the rural majority was equally united on other questions is more difficult to gauge. Again the basic problem is

[11] *A&R*, 2:52–53, 388–89, 802–04, 3:279–81, 967–68, and the statistical appendix.
[12] Bernard to the Lords of Trade, 5 September 1763, J. H. Benton, Jr., *Early Census Making in Massachusetts* (Boston, 1905), pp. 51, 59; *A&R*, 17:512–18.

the relative absence of formal votes in the House of Representatives, only seventeen being published during the twenty-five years covered by this study. What an analysis of this fragmentary record suggests, however, is that regional biases had little effect on questions of patronage and constitutional prerogatives. But on fiscal issues three separate and relatively distinct clusters of communities did emerge.[13]

Ironically, it was the West, not the East, which most defiantly preached the gospel of sound money, balanced budgets, and a frugal government. Hampshire County conservatism meant curbing inflation, damning the Land Bank, and, after 1750, resisting every attempt to soften the province's new specie currency. Nearly a dozen of the colony's older and more established farming communities shared the Connecticut Valley's abhorrence of easy money and budget deficits.

A slightly smaller group of communities took their cue from the province's maritime towns, particularly Boston and Salem. These towns, like the West, opposed the Land Bank and radical experiments in inflationary economics. Nonetheless the need to placate the inflationists in their own midst occasionally forced representatives from these communities to moderate their opposition to budget deficits and paper money. In 1740 representatives from the bulk of the province's commercial centers supported a three-year tax moratorium and a corresponding reliance on new emissions of paper. Again, in the 1750s, once the new specie currency had gone into circulation, Boston and its allies endorsed a partial continuation of paper money.

Yet for most provincial communities hard money was anathema and inflation, at worst, a necessary evil. These towns provided the bulk of the Land Bank's support, bitterly resented the conversion to a specie currency, and readily supported any measure

[13] See the statistical appendix.

promising more paper. And the province's easy money communities were, with few exceptions, midland or eastern shore farming towns. Massachusetts farmers—or at least their representatives—swelled the ranks of the radical inflationists. If nothing else, their program made a virtue of simplicity. On tax questions there was but one rule of thumb: whatever the levy, let Bostonians pay most of it. And economic prosperity, they argued, required nothing more than setting Massachusetts awash in a sea of paper money.

"The prudent, frugal, industrious honest farmers and husbandmen," wrote a disgruntled Bostonian in 1754, "live in plenty, peace and safety, not acquainted with the way and manner that others live. . . . They sleep quietly in their houses, their fields are well secured from danger, everyone sits quietly under his vines and fruit trees, and none can make them afraid." [14] Despite its mocking tone, this description of rural Massachusetts was not irrelevant. The vision of the farmer living in pastoral serenity and embodying the virtues of frugality, honesty, and self-reliance seemingly captured the essence of rural life. Untainted by commercialism, given to honest labor, and capable of producing and enjoying simple abundance, the farmer tilled his own land, ordered his own life, and was more than capable of defending his own rights.

Yet rural Massachusetts was obviously not serene. With alarming regularity the farmer—or at least the representatives who spoke for him—embroiled the province in a succession of crises, each more rancorous than the last and each designed to adjust the economic order. There were, no doubt, a number of explanations for the farmer's discontent, but the simplest and most basic was that the rural economy had failed to satisfy his aspirations. The

[14] *A Plea for the Poor and Distressed of Boston* (Boston, 1754), pp. 3–4.

farmer was of middling status in a society dominated by men like him, and yet seemingly he was denied the goods and luxuries his status ought to have brought. Frustrated in his own quest for material abundance, he was equally convinced that the opulence of the East and particularly of Boston was being achieved at his expense. In 1754 the farmer vented these frustrations, but the quarrel itself went back more than four decades.

By 1714 Massachusetts had already dabbled in the mysteries of a paper currency. Hesitantly, on a limited scale, and without quite perceiving the Pandora's Box it opened, the General Court had sanctioned the printing of government notes. The absence of an adequate medium of exchange, everyone had agreed, made trade sluggish and encouraged the recessions that periodically plagued Massachusetts. The notes had met an obvious need, and yet the results of the experiment were uncertain. A province and particularly a merchant community accustomed to a specie currency had driven the price of the paper down and the cost of silver and gold up. But it was not clear whether the government had printed too much or too little money, and while most of the province simply debated the merits of more paper, a dozen Bostonians whose fortunes were in land rather than trade proposed their own solution.[15]

"The difficulties," their prospectus began, "which the trade of this province labors under, by reason of the scarcity of money, having rendered it necessary that some expedient be found . . . to supply that deficiency: A scheme of a bank of credit founded upon a land security, has been accordingly projected." Seeing no other way to produce a medium, the Bank's directors had decided to provide it themselves. Land mortgaged to the Bank, rather than an unpredictable supply of gold and silver, would secure

[15] Andrew McFarland Davis, *Currency and Banking in the Province of the Massachusetts-Bay,* 2 vols. (New York, 1900, 1901), 1:25–67.

the notes and, incidentally, increase the capital holdings of the bulk of the population. True, the bankers themselves stood to make a tidy profit, but the province would have an adequate money supply and graciously the directors planned to turn over some of the proceeds to charity and Harvard College.[16]

The ink on the prospectus had scarcely dried when Joseph Dudley replied on behalf of the province's conservatives. Dudley was confident that the Privy Council would never allow the Bank to issue a note, but not content with this prospect, he lectured his fellow provincials on the folly of their ways. Were frugality and sober husbandry in fashion there would be no need for banks or paper money or schemes for depriving the industrious and rewarding the idle. But "the people, and especially the ordinary sort," had fallen into "great extravagance . . . far beyond their circumstances, in their purchases, buildings, families, expenses, apparel, and generally in their whole way of living: And above all, the excessive consumption of *rum* and *wine,* as one of the greatest sources and causes of the present distress." The decline of New England piety, not an inadequate money supply, Dudley told Massachusetts, was the root of the problem.[17]

Thus began the debate over the propriety of a private banking scheme. The debate itself marked a new epoch in the province's political and intellectual history. Once provincials had assumed that religion would cure economic ills and that the language and symbols of the jeremiad adequately defined the political process. Now all this changed. The debate created a new frame of reference, secularizing the political rhetoric and replacing the metaphors of the pulpit with those of the marketplace. But more important, the debate made a mockery of the notion that Christian charity and bonds of mutual affection knit together the

[16] *A Model for Erecting a Bank of Credit* (Boston, 1714), p. 2.
[17] [Paul Dudley], *Objections to the Bank of Credit* (Boston, 1714), p. 24.

Christian community. Massachusetts now adopted new categories to explain political reality, and the province, most men came to agree, was after all afflicted by tensions between rich and poor, creditor and debtor, farmer and merchant.[18]

Both sides bore some responsibility for these changes. But the Land Banker, convinced that his conservative opposition had wrapped itself in the cloak of orthodoxy, launched the boldest attack on the old order. Were not, he asked, hard-money men only protecting their own interests at the expense of the rest of the province? Did not the conservative policy of returning to a currency worth its face value mean, in concrete terms, increasing already exorbitant interest rates in order to benefit the province's creditors? It took little effort to generalize this argument, to suggest as John Colman did, that "the richest men are not always most beneficial to the commonwealth," or that the opposition to the Bank came principally from "some country gentlemen, who live on their farms, and others, men of plentiful fortunes, who do not feel the straits of the times, and therefore cannot," as Christian charity commanded, "sympathize so feelingly with their neighbors." [19]

Then in 1720 Oliver Noyes went further. Conservatives had blamed the province's ills on outrageous extravagance. The people, they charged, thirsted for what they could not afford and should not have wanted. "If we import from abroad, more than we can pay for . . . we shall," Dudley had warned, "unavoidably grow poor, and a million of *paper-money* won't help the matter at all." Noyes was unimpressed. "I must own," he conceded, "that we have been too extravagant in our buildings, clothing, furniture, and tables, and I confess it is a fault to exceed

[18] Perry Miller, *The New England Mind. From Colony to Province* (Cambridge, Mass.: Harvard University Press, 1953), pp. 305–23.
[19] [John Colman], *The Distressed State of the Town of Boston* (Boston, 1720), pp. 6, 8.

in these things; but *Solomon* tells us, *that there is nothing better under the sun than for a man to eat and drink, and enjoy the good of his labor:* So that I believe we ought not to be sordidly covetous, and deny ourselves the comfort of what we work for, but eat and drink as our circumstances will afford." [20] Grafted to a rhetoric already directed toward the least affluent segment of the society, this justification of material wants implicitly defined opulence for everyone as the society's goal. No one need feel guilty about wanting to dress his wife in imported silks and to adorn his table with pewter and silver. And if easy credit and paper money were the only means of guaranteeing shared abundance, then the government had a moral obligation to sanction, indeed to encourage, a private Land Bank that would invigorate the economy and allow everyone to enjoy the good life.

Initially the debate over the Land Bank was chiefly a discussion among Bostonians about conditions in the capital. When Bank opponents lamented the extravagance of a distressed people they were talking about Boston, and the ordinary sort who insisted upon living beyond their means were the capital's tradesmen, shopkeepers, and mechanics. The Bank's supporters always understood that success depended on defending the aspirations of these men while simultaneously reinforcing their hostility to the merchant community. Thus the justification of shared abundance was largely directed toward those who in good times had whetted their material appetites and now during a trade depression faced reduced standards of living. After 1720, however, the Bank's propaganda broadened this appeal and suggested that the province's forgotten husbandman, like the urban mechanic, could only benefit from a rapidly expanding economy fueled by an increasing money supply and easy credit. Noyes himself had fore-

[20] Dudley, *Objections to the Bank,* p. 23. [Oliver Noyes], *A Letter from a Gentleman* (Boston, 1720), p. 9.

shadowed this development when he argued: "the country will by and by feel as great, if not greater mischiefs from this want of a medium than we [in Boston] have felt, and in matters of greater consequence," for when there is no more paper money, "(which will not be long . . .) they must sell their produce for shop goods, or keep them and eat them all themselves; and that we can't allow . . . for then we must starve, and rather than do so, we shall be so wicked as to borrow of our country friends and never pay." [21] John Wise, writing in 1721, expanded this argument and focused on the farmer's own rising expectations.

Wise not only approved of abundance, he reveled in it. Why, he asked, did luxuries abound if not to be enjoyed and "to furnish a generous people, that would banish sordidness, and live bright and civil, with fine accomplishments about them?" Only if Massachusetts was prepared to live on ground nuts and clams and to rely on fur pelts for its clothing could it hope to become self-sufficient and renounce foreign imports. "But if we intend to live in any garb, or port, as becomes a people of religion, civility, trade and industry, then we must still supply ourselves from the great fountain." But more important than abundance itself was the distribution of the amenities it brought. As long as the economy satisfied the material aspirations of only a few, envy would breed social and political turmoil. And in Massachusetts, Wise declared, the "abundance . . . [enjoyed by the province's farmers] if not gone behind hand . . . [has] stood at a stay; or with all their hard labor, and hard fare . . . [has] turned like the door on the hinge, as though [farmers were] sluggards." And to keep the farmer "in a thread-bare coat, and starve him of his profits . . . will . . . much dis-animate . . . the means of your plenty, your safety, and flourishing condition." [22]

[21] Noyes, *A Letter*, p. 10.
[22] [John Wise], *A Word of Comfort to a Melancholy Country* (Boston, 1721), pp. 23, 33–34, 38.

Yet for Wise this was scarcely an unresolvable dilemma. One need only recognize that in Massachusetts the farmer's economic plight reflected neither a lack of personal piety nor a God-given destiny, but rather the province's attempt to maintain a specie currency. Why had farmers suffered from "penurious markets and prices?" The answer was obvious: "The fault has been in the medium of trade, on which they have depended." In short, an insufficient money supply had disrupted the economy, depressing agricultural prices and inflating the value of those imported luxuries by which provincials measured personal affluence. And since specie was scarce, Wise declared, let Massachusetts rely on paper notes which "allow of a quicker dispatch, and fuller price, and with more equity, and thus it ought to be; and this animates the farmer; keeps him to his plough; brightens and enlivens all his rural schemes; reconciles him to all his hard labor, and makes him look fat and cheerful." [23]

Wise was never more radical. In his hands, money, like government, became an instrument to be employed at man's convenience. In some societies exclusive reliance on gold and silver fulfilled a useful function by stabilizing the economy. But in a predominantly rural and politically dependent community like Massachusetts, Wise believed, a specie currency was palpably absurd. Then too, since money was simply a convenient instrument for managing the distribution of economic resources, it could be employed to structure the economy itself. If the society's goal was shared abundance, then let the provincial government sanction a Land Bank designed to bring affluence to rural Massachusetts.

The Bank, however, never issued a note. And while trade recovered, the rural economy continued much as before. The farmer tilled his land and fed his family while he watched the

[23] Ibid., pp. 23, 34.

East grow richer and its merchant community more opulent. Despite all his efforts the gap between city and farm only widened. But the debate had taught the farmer one thing: his prosperity obviously depended on a bountiful supply of paper money. Inflation, he had been told, would spur the rural economy, creating new sources of cash and credit and increasing the availability of the goods he wanted. Not only was his poverty an unnatural state of affairs, but the government could banish, as if by magic, the cause of his distress. All Massachusetts need do was print an abundant supply of money.

The farmer learned this lesson well. Rural-dominated assemblies never tired of printing money. By 1736, when Jonathan Belcher and a conservative Council finally applied the brakes, £250,000 was in circulation. Then in 1739 John Colman, responding to England's edict that Massachusetts retire its entire paper currency, revived the idea of a private Land Bank. Conservatives like Douglass were appalled. "You desire to know," he wrote in a mock letter to a London merchant, "the nature of our landed interest, which . . . [the Land Bank has] set up in competition with the trading interest. . . . Our *freeholders* generally are laboring men, who earn less, and fare worse, than many in *Boston*. . . . Indulge me here, to cast a veil, over the nakedness of our country: This country seems designed by nature for trade, not for produce: We import provisions at much easier rates from the southern provinces, than we can afford to raise them here." Not content with mocking the farmer's poverty, Douglass went on to charge:

> The truth is shortly this; the debtor part of the country (which is vastly the most numerous) are contriving to baulk their creditors by reducing the denominations of money (by their huge and ill-secured emissions) to a small or no value; that they who have laudably acquired fortunes by industry and frugality, may reap

no benefit thereof, but be upon a level with the idle and extravagant.[24]

Thus in a single stroke Douglass reduced an entire rural population to the status of debtors, men so morally base that they could corrupt the entire economy in their quest for idle and extravagant luxuries. A week later a spokesman for rural Massachusetts issued the traditional rejoinder. "In . . . answer to your desire *to know the nature of our landed interest,*" a second public letter to the same London merchant replied, the previous author

> ought to have told you, "that it is almost ruined by our trade, as our merchants manage it." It's true, *sir,* our fore-fathers spent their blood and treasure . . . in subduing this wilderness, and its savage inhabitants; and the land being cultivated is generally exceeding good, for so cold a climate; the people orderly, virtuous, and industrious, but the want of money . . . has brought them to the pass our author speaks of. Though he has his own ends in casting his veil over their nakedness; otherwise he might have discovered the means which made them so, which would be little to his credit. The truth is this, that the import too much encouraged, or export too much neglected and discouraged, has built up a few on the ruins of many.[25]

Few farmers demurred. Again, or so they thought, they stood at Armageddon, challenging the province's merchants, defying their intemperate governor, and defeating any politician who refused to champion the new orthodoxy.

It was not, however, the Land Bank but the supply bill Robert Hale drafted in September 1741 that most clearly marked out the path rural radicalism intended Massachusetts to follow. The

---

[24] [William Douglass], *A Letter to* —— —— *Merchant in London* (Boston, 1741), pp. 8–9.
[25] *A Letter to the Merchant in London to Whom Is Directed a Printed Letter,* pp. 16–17.

bill would have emitted £36,000 in new tenor notes, established an official depreciation rate specifically benefiting those caught in the credit squeeze, and increased agricultural prices by allowing the farmer to pay his taxes in commodities. The Treasury, in effect, would become a depot for farm surpluses which it could dispose of only when the market price equaled rates established by the General Court. What rural radicalism prescribed was a healthy dose of inflation and special favors for the province's rural population. Taxes would no longer drain the interior of its limited currency. Crops once unmarketable, particularly corn, rye, and barley, would be given new value, thus freeing the cash the farmer earned from his few commercial exports. Indirectly, of course, the mercantile community would subsidize these programs. Tax assessments in the East, where specie and paper were more abundant, would naturally rise in order to compensate for the real revenues lost by accepting commodities in lieu of taxes.[26]

The compromise measure Shirley eventually signed embodied some, but not all, of this program. Thirty thousand pounds in new tenor notes were issued, and the farmer, for the first time since 1727, was allowed to pay his taxes in commodities. The compromise fulfilled some of the farmer's demands.[27] The war, which began in earnest in 1744, temporarily satisfied the rest. A steady stream of British contractors supplied the province with a new source of specie, and the Louisbourg expedition furnished new markets for agricultural products. Not for almost a decade did the old antagonisms erupt again—not until Shirley and Thomas Hutchinson cajoled, wheedled, and finally compelled a reluctant Assembly to return the province to a specie currency. The reaction of rural Massachusetts was predictably violent.

[26] *MHJ*, 19:105–11.
[27] *A&R*, 2:1077–83.

Farmer representatives who had backed the measure were swept out of office, and even Hale, who had supported hard money out of personal loyalty to Shirley, was unceremoniously retired by Beverly's irate voters. Only representatives from traditionally conservative farming communities escaped unscathed. For the next five years the rural majority nursed its grievances, then suddenly, petulantly, and not a little irrationally, it took its revenge.

The 1754 term began innocently enough. Shirley, buoyed up by the prospect of a new war with France, contemplated a productive year. He addressed the General Court on May 30, requesting improved local defenses, an adequate budget, and a new source of revenue. The speaker obligingly appointed a committee to review the province's fiscal conditions, and by June 1 the committee reported its first recommendation. Its proposal was simple enough. Previously rum bought in more than thirty-gallon lots had not been taxed, and this loophole, the committee suggested, could be plugged by an expanded excise on the consumption, as well as the retail sale, of rum.[28]

In his election sermon preached three days before, Jonathan Mayhew had warned the Assembly that Boston's taxpayers were growing restive. "Heaven," he suggested, "will be justly and greatly provoked, unless some pity and relief is afforded. . . . Poor *BOSTON!* once the glory of British America, what are thou coming to! What rather, art thou come to already!"[29] Whatever Boston had come to, the committee had decided it was still rich enough to absorb another tax. The extra revenue the governor had requested would come from the province's maritime towns which both distilled and consumed the bulk

[28] *MHJ,* 31:14; *A&R,* 8:673–79.
[29] Jonathan Mayhew, *An Election Sermon* (Boston, 1754), p. 48.

of the province's rum. By June 7 the House had engrossed an excise bill incorporating the committee's suggestion, and by June 16 the Council had reluctantly enacted the measure.

William Shirley had survived thirteen years as governor by making few mistakes. He could justifiably pride himself on his ability to mold public opinion by championing causes most provincials supported. Now, however, this gift betrayed him. Perhaps the furor that reports of the excise had already raised in Boston alarmed him. Or perhaps he was genuinely unhappy about the bill's provisions. Whatever his reasons, he refused to sign the excise, and told the House he would reserve judgment until after the representatives had consulted their constituents. Reluctantly the House ordered the excise bill printed and sent to the towns for their consideration. In a surly mood the representatives departed Boston, not to return until the following October.[30]

On the surface Shirley's gambit seemed eminently successful. Pamphleteers excoriated the House for enacting the measure, praised Shirley for his prudent stewardship, and railed against the farmer for again forcing the province's mercantile centers to subsidize the central government. In a letter to Shirley a grateful Plymouth thanked the governor for his past diligence, trusting "that in the important affair of the . . . excise your excellency will continue the same equal regard, and not suffer the maritime towns to be burdened, more than the inland towns (as they must we comprehend unavoidably be) if the . . . bill should pass into a law."[31] In August Boston became the first town to condemn the excise, and by October every major seaport and a dozen farming communities had joined the capital in calling for the measure's defeat.[32]

---

[30] *MHJ*, 31:46.

[31] *Records of the Town of Plymouth*, 3 vols. (Plymouth, Mass., 1903), 3:63–65.

[32] Kenneth Colegrove, "New England Town Mandates," *Publications of the*

The public attack on the excise echoed Shirley's charge that the measure was unconstitutional and "inconsistent with the *natural rights* of every private family in the community." But constitutional arguments aside, the excise openly invited hostility. The clause taxing private consumption began, "every person consuming, using or any way expending in his or her house, family, apartment or business . . . any wine [or] rum . . . except . . . purchased . . . of a taverner, innholder or retailer and in a quantity less than thirty gallons . . . shall pay the duties following," and then spelled out the procedures tax collectors could employ to verify the citizen's calculation of how much he and his family had imbibed in the last year.[33] Anti-excise pamphleteers condemned the invasion of the sanctity of the home, ridiculed the oath every citizen would have to swear, and drew grim pictures of honest women sacrificing their virtue to satisfy hounding tax collectors.

In a referendum, a majority of the province would probably have voted against the excise. Yet the apparent success of the campaign against the measure was in part an illusion. The opposition was concentrated in the East, and the public attacks, more often than not, reflected eastern and particularly Boston attitudes. In the interior the excise apparently generated little controversy. Some farming communities simply avoided the issue, while others, like Framingham, judged the excise to be "reasonable and for the interest of the province." [34] Remote from Boston and consequently untroubled by the propaganda emanat-

---

Colonial Society of Massachusetts 21 (1919): 535. Colegrove lists five towns in favor of the excise and twenty-one against. My own search through the extensive collections of town histories in the Yale University Library added only four towns to this list; Watertown endorsed the excise while Beverly, Duxbury, and Reading disapproved of the bill. At least two towns, Topsfield and Wenham, did not even consider the measure at their summer meetings.

[33] *MHJ*, 31:46. Massachusetts Archives (State House), Boston, Mass., 119:664–67.

[34] William Barry, *A History of Framingham* (Boston, 1847), p. 48.

ing from the capital's printing presses, rural Massachusetts appeared undisturbed by the furor the excise had raised.

The task facing the leaders of the coalition that had created the crisis was to dampen the East's hostility while reinforcing the solidarity of their farmer coalition. In July a long, often rambling pamphlet attempted to accomplish these diverse goals. Probably written by William Fletcher, *The Good of the Community Impartially Considered* began by pursuing the argument which anti-merchant pamphleteers had traditionally employed to divide public opinion in the province's maritime communities. The excise, Fletcher correctly pointed out, had not raised the tax on rum. Nor did it affect those who bought their refreshments retail. In fact all the excise did was tax those who could afford to buy their liquor wholesale. Turning to the author of an anti-excise pamphlet, Fletcher charged, "I am really afraid, sir, the most discerning sort of men will think you are aiming to throw the burden of the taxes upon the poorer sort of people, while you yourself are desirous of *wallowing freely* in all the luxuries of life."[35] Fletcher's message was clear: if any man could afford to pay more taxes, it was clearly the citizen affluent enough to buy his rum by the hogshead instead of by the dram. And just as obviously most city dwellers had little reason to resent an excise which taxed only the rich.

Fletcher's appeal to the farmer was scarcely more subtle. The interior, like the seacoast, consumed prodigious quantities of alcohol, but instead of rum farmers drank beer and homemade cider pressed from the fruit of their orchards. This simple fact had made the excise controversy possible, and now Fletcher counted on the same logic to convince the province's farmers

[35] [William Fletcher], *The Good of the Community Impartially Considered* (Boston, 1754), pp. 4, 5. The parallels between this work and Fletcher's speech on the 1754 impost bill (see note 1 above) were used to assign the authorship. See also *The Review* (Boston, 1754), p. 5.

that a special tax on rum was in their best interest. The excise, he suggested, would encourage the East to drink less rum and more cider, thus increasing the commercial importance of the farmer's orchards. And if some provincials insisted on satisfying their expensive appetites, then the resultant revenue would reduce land and poll taxes. Nor did Fletcher understand why some should object to swearing oaths. Had not, after all, the 1749 Currency Act required an oath? What was good for the goose was obviously good for the gander. And lest any farmer misunderstand just what the excise intended, Fletcher reminded him that the increased revenue would come from "our being able to get the excise paid on those vast quantities of rum, that are consumed in the eastern parts of this province." Still, Fletcher suspected that the anti-excise propaganda, by appealing to the farmer's sense of constitutional orthodoxy, had eroded away the measure's support. To reinforce the solidarity of the rural coalition in the House, Fletcher reminded the interior's representatives that "the business of a representative is to consult the good of the whole body, and to take particular care that the town he represents, does not pay a greater proportion of the charges of government than it ought to do . . . I take [this] to be the proper business of a representative, and not to follow the humor of his constituents, when it is evidently contrary to the good of the community; and I hope everyone of them are thoroughly sensible that this is their duty." [36]

And rural Massachusetts did triumph. In February the excise for Suffolk County was sold for £2420 and in Essex for £1241. Between them the province's two most maritime counties contributed 65 percent of the new tax.[37] By then Boston, joined by Marblehead and Gloucester, had retained Christopher Kilby to plead in England for the bill's disallowance. In a final appeal to

[36] *The Good of the Community*, pp. 36, 47.
[37] *A&R*, 3:82.

the country Boston asked the farmer to support the capital's petition to the Privy Council:

> This is no private cause of the town of *Boston;* it is the cause of the whole province: The town has deserved highly of all the freemen of the government, for the noble stand they have already made; our brethren in the country begin to be sensible of this, and they will be more so, the more thoroughly they understand the affair. . . . May the pulse of liberty still beat with a generous warmth, and press through all obstructions.[38]

The excise controversy closed an era. The following summer the House revised the excise, replacing the tax on the consumption of rum with a lesser levy on its distillation. In the next decade different quarrels emerged, reminding the country and city of their common bonds and dampening much of the farmer's hostility toward the East. The province, of course, continued to import too much, and the farmer made little permanent progress towards a commercialized rural economy. But as long as the new war provided temporary markets for his crops, the farmer seemed unconcerned about the future. And by 1765 the General Court had commemorated this lessening of tensions in the only way that really mattered. At the expense of the far West, the Assembly had redistributed tax burdens, cutting Boston's share of the provincial tax by a fourth and lessening the levies imposed on most midland and eastern shore farming communities. Men still quarreled. They still thought their own taxes too heavy and their neighbors' too light. They still haled one another into court with alarming regularity. And local politics continued to be a series of crises interrupted by moments of political exhaustion. But the mood of the province had changed.

[38] *The Eclipse* (Boston, 1754), pp. 6–7. See also Boston, *Report of the Record Commissioners*, 14:359; Samuel Roads, Jr., *The History and Traditions of Marblehead* (Boston, 1880), p. 63; *A&R*, 3:825–33.

In the Assembly political alignments became even more diverse until a new, largely external challenge created its own antagonisms and new divisions.

Yet the excise controversy also testified to the nature of the government which provincials said they fought to preserve when they stood on Lexington green two decades later. Whether its desire for revenge had been irrational or not, rural Massachusetts had got what it wanted. The Assembly had deliberated, negotiated, and then made the excise law. Neither the province's governor nor its merchant community had been able to dissuade the rural majority. For most of the eighteenth century, the Assembly had made most of the farmer's demands public policy. Only in 1749 could the farmer legitimately claim he had been betrayed; and there were enough new faces in the next Assembly to remind most politicians of the cost of openly flouting their constituents' demands. What was evident, too, considering the bitterness of the 1749 contest, was that most men accepted political action as the only legitimate means of expressing dissatisfaction. Though some had feared rioting would accompany the return of a specie currency, the transition had been peaceful. The opposition, after all, had sought adjustment only in the political arena. Of equal importance was the absence of any overt attempt to reorganize the government. Even in 1741, when antagonisms ran deepest, the Assembly continued to be dominated by men who had inherited wealth and social position. Despite the bitterness which often divided farm and city, the spokesman for rural Massachusetts was obviously content to allow men from the maritime East to dominate the House and enjoy the fruits of personal political power. All he asked was that public policy reflect his own interests—and this he got.

In 1748 Otis Little, a sometime politician and land speculator, dwelt briefly on the virtue of his country's government. He had invested heavily in Nova Scotia land, and now he suspected that England intended to stifle America's economic development. For the most part, Little's pamphlet simply catalogued the bountifulness of the American continent, but en route to his main argument he paused to allay a suspicion he thought nagged English minds. There was no reason, he counseled, to fear that Americans would desire independence. "No motive could be urged of sufficient weight to induce them to a revolt; neither love of liberty, *force of oppression, burden of taxes,* or desire of becoming more powerful, could possibly influence them to struggle for independency . . . As to any discontents that might arise from oppression, or the burden of taxes, they are subject to none but such as result from the laws of their own making, an indulgence they esteem themselves secured of under a protestant king, and which gives them a share of power equal to their desires." [39] This short aside merely summed up what most provincials assumed was the natural state of political affairs. The inhabitants of Massachusetts had been imposing their own taxes and making their own laws for over a century and took it for granted that they would continue to do so.

[39] Otis Little, *The State of Trade in the Northern Colonies* (Boston, 1749), pp. 10–11.

Statistical Appendix:
A Method
for Our Madness

MY DECIPHERING OF THE POLITICAL CULTURE OF MASSACHU-
setts has embodied a number of experiments, not the
least of which was the use of statistical analyses to describe and explain political patterns. The following essay reports
on this experiment by presenting the relevant data, discussing
some of the strengths and many of the dangers inherent in this
kind of undertaking, and suggesting how we might proceed in
our attempt to broaden the historical imagination by building
statistical models.

At the outset, however, let me confess that a basic problem of
presentation has haunted this aspect of the enterprise from its in-
ception. Initially three very different alternatives were considered.
The first was to repress the methodological aspects of the work
altogether and simply report the condition of eighteenth-century
Massachusetts as I saw it. That, after all, is the traditional way of
writing history. The scholar collects his data, mines it for relevant
insights, and then presents his findings in a coherent and literate
explanation of what has occurred in the past. Hence the reader,
whatever his interests, confronts a polished narrative which, for

all he knows, was arrived at by magic—what we, in moments of weakness, refer to as intuition. It has always seemed to me that this approach robs our enterprise of its excitement. Most of us who become historians do so not because we particularly enjoy reading history books (our own excepted); rather we are attracted to the task of historical reconstruction because it challenges us to gather a coherent picture from the fragmented clues the past chose to leave us. To hide this, the major part of our work, from each other and from the more general reader is to deny the creativity of our endeavors.

The second alternative thoroughly mixes method and result. If the results depend on a particular statistical analysis, then the analysis must be presented alongside the accompanying interpretation. I had intended to follow this strategy until it was forceably demonstrated that my methodology stuck out like a sore thumb. More than that, the methodology, as originally reported, was incomplete. I could hardly, given the structure of the study, speculate on methodological problems and discoveries at the same time that I attempted, for example, to discuss the nature of political alignments within the Assembly. Obviously something had to give.

And so a third alternative was employed. The reporting of results and the discussion of methodological problems have been separated to allow each its proper place. To do so, however, involves another danger. Since the one can be discussed without the other, is it not possible that the results as already reported do not really depend on the analytic techniques about to be described? For those who believe statistics have no place in the writing of history no denial of this proposition will prove persuasive. Let me try anyway. The discussions of political leadership and alignments presented above in chapters 2, 3, 9, and 11 depend absolutely on the methodology described below.

The Social Prerequisites of Leadership (*Chapter 2*)

DESIGNATION OF LEADERS

It has long been assumed that a legislature's committee system probably offers the best data for identifying that group's leaders. The problem, however, is that most modern legislatures have standing committees which require, on the one hand, ranking the various committees according to their relative importance and, on the other hand, deciding in advance the precise size of the leadership group one seeks to isolate. The absence of standing committees in the Massachusetts Assembly allowed me to avoid this problem, largely because the Assembly's ad hoc committee system created an enormous amount of data (it was, for example, not uncommon for the speaker of the House to create upward of a thousand assignments in a single year). Assuming for the moment that all committee posts were of equal weight, I then asked, "Were committee assignments distributed equally among the Assembly's membership?"

Statisticians have developed a battery of simple yet potent tests for estimating the degree of inequality inherent in such distributions. Probably the most useful is the Lorenz curve, which geometrically represents the extent to which a distribution departs from the idea of equality. Constructing the curve itself is a rather simple process. The first step is to rank the members of the population according to their respective share of the value being distributed—in this case, committee assignments. This ranking is then plotted on a graph whose horizontal axis represents the accumulated percentage of the population and whose vertical axis represents the corresponding accumulated percentage of the value being distributed. For example, if there were 100 representatives and 1000 committee assignments, each representative

would equal 1% of the population and each committee assignment 0.1% of the value being distributed. The first point on the
curve would designate the representative with the fewest committee assignments (committee assignments = 0). The point
would signify 1% of the population and 0% of the value being
distributed. The second point—say a representative with 3 assignments—would be 2% of the population (1% + 1%) and 0.3%
of the value being distributed (0.0% + 0.3%). The third point
—a representative with 7 assignments—would designate 3% of
the population (1% + 1% + 1%) and 1% of the value being
distributed (0.0% + 0.3% + 0.7%). Each succeeding point
would be similarly plotted until the last point designated 100%
of the population and 100% of the value being distributed (see
figure 1).

Once the curve is plotted, a number of important definitions
are possible. If you move along the horizontal axis to the 50%
mark, then turn and move vertically till you meet the curve, and
finally turn again and move horizontally until you meet the
vertical axis, you can determine what percentage of committee
assignments the bottom half of the Assembly received as a group.
If the distribution was equal, then 50% of the membership
would have received 50% of the assignments. In fact, if complete
equality characterized the distribution, the line connecting the
various points would be straight and would run at a 45° angle
from the origin. This line is called "the line of complete equality."

As figure 1 suggests, committee assignments in the 1749 Assembly were not equally distributed; the bottom 50% of the population received only 8.7% of the committee assignments. Conversely, 51.7% of all the assignments went to the twelve most
active representatives. This group of representatives constituted
the minimal majority (the smallest number of individuals who
taken together controlled at least one-half of the value being dis-

FIGURE 1.

Accumulative Distribution of Committee Assignments, 1749, Showing
the Designations of Leaders, Sub-leaders, and Back-benchers

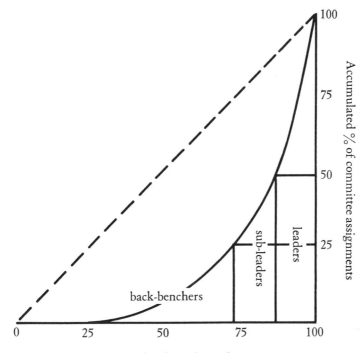

Note: This type of distribution is a Lorenz Curve. The broken
line represents what the distribution would have been if all men had
held an equal number of assignments. The area between the broken
line and the solid line reflects the distribution's inequality.

tributed). Graphically this group was found by starting at the top of the vertical axis and then moving down to the 50% mark, turning and moving horizontally to the curve, and finally turning again and moving vertically to the horizontal axis. In turn, this minimal majority became the criterion for designating the Assembly's *major leaders*. Hence the designation of major leaders depended on a rather arbitrary criterion, the concept of a minimal majority, which has nothing to recommend it other than common sense and convenience. But it should also be noted that the size of this leadership group was not predetermined. Theoretically, at least, the size of this group could range roughly from 1% to 49% of the population. *Sub-leaders* were designated as that group of representatives (after ranking) which received the next 25% of the committee assignments. Graphically this was that group of representatives occupying the 25%–49% range on the vertical axis. In sum, then, the Assembly's leadership was defined as that group of representatives which received more committee assignments than any representative outside the group and which collectively occupied 75% of all the available places.

The basic notion underlying all statistical analyses is that of regularity. What is present one time should reappear every time the experiment is conducted. Hence I asked, "How typical was the 1749 distribution of committee assignments?" To answer this question one need only superimpose on the same graph Lorenz curves drawn for a large number of Assemblies. Regularity would be established if the curves fell practically on top of one another. It is also possible to perform this task mathematically. A quick way to estimate the degree of inequality in any distribution is to focus on the area between the line of complete equality and the actual curve depicting the data (see figure 1). The larger this area, the greater the inequality. A slightly better measure focuses on the equal-share point—that point on the curve which defines who gets more or less than an equal share of the value being distributed. Here the resultant measure is known as the Schutz coefficient. The Schutz coefficients for the twelve Assemblies analyzed for this study are shown in table 1 and suggest the

TABLE 1

Schutz Coefficients

Year	Coefficient
1739	46.7
1740	43.5
1741	39.8
1748	40.7
1749	43.8
1750	44.9
1751	43.1
1752	45.3
1753	46.2
1754	46.5
1755	42.9
1756	44.4

extraordinary regularity of the distribution of committee assignments. A second and somewhat tautological approach is to focus on the relative size of the designated leadership groups in each of the twleve Assemblies (see table 2).

A third approach is to examine the kinds of committees on which leaders served. Initially I assumed each committee was of equal weight. But inspection of the committee assignments of the Assembly's leaders suggests that this assumption is not entirely valid. Indeed the Assembly's "major leaders" monopolized committees dealing with fiscal and monetary policy and political spoils and official delegations. The sub-leaders received the few remaining posts in these areas while spending most of their time dealing with private petitions. Ordinarily a back-bencher was

TABLE 2

Size of Leadership Groups

Year	Major Leaders N (%)	Sub-leaders N (%)	Back-benchers N (%)	Total Active Member-ship*
1739	8 (12.4)	9 (13.8)	48 (73.8)	65
1740	9 (12.9)	14+ (20.0)	47 (67.1)	70
1741	13 (16.1)	12 (14.8)	56 (69.1)	81
1748	12 (15.8)	14 (18.4)	50 (65.8)	76
1749	12 (14.1)	13 (15.3)	60 (70.6)	85
1750	11 (14.2)	16+ (20.8)	50 (65.0)	77
1751	9 (15.0)	10 (16.7)	41 (68.3)	60
1752	10 (14.3)	11+ (15.7)	49 (70.0)	70
1753	10 (12.0)	14 (16.9)	59 (71.0)	83
1754	13 (14.5)	13 (14.5)	64 (71.0)	90
1755	13 (14.5)	16 (17.8)	61 (67.7)	90
1756	15 (14.6)	17 (16.5)	71 (68.9)	103

* There are two ways to calculate these percentages: using the total elected membership as the total N; and using the number of members probably in attendance sometime during the term, i.e., the "total active membership." This latter method has been used for plotting the Lorenz curves, calculating the Schutz coefficients, and constructing table 2.

+ Group slightly larger to avoid distinguishing between representatives with same number of committee assignments.

appointed to a committee only when the issue, usually a private petition, involved his community. Hence, having begun by assuming all committee assignments to be equal, I now possessed a rough ranking of committees if I assumed that those individuals with the most committee assignments were the Assembly's most important members. The symmetry of the argument thus offered an indirect verification of the initial measure of legislative importance.

Yet it was still possible that the Assembly's real leaders seldom served on committees, having left the routine work to their subordinates. Inspection of the lists of designated leaders, however, revealed that the men who dominated the Assembly's committees were the political figures colonial historians have long considered dominant in provincial politics—Hutchinson, Otis, Choate, Allen, Williams, Brattle, Chandler, Bowdoin, Hale. The handful of committees elected by the House similarly illustrated the relationship between committee service and political status. On the 1741 committee elected to sign bills of credit, for example, sat Choate, Watts, Hale, and Cotton. Choate, Watts, and Hale ranked first, second, and third, respectively, in terms of number of committee appointments received. Cotton ranked fourteenth but at the time was clerk of the House, a position which restricted his opportunities for committee work. One final test of the usefulness of committee service as a measure of legislative leadership was provided by the records of the six men who won election as Speaker of the House and for whom sufficient data are available. All six consistently qualified as House leaders in terms of number of committee assignments received (see table 3).

TABLE 3

Percentile Ranking of Speakers of the House before Election

Speaker	Years as Speaker	Years for Which There Are Data	Mean Percentile
Thomas Cushing	1743–45	3	95
Thomas Hutchinson*	1746–48	1	98
Joseph Dwight	1749	2	84
Thomas Hubbard	1750–58	2	95
Samuel White+	1759	6	76
James Otis, Sr.	1760–61	9	95

* Hutchinson served for three-fourths of his term in 1740. His service has been prorated to give this percentile.
+ White, during his first two years in the House, served on a total of five committees. The following year, however, he was the highest ranking leader. This suggests that his low ranking the previous two years was a product of absenteeism. Subtracting these two years, his mean percentile is 98.

Let me repeat, such comparisons, while they increase confidence in the analysis, cannot objectively establish its validity. No doubt some error exists which, in turn, will influence every subsequent analysis in which leadership designations are used. Moreover, the measure itself does not define what leadership means. All that is inferred here is that a leader was important, visible, and highly active.

LEADERSHIP ATTRIBUTES

To infer what makes one representative a leader and another a back-bencher is essentially a problem in collective biography and as such involves a rather obvious dilemma. Ordinarily, to explain any particular pattern requires a large number of individual attributes or variables. Unfortunately, the more variables or attributes introduced into the analysis, the greater the problem of understanding how any single attribute contributes to the overall pattern.

The first question asked of the Massachusetts data was simply, "Was seniority or previous experience important?" As the data for the 1754 Assembly suggests, most inexperienced representatives were in fact back-benchers, but at the same time two representatives became major leaders in their freshman terms (see table 4). Table 5, which deals with freshman representatives for a three-year period, makes the point even clearer: most leaders did not serve an apprenticeship; rather, they began their careers at the top of the legislative hierarchy.

Because previous experience was not a necessary condition for achieving a leadership position, it seemed safe to assume that the Assembly did not distribute committee assignments according to a special, peculiarly legislative set of values. Rather, those same attributes which earned a man deference outside the House

TABLE 4

Distribution of Legislative Experience, 1754

Number of Previous Terms	Leaders	Back-benchers	Total
5 or more	16	15	31
3–4	6	18	24
1–2	2	35	37
0	2	15	17
Total	26	83	109

chamber also entitled him to deference within the Assembly. Indeed the House, in this special case, was a political microcosm exhibiting the same values as were present in the larger political community.

Collecting sufficient data about the 526 men who served in the twelve Assemblies to answer the question "What separated the leader from the back-bencher?" was at first thought to require a major research effort. Before this effort was launched, however, three easily collected variables were used in a preliminary analysis in order to test the soundness of my approach. The three variables were: (1) whether the representative had attended Harvard or

TABLE 5

Mobility of Freshman Members
1748–51

1st Term Ranking	Highest Ranking	Members
Major leader	Major leader	5
Sub-leader	Major leader	4
Sub-leader	Sub-leader	3
Back-bencher	Major leader	2
Back-bencher	Sub-leader	6
Back-bencher	Back-bencher	80
Total		100

Yale, (2) whether he held a judicial appointment, and (3) whether his constituency was in the eastern shore region. This last category requires some explanation. Originally I sought a simple variable uniquely measuring the impact of the province's merchant community on the Assembly's leadership. An obvious choice would have been whether or not a constituency was a seaport. Unfortunately, as I quickly discovered, a number of eastern shore farming communities—Braintree, Roxbury, and Cambridge, to name three—were sometimes represented by merchants who maintained their businesses in Boston while living in the country. Hence a compromise was devised: rather than making a separate variable "seaports," these mercantile centers were lumped with the eastern shore's farming settlements.

The results of this preliminary analysis using three variables were startling. Despite their seeming crudeness each attribute proved a significant predictor of Assembly leadership (see table 6). Next, two cross-checks were performed. To see whether or not lumping the province's seaports with the eastern shore's farming communities depressed the region's leadership ratio, a new analysis was performed separating the two. The results were nearly identical, in part because of the number of merchants representing farming communities, and in part, as it later turned out, because these rural communities attracted a number of lawyers with provincial ambitions. If a lawyer lived in Braintree or Lynn or Cambridge, for example, he could practice before six major county courts—Suffolk, Essex, Middlesex, Barnstable, Bristol, and Plymouth—while winning election to the House from a relatively small and unimportant farming community.

The second cross-check involved the relative ranking of representatives who had attended Harvard, 62 representatives in all (see table 7). This analysis isolated the importance of inherited prestige in distributing legislative status and, by implication, gen-

TABLE 6

Leadership Profile,
Massachusetts Assembly

	Number of Members	*Leadership Ratio**
Region		
Eastern Shore	137	40
Connecticut Valley	46	19
Other	343	11
Judicial Experience		
With judicial experience	181	41
Without judicial experience	345	8
College Experience		
With college experience	70	60
Without college experience	456	13

* The leadership ratio is the percentage of men in any category who became House leaders.

eral political status. With this finding in hand, no attempt was made to add more variables to the analysis.

TABLE 7

Leadership Profile,
Harvard Graduates

	Number of Members	*Leadership Ratio*
Ranked in top half of Harvard class	44	73
Ranked in bottom half of Harvard class	18	28

When taken together, these three explanatory variables proved remarkably powerful predictors of what one needed to become a leader. Of the 262 representatives devoid of all three attributes —a college education, a judicial appointment, and an eastern shore constituency—only 8 became House leaders. Conversely, the more attributes a representative possessed, the greater his probability of achieving a leadership position (see table 8). The

TABLE 8

Inclusiveness of Attributes

Number of Attributes	Number of Members	Number of Leaders	Leadership Ratio
3	20	15	75
2	84	48	57
1	160	30	19
0	262	8	3

fact that a quarter of those with all three attributes did not become leaders suggests that even this model only partially explained the leadership pattern. Finally, by displaying the same data in yet a third form, it was possible to rank the three attributes as to the probable importance of each one's contribution to the leadership equation (see table 9).

Again, how valid are such results? Statistically, the model explained most of the variance, particularly when the proposition read, "What attributes were necessary to achieve a leadership position?" Nevertheless, a major problem remained. None of the three variables directly measured wealth. Moreover, if wealth was in fact important, then at least one of the variables had to be partially synonymous with financial status. Perhaps only rich men could become justices of the peace. Or perhaps

TABLE 9

Relative Importance of Attributes
of Assembly Leaders

Educational Experience	*Judicial Experience*	*Eastern Shore Constituency*	*Leadership Ratio*
x	x	x	75
x	x		62
x		x	60
	x	x	44
x			36
	x		19
		x	14
			3

most sons of rich men attended Harvard, where they ranked in the top half of their class.

Why not introduce a wealth variable into the analysis? To be sure, some financial information about almost all the 526 men in the sample was available. But it was of widely varying credibility. Moreover, the wealthier and more visible the representative, the more likelihood there were sufficient data to measure his wealth. There is yet another aspect of this problem. The three variables used in the analysis were quite discrete and reasonably accurate. Suppose a wealth variable of questionable accuracy was introduced. Whether the results reflected a valid pattern or a measurement error would not be known. There are, to be sure, ways of controlling this problem. But where truly questionable data are used, truly questionable findings result.

What I am suggesting, then, is that the analysis using these three variables does not answer every question. I know more about the attributes a leader required than about the attributes which differentiated men of equal status; what I cannot do here, for example, is explain why James Bowdoin became a House leader and his brother William did not, despite the near identity of their measurable attributes. Nor do these results directly measure the impact of wealth, although we have always suspected that men of means enjoyed a large advantage in eighteenth-century politics. On the other hand, the model does create guidelines for further discussion. However one wishes to describe eighteenth-century attributes of leadership, he must in the process explain why men who ranked in the top half of their Harvard class received significantly more committee assignments than those who ranked in the bottom half of their class.

The Nature of Leadership (*Chapter 3*)

LEADERSHIP COHESION

Having suggested that inherited social status was the mark of leadership, both within and outside the Assembly, the obvious question became, "Was this leadership group drawn from the colony's gentry also a political oligarchy bent on preserving the privileges wealth and social status conferred?" To answer this question by statistical analysis is all but impossible given the paucity of data reflecting the leaders' policy preferences. All that we possess, in fact, are seventeen roll calls recorded over a sixteen-year period, 1740–1756. Indeed the very scarcity of these votes is an implicit warning about the relevancy of such data. Obviously the House did not ordinarily decide questions by a public telling of the yeas and nays. Just as obviously, men voted differently on a public roll call if for no other reason than the fact that the uniqueness of the situation made them more self-conscious.

Hence to use these roll calls as data required a certain amount of bravado as well as a procedure which minimized the danger of wayward inference. I will not repeat this observation, though it explicitly guided every step of the analysis described here and below, in the section on political alignments.

Traditionally the first question asked of the votes of any coherent group of legislators has been, "Do they testify to the group's cohesiveness?" In short, does the group vote together when its interests are seemingly at stake? Thus, one approach to the political nature of the Assembly's gentry leadership was to measure its voting cohesion, particularly on the seven roll calls dealing with basic economic issues—taxes, inflation, the Land Bank—issues on which a conservative oligarchy theoretically should have achieved its greatest solidarity. (An eighth economic vote was excluded from the analysis because only five leaders voted—which may or may not be significant.) The leadership cohesion—as measured by the percentage of the group voting with the group's majority ($50\% \leq$ cohesion $\leq 100\%$)—on these seven roll calls ranged from a low of 56% to a high of 70%. More intriguing, three times a majority of the Assembly's leaders endorsed policies traditionally ascribed to the province's agrarian majority.

While economic votes did not yield high cohesion scores, a second subset of the roll calls did: on five votes involving political rewards or imperial policies on which the administration had staked its prestige, cohesion scores ranged from a low of 64% to a high of 94%. The difference between these two subsets is best reflected graphically. Figure 2 suggests that most House leaders separated legislative issues (decided by roll call votes) into two distinct categories. Whereas those votes dealing with the basic structure of the economy did not produce group solidarity, those votes involving political spoils and support for a governor responsible for dispensing patronage did.

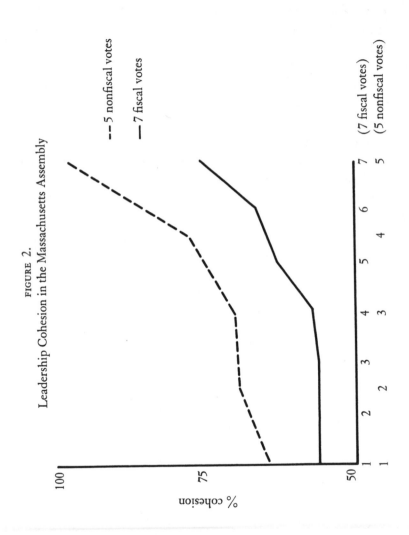

FIGURE 2.
Leadership Cohesion in the Massachusetts Assembly

The importance of this perspective became more apparent when the cohesion of the rank and file was similarly analyzed. Figure 3 indicates that the back-bencher, when confronted by the same roll call votes, seldom distinguished between fiscal policies and issues involving political largess.

LEADERSHIP INFLUENCE

At this point in the study it became necessary to confront the problem of defining what leadership meant in the eighteenth century other than visibility and activity. If influence is defined as the ability of one citizen to induce other citizens to act in some way they would not have otherwise acted, the roll calls provide one measure of the leadership's influence with the Assembly's rank-and-file majority. Using the twelve votes discussed above, three hypotheses were ventured:

1. When confronted with a united leadership, the back-bencher tended to vote as the leadership did.
2. When confronted with a united leadership, the back-bencher tended to vote contrary to the leadership's preferences.
3. The null hypothesis; that is, most back-benchers cast their votes without reference to the leadership's position or unity.

When the leadership's and rank-and-file's cohesion scores for the twelve roll calls were plotted on a scatter diagram, it became obvious that only the null hypotheses described the data (see figure 4). Nor did a meaningful pattern emerge when the seven roll calls dealing with fiscal issues were plotted separately (see figure 5). On the five roll calls involving political spoils and imperial policies, however, a slight tendency on the part of the back-bencher to vote contrary to the leadership did appear (see figure 6).

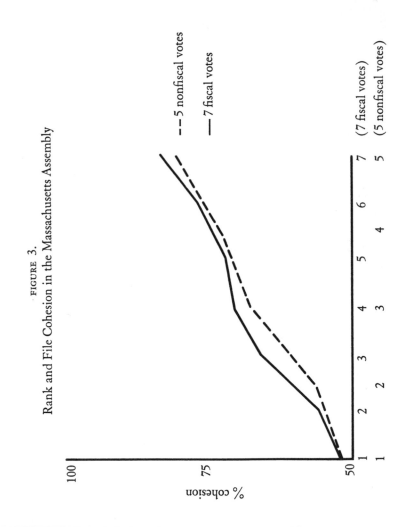

FIGURE 3.
Rank and File Cohesion in the Massachusetts Assembly

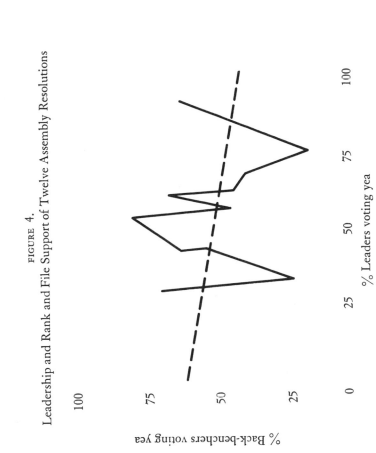

FIGURE 4.
Leadership and Rank and File Support of Twelve Assembly Resolutions

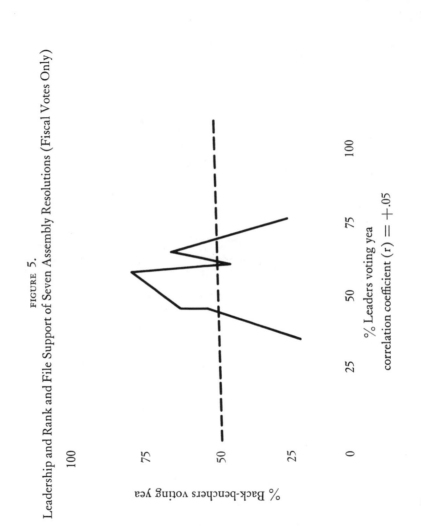

FIGURE 5.
Leadership and Rank and File Support of Seven Assembly Resolutions (Fiscal Votes Only)

FIGURE 6.

Leadership and Rank and File Support of Five Assembly Resolutions (Nonfiscal Votes Only)

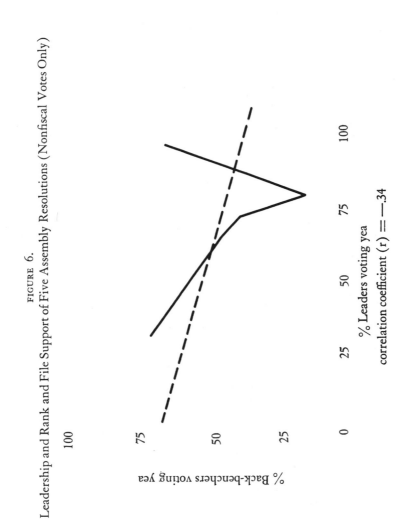

% Leaders voting yea

correlation coefficient (r) = −.34

% Back-benchers voting yea

Unfortunately figure 6 involves a problem beyond the questionable nature of the data. Five points on a graph are painfully few. Note, for example, that if the last vote is eliminated or changed, a very different pattern would emerge. The regression equation $(y = a + bx)$ defines the best-fitting straight line for predicting rank-and-file percent *yea* (y), knowing leadership percent *yea* (x). The *a* equals the point where this line intercepts the y axis; and the *b* equals the slope of that line (the amount of increase in y related to a decrease in x).

There are several criteria for assessing the usefulness of graphs like figure 6. The r^2 reflects how much of the variance the regression explains; or, in other words, whether one can predict y (rank-and-file percent *yea*) knowing x (leadership percent *yea*). If one seeks genuine predictability, then r^2 should obviously come close to being 1 (100% of the variance explained). If one seeks instead to describe a strong but not complete degree of association between two variables, then r^2 should be at least 0.5. If one seeks merely to demonstrate the presence of association (or covariation), then the appropriate size of r^2 can vary depending on how much association is deemed significant. Nonetheless, it seems clear that except when working with relatively large samples, an r^2 of less than 0.3 is all but meaningless. Hence I concluded that a House leader's influence was not often associated with an ability to persuade the rank and file to abandon prior policy commitments.

Patterns of Participation: The Council (*Chapter 9*)

Because it was a smaller, more homogeneous, and far less public body, the Council contributed little to this study of eighteenth-century political attitudes and procedures. There was, however, one significant kind of data which only the Council provided:

a detailed roster of attendance. In turn, these rosters, coupled with the Council's lists of those appointed to joint House-Council committees, provided a rather unique and revealing portrait of the Council at work.

In a body of near equals, an individual's influence ought to be roughly proportional to his effort. This, at least, was the basic assumption employed to examine patterns of influence and participation within the Council. For the analysis portrayed in figure 7 the number of sessions attended was used as a rough measure of effort, and the number of joint committee assignments became an index of influence. (The Council's official minutes list only the members of joint committees. The upper chamber, however, also appointed legislative committees though with less regularity than the Assembly. The Council's rough-copy minutes list some, but not all, of these assignments. Where possible, legislative and joint committee assignments were compared, and the results suggest that legislative committee posts were distributed in the same pattern as were joint committee assignments.) To correct for the crudeness of the measures, each was trichotomized into above average, average, and below average. Theoretically, a councilor who had attended an average number of sessions should have received an average number of committee assignments if influence was proportional to effort. And in fact, of the twenty-five councilors in good health and available for committee duty, only seven received either more or fewer committee assignments than their attendance rates would indicate. At this point the analysis focused on the seven exceptions, noting that those with special expertise and status (Cushing, Sewall, Lynde) received more committee assignments than they should have; while the novice Hancock and the sometimes bumbling Royal and Cheever received less than their fair share of committee posts. Wendall was a true exception. The conformity of the data to the

FIGURE 7.
Classification of Councilors by Committee Assignments and Attendance

	below average	average	above average
above average	Cushing	Sewall	Hutchinson Osborne Watts Erving Brattle Bowdoin
average	Lynde	Danforth Chandler Pynchon Lincoln Cutt Bradford	
below average	Pepperrell Waldo Leonard Hill Pickman Hooper	Cheever Hancock	

COMMITTEE ASSIGNMENTS

ATTENDANCE

expected pattern suggested particular attention ought to be given to those who regularly attended and just as regularly exercised a special kind of influence. As I suggested in chapter 9, this group of men, like its counterpart in the House, was comprised of professional politicians whose chief function was to provide the expertise which effective decision-making required.

Political Alignments (*Chapter 11*)

TAX DISCRIMINATION

One way to study the distribution of influence and power is to ask, "Who makes the decisions?" A second, equally effective, approach is to ask, "Who benefits from such decisions?"

Throughout the eighteenth century, Boston bitterly complained that it benefited least from the distribution of the provincial tax burden—a complaint which ought to be susceptible to statistical analysis. In fact, eighteenth-century taxing procedures considerably eased the analytic problem because the General Court taxed not individuals, but communities, assigning to each a fixed proportion of the provincial tax bill. There was, however, one major data problem: the only reliable census dates from 1765, yet after 1756 the General Court began a program of tax adjustment. To calculate tax rates for the 1750s, then, it was necessary to assume that the relative size of Massachusetts towns did not drastically change between 1756 and 1765. To some extent, grouping towns from a given region of the province should help control for all but the most major kind of population shifts.

Taking each town's assessed share of the 1756 province tax and dividing this figure by the number of adult males (rateable poles) in 1765 yielded an average assessment per individual for each town. These figures were then averaged by region; they appear in table 10. The three middle-sized seaports were Ipswich,

TABLE 10

Comparative Tax Rates, 1756

Community Type	Average Assessment in Shillings	Tax Inequity Score
Boston	61	−94
Eastern Shore Farming	22	−9
Newbury	20	−4
Middle-sized Seaport	19	−2
Midland Farming	18	+1
Salem	17	+2
Maine	16	+5
Connecticut Valley	15	+7
Near Frontier	13	+12

Marblehead, and Gloucester. The tax inequity score transformed these average assessments into a more standard index. Tax equity was defined as 0. For each standard deviation of a town's rate above the mean rate, its tax inequity score *decreased* 15 points. Those towns burdened with discriminatory assessments had negative tax inequity scores. Thus Boston's average tax rate was 6.24 standard deviations above the mean, and its score was −94 (0 minus the product of 6.24 times 15).

Table 11 documents the extent and direction of the tax adjustment program which substantially reduced Boston's tax burden.

LEGISLATIVE ALIGNMENTS

A third approach to questions of power and influence is to ask, "Who sided with whom?" How, in short, did the Assembly divide politically? Once again the major problem is the paucity of data, since all that we have are the seventeen roll calls published during this period. Hence any analysis of voting in the Assembly necessarily had to deal with the voting records of com-

TABLE 11

Comparative Tax Rates, 1764

Community Type	Average Assessment in Shillings	Tax Inequity Score
Boston	38	−75
Eastern Shore Farming	19	−9
Salem	17	−3
Newbury	16	0
Midland Farming	16	0
Middle-sized Seaport	16	0
Connecticut Valley	16	0
Maine	14	+5
Near Frontier	14	+5

munities (the total voting record of their various representatives over a sixteen-year period) rather than with the preferences of individual representatives. And since chronic absenteeism always plagued the House, only slightly more than a third of the province's two hundred townships (through their representatives) voted often enough to be included in the analysis.

Initially one hundred towns, each having voted on at least five roll calls, were included in the analysis. Preliminary inspection of the data, however, indicated that meaningful patterns were possibly being obscured or distorted because a large group of towns were not recorded on a wide enough range of issues. A stricter but no less arbitrary criterion was then employed. A town was included in the sample only if it met the following three conditions:

1. voted on at least eight roll calls
2. voted on at least four roll calls involving fiscal policies
3. voted on at least four roll calls not involving fiscal policies

In all, sixty towns fulfilled these conditions.

The initial examination of all sixteen roll calls—one of the original seventeen being dropped since it replicated a vote taken fifteen minutes earlier in the House—employed two types of analysis: cluster analysis and Guttman scaling. Neither analysis produced meaningful clusters or scale types. (Here it should be noted that scale analysis could have only identified voting patterns rather than true issue dimensions, because the data were town, rather than individual, voting records.) To some extent this result was foreshadowed by the analysis of leadership and rank-and-file cohesion which, in using this same roll call set, had isolated two basic groups of votes: issues involving fiscal policy, and issues involving imperial policy and the creation of political spoils. A third group of votes dealing with the Assembly's constitutional prerogatives accounted for the remaining roll calls.

The roll calls were then partitioned into three subsets, which necessitated a redrawing of the original sample of townships as follows.

1. Fiscal policies: voted on at least four of the six roll calls (1, 2, 3, 4, 5, 8)—67 towns fulfilled this condition
2. Patronage, government salaries, questions of imperial policy: voted on at least four of the five roll calls (9, 10, 12, 13, 15) —58 towns fulfilled this condition
3. Privileges of the House: voted on all three roll calls (7, 14, 16)—41 towns fulfilled this condition

Two roll calls (6 and 11) dealt with taxing and were not included, because a clear anti-Boston bias on this issue had already been established. (The numbers in parentheses refer to table 12.)

Each subset was then analyzed to see whether it scaled or produced meaningful clusters. This time the fiscal policy subset did yield clusters of towns with similar voting records. Two patterns

TABLE 12

Roster of Roll Calls

No.	Year	MHJ Citation	Issue	Yeas	Nays
1	1740	17:256–58	Whether the House will now proceed to make any supply of the Treasury with bills of credit to be drawn before the year 1742	19	53
2	1740	18:47–48	Whether the persons concerned in the scheme of John Colman, Esq., and others be strictly forbidden issuing any bills	37	59
3	1741	18:185–86	Whether the House will now . . . appoint a committee to take under consideration the proclamation . . . of . . . the governor and Council, respecting the . . . [Land Bank]	42	28
4	1751	27:195	Whether the . . . paragraph [emitting a new form of paper notes] in the engrossed bill shall be taken out of said bill	33	46
5	1751	27:224	[Same as Roll Call 4]	31	28
6	1751	28:46	Whether . . . [the engrossed tax bill] pass to be enacted	36	26
7	1753	30:18	Whether the province treasurer shall . . . be obliged to enter into bonds with two sufficient sureties to a committee annually to be appointed by the Court for the faithful discharge of his trust in that capacity	71	13

Table 12—*Continued*

No.	Year	MHJ Citation	Issue	Yeas	Nays
8	1753	30:88	Whether the bill [inflating the value of the paper currency still in circulation] should pass to be engrossed	53	25
9	1754	30:153	Whether any grant [to the governor] shall be made in consequence of . . . [his] message	41	44
10	1754	30:260	Whether the House would make addition to the said grant [to former Treasurer William Foye]	23	42
11	1754	31:38	Whether the [excise] bill should pass to be enacted	52	17
12	1754	31:152–53	Whether it be the mind of the House that there be a general union of his majesty's colonies on this continent	41	37
13	1754	31:182	That the consideration of the report of a general union be suspended until the members have had an opportunity to consult their constituents	48	31
14	1755	32:60	Whether the House accept the . . . report [appropriating money to defend Speaker of the House Thomas Hutchinson against a suit brought by Daniel Fowle]	57	28

Table 12—*Continued*

No.	Year	MHJ Citation	Issue	Yeas	Nays
15	1755	32:116	Whether it be the mind of the House that any method be taken to raise a number of men to reinforce the army destined for the Crown Point expedition	39	12
16	1756	32:375	Whether excise farmers or collectors shall be members of the General Court	11	42

were identified as particularly likely: an inflationist pattern composed of what I thought to be the inflationists' stand on each roll call; and a seaport pattern composed of the stand a majority of the province's seaports took on each of the six roll calls. The first pattern became *rural radicalism* and the second moderate or *maritime conservatism*. The third pattern, *Hampshire County conservatism,* was discovered by accident. The computer printout from the cluster analysis performed on all sixteen roll calls was so arranged that the remarkably high level of agreement on all issues among Hampshire County towns was readily apparent. On closer inspection I noted that on fiscal issues a number of farming communities as well as one seaport had voting records similar to those of the Hampshire County delegation. The results of this analysis are given in table 13.

Of the several criteria available for measuring the reliability of such findings, the simplest was the amount of variation accounted for by this particular group of voting patterns. Representatives from 67 towns voted often enough to have their community's voting record included in the analysis. Yet 3 of these towns regularly sent more than one representative to the General

TABLE 13

Regional Distribution of Voting Records
(Fiscal Issues Only)

Community Type	Rural Radicalism	Maritime Conservatism	Hampshire County Conservatism	Unexplained
Midland Farming	16	4	4	7
Eastern Shore Farming	8		2	3
Maine	4		1	
Near Frontier	1		1	3
Seaport	1(2)*	3(7)*	1	2
Connecticut Valley			6	
Total	30(31)*	7(11)*	15	15

* Figures in parentheses result when Boston is allotted four and Salem and Ipswich are allotted two votes.

Court—Boston four and Salem and Ipswich two each. Hence it became necessary to perform a double set of calculations, one for towns and a second for representatives. Of the 67 towns, 52 deviated from one (and only one) of the three patterns on no more than a single vote. In other words, when the criterion for inclusion in a category was set at "deviation ≤1," 77.16% of the towns proved classifiable. When the same analysis is performed giving Boston four and Salem and Ipswich two votes, the figure rises slightly, 57 out of 72, or 79.2%. Obviously I would like these figures to be higher, say 90% of the towns proving classifiable (whichever method of calculation is employed). Still these three patterns—rural radicalism, maritime conservatism, and Hampshire County conservatism—produced significantly better results than any other cluster of voting patterns.

I also gauged the reliability of this particular group of voting patterns by counting the number of times a representative from a classifiable town deviated from the pattern best fitting his community's total voting record. Of the 257 votes cast by the representatives from the 52 classifiable towns over the six roll calls, 29 votes or 11.2% deviated from the predicted pattern.

Ultimately the credibility attached to this analysis depended on its ability to explain other data and related political decisions, particularly the 1748–49 contest over returning the province to a specie currency. While the House never published the 1749 vote on the bill, an embittered James Allen later revealed the names of the forty representatives who had supported the bill. If the classification of fiscal attitudes above is in fact a rough approximation of political alignments within the Assembly, then two predictions should be borne out by Allen's list. First, most representatives from communities with conservative voting records should have supported a specie currency, and most of their colleagues from radical communities should have belonged to the opposition. Second, representatives from radical farming constituencies who voted for redemption should have faced stiffer fights for re-election than did men from conservative farming communities who similarly supported the administration on this issue.

Before testing these hypotheses, however, it was necessary to reconstruct the roll call. Allen reported who voted for the bill; I still did not know who voted nay and who was either absent or abstained. Thomas Hutchinson's account of the passage of the bill indicates the final tally was 40 yeas and 37 nays. The 1748–49 House contained 103 members. As speaker, Hutchinson did not vote. Nor did Allen who had been expelled. Similarly the 9-man Hampshire County delegation was absent, leaving 51 members who either were absent or voted nay. If those who were absent were as likely to support a specie currency as their colleagues who remained in Boston, then 37/51 of each category of representatives who did not vote yea probably voted nay.

Representatives from sixteen farming communities with classifiable voting records supported a species currency. Eight were
communities with consistently conservative (Hampshire County
conservatism or maritime conservatism) voting records. The
other eight representatives were from communities classified as
loyal to rural radicalism. As tables 14 and 15 indicate, both hy-

TABLE 14

Probable Voting Patterns, 1749 Currency Act
(Eastern Shore Farming and Midland Farming Only)

Voting Type	Yea	Probably Nay
Rural Radicalism *	8	11
Maritime or Hampshire County Conservatism	8	1

TABLE 15

Election Records of Representatives
Supporting 1749 Currency Act
(Eastern Shore Farming and Midland Farming Only)

Voting Type	Reelected May 1749	Not Reelected May 1749
Rural Radicalism	3	5
Maritime or Hampshire County Conservatism	7	1

potheses are borne out; men from the conservative communities
overwhelmingly supported the bill and, with one exception,
returned to the House in May 1749. Their colleagues from more
radical communities did not fare nearly so well.

Conceivably, however, the difference in return rates might reflect a community's political stability rather than its voters' pleasure or displeasure over a specie currency. For example, communities with conservative voting records might normally have re-elected their representatives, while the more radical communities might have rotated the office of representative. To test for this possibility, return rates for previous elections were calculated for the immediate five- and ten-year periods. Over both periods each subset of communities had nearly identical return rates (see table 16).

Occasionally the systematic testing of a proposition proves serendipitous. Table 16 gives the election returns for all 34 farming communities from the midland belt and eastern shore with classifiable voting records for a ten-year period. In studying the table one should remember that we know more about these 34 towns than any other farming communities inasmuch as their representatives voted both regularly and consistently enough to yield a classifiable voting record. Presumably, then, these 34 towns reflected basic political currents in Massachusetts. If such an assumption can be accepted, then a number of interesting patterns emerge from the data. First, the 1739 election marked a major convulsion in provincial politics: 23 of the 34 towns replaced their representatives. Moreover, given the subsequent roll calls, this election split rural Massachusetts into two groups, one essentially radical and the other conservative. Then in 1741, when the election turned on the question of the Land Bank, rural towns previously content with their conservative representatives relaxed their opposition to inflation. For the next eight years political alignments remained remarkably stable; then in 1749, the previously united radical group split on the issue of a specie currency and loyalty to the administration. In the following election there was again evidence of selective retribution, as only those

TABLE 16

Return Rates, 34 Classifiable Eastern Shore Farming and Midland Farming Towns

Voting Type	1739	1740	1741	1742	1743	1744	1745	1746	1747	1748	1749
Number of representatives not returned each election											
Rural Radicalism (N = 24)	15	9	7	9	9	9	6	5	4	8	8
Maritime or Hampshire County Conservatism (N = 10)	8	2	7	1	2	3	3	1	1	3	2
Percent representatives not returned each election											
Rural Radicalism	63	37	29	37	37	37	25	21	17	33	33
Maritime or Hampshire County Conservatism	80	20	70	10	20	30	30	10	10	30	20

Voting Type	10-Year Average	5-Year Average	1749
Aggregate non-return rates, all 34 towns			
Rural Radicalism	34%	27%	33%
Maritime or Hampshire County Conservatism	33%	22%	20%
Aggregate non-return rate, 16 towns with representatives supporting 1749 Currency Act			
Rural Radicalism	35%	25%	63%
Maritime or Hampshire County Conservatism	31%	20%	13%

representatives who had turned apostate were singled out for political retirement.

A Legislative Model

One by-product of the attempt to use statistical techniques to analyze historical data has been the assumption by many that the mere act of counting controls bias and error. Believing that they have achieved objectivity while their colleagues continue to wallow in prejudice and sentimentality, these quantifiers are the latest to lay claim to the Rankean dream of telling it like it was, of standing above the battle in order to resolve the quarrels that have so long divided the historical craft. The justification for such optimism, the quantifier suggests, can be found in the canons of a behavioral science; he has forgotten, perhaps, that most behavioral research has abandoned that mindless positivism once characteristic of social inquiry.

Nonetheless, the behaviorist does occasionally speak of subjective and objective validity, but he does so in a rather special and revealing way. Subjective validity, which refers to the internal consistency of a given analysis, essentially asks, "Are the results of this experiment, given the theoretical assumptions made and the data employed, logical and in that sense valid?" Objective validity, in its simplest form, is established when repeated performances of the same experiment produce roughly identical results. To repeat an experiment, however, requires new data, and this is precisely what historians cannot supply.

To a limited extent, however, it is possible to approximate this kind of verification. Although new information cannot be created, it is possible to analyze analogous data and then compare results. James Allen's unofficial account of who supported a specie currency presented just such an opportunity once I reconstructed the roll call.

The statistical analysis presented to this point has made two major claims: (1) that the number of committee assignments a representative received is an adequate measure of his importance within the Assembly; and (2) that for a limited number of communities it is possible to predict how their representatives responded to fiscal issues. In the text I also suggested that a certain amount of regional cohesion characterized alignments within the Assembly and that the more experienced back-benchers ought to have been more receptive to administration pressure than their less experienced colleagues. Allen's list of who supported a specie currency allows a systematic, though incomplete, evaluation of these assumptions.

One test of the value of a model is the extent to which it accounts for the variation within the data—in short, how well it helps reduce the amount of error in our analysis (in this sense variance explained is equivalent to the proportional reduction of error). Figure 8 portrays the 1749 vote on a specie currency using categories derived from the assumptions described above; that is, figure 8 is visual representation of the legislative model I am seeking to test. Ideally I would want everyone in a given box to behave in exactly the same way (for example, all leaders —box a—to vote for the measure). That, obviously, is not the case. But exactly how well does the model work? To what extent does it take the guesswork out of deciding how a particular representative voted (without, of course, looking on Allen's list to see how he voted).

If I know nothing more about the 1749 currency vote than the final tally, then the best way of guessing how any individual representative voted is to say that he voted yea. I would then be right 40 times and wrong 37 times; in short, I would be

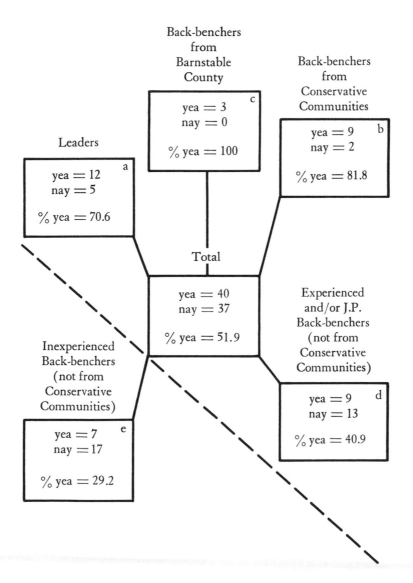

FIGURE 8.
Analysis of Vote for 1749 Currency Act

Back-benchers
from
Barnstable
County

yea = 3
nay = 0

% yea = 100

c

Back-benchers
from
Conservative
Communities

yea = 9
nay = 2

% yea = 81.8

b

Leaders

yea = 12
nay = 5

% yea = 70.6

a

Total

yea = 40
nay = 37

% yea = 51.9

Experienced
and/or J.P.
Back-benchers
(not from
Conservative
Communities)

Inexperienced
Back-benchers
(not from
Conservative
Communities)

yea = 7
nay = 17

% yea = 29.2

e

yea = 9
nay = 13

% yea = 40.9

d

right 51.9% of the time. The task is to improve on this initial method for guessing who supported the measure. We must also recognize that the maximum amount of improvement will be 48.1 percentage points (100% — 51.9%). Using the model portrayed in figure 8, I segmented the guessing procedure by saying that all leaders, all back-benchers from conservative communities, all back-benchers from Barnstable county, and all experienced and/or J.P. back-benchers from nonconservative communities voted yea, and the rest of the back-benchers voted nay; in terms of figure 8, everyone in boxes *a, b, c,* and *d* voted yea, and everyone in box *e* nay. When I used this procedure I was wrong only 27 times (5 in box *a,* 2 in box *b,* 0 in box *c,* 13 in box *d,* and 7 in box *e*); or conversely, I was correct 64.9% of the time. We are now in a position to estimate the power of the model. Obviously I have improved the rate of success from 51.9% to 64.9%; in short, I improved my ability to guess how each representative voted by 13 percentage points out of the 48.1 possible percentage points. Thus we now have a 26% (13.0%/48.1%) better guess. Inspection of figure 8 indicated that one of the prime sources of error is box *d,* the experienced and/or J.P. back-benchers from nonconservative communities. For the moment let us admit we have failed to explain the behavior of this group and remove them from the analysis. Figure 9 accomplishes this task and allows us to recalculate the power of the model. I again began by guessing that all 55 representatives voted yea and then calculated that I would be right 56.4% of the time. In this case the maximum amount we could improve our guessing procedure was 43.6 percentage points. Again I segmented the guessing and said that everyone in boxes *a, b,* and *c* voted yea and everyone in box *e* nay. This time I was wrong only 14 times or right 74.5% of the time. Here I improved my rate of success from 56.4% to 74.5% or by 18.1 percentage points. Hence I made a 41.3% (18.1%/

43.6%) better guess. We can conclude then that the model is more powerful when it restricts itself to predicting the behavior of leaders, conservative back-benchers, a small county delegation led by an imposing professional (Otis), and inexperienced back-benchers from nonconservative communities, than a more general model which includes experienced and/or J.P. nonconservative back-benchers. We might also conclude that it was this latter group which was most often the subject of conflicting cross pressures.

What has been learned? First, my initial assumptions about legislative behavior do substantially improve our ability to predict the behavior of at least some representatives. Second, these assumptions (or this model) only explain a portion of the variance: in short, the model must be added to, subtracted from, or rearranged. Perhaps improvement will come when more information is discovered or when better, more powerful techniques are invented for manipulating the data we have. Until then, we might build on this admittedly imperfect answer which nonetheless broadens our understanding of how men behaved in the eighteenth century.

Our madness is not in attempting to meld history and numbers, but rather in forgetting who we are and the ultimate uncertainty of our endeavors.

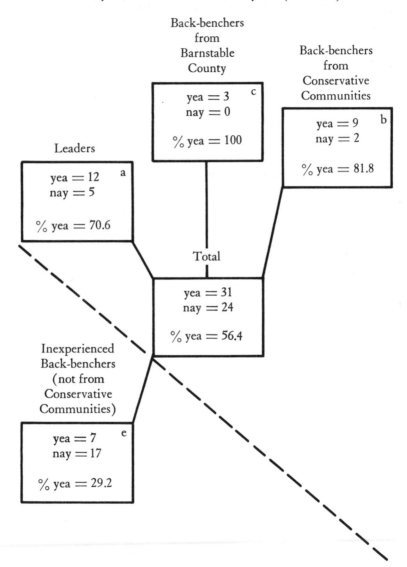

FIGURE 9.

Analysis of Vote for 1749 Currency Act (Modified)

Bibliographic Note

I HAVE USED THE OPPORTUNITY THIS BIBLIOGRAPHIC NOTE AFFORDS to describe the kinds of material I examined, to discuss the work of other men which contributed to my own understanding of both provincial Massachusetts and modern political behavior, and—as I attempted in the statistical appendix—to reproduce at least something of the analytic process which resulted in my portrait of eighteenth-century Massachusetts.

The Business of Government (*Prologue*)

In seeking to describe the boundaries of their discipline, political scientists have spent considerable time defining the attributes of a political system; see, for example, David Easton, "An Approach to the Analysis of Political Systems," *World Politics* 9 (1957): 383–407, and Robert A. Dahl, *Modern Political Analysis* (Englewood Cliffs: Prentice-Hall, N.J., 1963), pp. 4–13. What scholars like Easton and Dahl really seek is a dual definition which first decides which acts are essentially political and then assesses the importance of the political sphere for the ordinary citizen. More than that, they seek a definition which has universal applicability, one that is not rooted in the American experience or even in that of the western world. Unfortunately, a usable, all-purpose definition is still beyond their reach. Hence we are forced to rely on temporary, common-sense expedients which, with remarkably few exceptions, result in defining the political system as the activity of public institutions and public officials (formal as well as informal). In short, the political system is the business of government. Similarly, the impact that system has on the life of the ordinary citizen is largely reflected in the scope and effectiveness of this governmental activity.

Three separate, though not distinct, political systems held sway in eighteenth-century Massachusetts. The first was the town, a remarkably homogeneous and close-knit assembly of neighbors which, as Michael Zuckerman in his *Peaceable Kingdoms* (New York: Knopf, 1970) points out, was often a political world unto itself, immune to and unconcerned about what happened elsewhere. Second was the now largely forgotten county government, responsible for regional services, taxes, and justice. Third was the provincial government personified by the General Court. It is this provincial political system which has held central stage in my study.

The activity of this central government is preserved in two remarkably rich and well-edited compendiums of public records: *The Journals of the House of Representatives of Massachusetts,* 39 vols. (Boston: the Massachusetts Historical Society, 1919–   ) and *The Acts and Resolves, Public and Private, of the Province of the Massachusetts Bay,* 19 vols. (Boston: Commonwealth of Massachusetts, 1869–1922). Both allow a systematic analysis of the bills introduced and passed, the executive actions considered and taken, and the kinds of petitions both individuals and communities annually sent the Assembly. The Massachusetts Archives (State House, Boston) supplement these records. Two contemporary accounts provide further evidence of the scope of governmental activity: William Douglass, *A Summary, Historical and Political of the . . . Present State of British Settlements in North America,* 2 vols. (London, 1760), and Thomas Hutchinson,

The History of the Colony and Province of Massachusetts-Bay, ed. Lawrence Shaw Mayo, 3 vols. (Cambridge: Harvard University Press, 1936).

Some note must also be taken of the discrepancy between my own account of governmental activity and that supplied in Oscar and Mary Flug Handlin, *Commonwealth: A Study of the Role of Government in the American Economy: Massachusetts, 1774–1861* (New York: New York University Press, 1947). The Handlins' study deals with the development of the Massachusetts economy between 1774 and 1861 and is limited to "the delineation of the developing conception of the role of government in the economy." Within the limits of this context they conclude, "The laissez-faire argument found no place in Massachusetts thinking" (pp. xii, 262). I suspect differences between this conclusion and my own conception of eighteenth-century Massachusetts as an archetype of the classical economic state are differences of perspective and semantics. To some extent the Revolution itself created many of the attitudes the Handlins portray. Prior to 1776 Britain inhibited government action designed to develop the provincial economy. Once these restrictions were removed and the economy faced a severe crisis, the government sanctioned programs which a decade earlier would have been neither legal nor intellectually attractive. But more important, in the eighteenth century the provincial government's attempt to develop the economy never reflected the total concept of community planning embodied in the seventeenth century's concepts of the just price and the regulated economy. Nor did these efforts reflect the twentieth century's attempts to restructure the economic order through progressive income taxes, special advantages for labor unions, or complex programs of tax incentives for capital investments. What is evident, too, particularly from the perspective of the Puritan's attempt to build a single-minded, cohesive community, is that in the eighteenth century the central government no longer concerned itself with the social order.

The Legislative Task (*Chapter 1*)

Since the General Court was in fact the central political system, it proved possible to explore the texture of the political process, to ask, in effect, not why decisions were made, but rather how. The principal theoretical model was adapted from Nelson W. Polsby's "The Institutionalization of the U.S. House of Representatives," *American Political Science Review* 62 (1968): 144–68. A highly institutionalized legislature, such as the federal House of Representatives, is characterized by a stable membership, a set of special legislative values, and a complex, internally coherent bureaucracy which determines the flow and pace of legislative activity. Thus in highly institutionalized legislatures most members will have substantial tenure, a seniority system (either formal or informal) will be relied upon to define the group's leaders, and standing committees with well-defined spheres of activity will organize the legislative calendar. In such a legislature, moreover, there will be a trade-off between individual freedom and institutional stability. Finally, new men will necessarily start at the bottom of the ladder because, coming fresh from the outside world, they will have to learn an entirely different set of values and procedures. Hence a logical question to ask is, "How institutionalized was the Massachusetts House of Representatives?"

Again the data were drawn largely from the Assembly's journals and, to a lesser extent, from the *Acts and Resolves*. The only surviving copy of the Assembly's rules dates from 1775 (Massachusetts Archives, 283:257–61). Internal evidence suggests, however, that these rules had changed little during the preceding decades. Several letters from Francis Bernard to Richard Jackson also reflect on House procedures (Bernard Papers, Harvard College Library, Cambridge, Mass.).

To prove the absence of either parties or organized factionalism in the House is all but impossible. The Otis Papers (Massachusetts Historical Society, Boston, Mass.) offer the best indirect testimony. Otis, who knew few peers as a legislative tactician, was often embarrassingly explicit about what the exercise of political power entailed. Yet Otis never admitted to being a member of a party or faction, and indeed in his lexicon parties were clearly something to which desperate opponents resorted.

Although I did not focus on comparative aspects of legislative procedures, a variety of works dealing with other eighteenth-century legislatures proved to be of considerable value, particularly Archibald S. Foord, *His Majesty's Opposition, 1714–1830* (Oxford: Clarendon Press, 1964); Charles S. Sydnor, *Gentlemen Freeholders, Political Practices in Washington's Virginia* (Chapel Hill, 1952); Stanley M. Pargellis, "The Proceedings of the Virginia House of Burgesses," *William and Mary Quarterly,* 2d ser. 8 (1927): 73–86, 143–57; and Jack P. Greene, "Foundations of Political Power in the Virginia House of Burgesses, 1720–1766," *William and Mary Quarterly,* 3d ser. 16 (1959): 485–506.

Among the welter of works dealing with modern legislatures, I found the following particularly helpful: John Wahlke et al., *The Legislative System* (New York: Wiley, 1962); James David Barber, *The Lawmakers* (New Haven: Yale University Press, 1965); David B. Truman, *The Congressional Party* (New York: John Wiley & Son, 1959); Robert L. Peabody and Nelson W. Polsby, eds., *New Perspectives on the House of Representatives* (New York: Rand McNally & Co., 1963); and Roland Young, *The American Congress* (New York: Harper & Row, 1958).

The Social Prerequisites of Power (*Chapter 2*)

This chapter depends almost exclusively on the analysis presented in the statistical appendix. The list of provincial justices was taken from William H. Whitmore, *The Massachusetts Civil List for the Colonial and Provincial Periods* (Albany, 1870). Yale graduates were recorded in Franklin Bowditch Dexter, *Biographical Sketches of the Graduates of Yale College* (New York, 1885). Clifford K. Shipton's monumental *Sibley's Harvard Graduates,* 15 vols. (Boston: the Massachusetts Historical Society, 1873–) provided the necessary Harvard class lists as well as an invaluable guide to the sources available for a study of the politics of Massachusetts. Shipton's "Ye Mystery of Ye Ages Solved, or, How Placing Worked at Colonial Harvard and Yale," *Harvard Alumni Bulletin* 57 (1954): 258–59, 262, documents the importance of class ranking in the eighteenth century.

The Professional Style (*Chapter 3*)

Political scientists have produced a remarkably rich literature dealing with the nature of political power and influence. For this study I relied first on Robert Dahl's insight that influence is the ability of one citizen to induce other citizens to behave in some way they would not otherwise behave; see his *Modern Political Analysis,* pp. 39–54. To this notion was added the argument that influence relationships are reciprocal, that is, those who obtain influence must supply something in return. Without this added dimension, discussions of the role political deference played in the eighteenth century are all but meaningless. The concept of the professional politician was also adopted from Dahl; see his *Who Governs?* (New Haven: Yale University Press, 1961), particularly pp. 223–325.

Much of the theoretical literature I consulted has now been collected into an excellent book of readings; see Roderick Bell et al., *Political Power* (New York: The Free Press, 1969). Trying to apply this rich theoretical literature in a historical context makes abundantly clear how silent the historical record is on questions of power and influence. I must confess, in fact, that my description of a professionalized ethic resulted largely from my intuitive reading of the surviving political correspondence. In this connection the most usable collections were the Otis and Williams Papers at the Massachusetts Historical Society, *Collections of the Massachusetts Historical Society,* 6th ser. 10 (1899) [The Pepperrell Papers], a scattering of letters to Samuel Waldo in the Massachusetts Archives, vol. 53, and a series of letters from Thomas Hutchinson to the Earl of Loudoun, Henry E. Huntington Library, San Marino, Calif.

In attempting to reconcile the obvious disparity between what was dominant political theory in the eighteenth century and what I saw as a necessarily covert professional ethic, I relied on Gabriel A. Almond and Sidney Verba's *The Civic Culture* (Boston: Little, Brown, 1965) which, using data from five modern nations, suggested how such a disjunctive system of values might influence political behavior. Yet even this addition to the theoretical framework still left the concept of a professional politician somehow dangling. This was brought home to me when I was asked, "Was John Winthrop a professional politician?" My immediate and intuitive response was "No!" Unfortunately I was unable to defend my answer. Shortly thereafter I encountered Guy E. Swanson's *Religion and Regime: A Sociological Account of the Reformation* (Ann Arbor: University of Michigan Press, 1967). Swanson argues that because professional politicians seek particularistic, self-serving ends, certain kinds of values which deny the primacy of the state and community must be present. The growth of these, what Swanson would consider modern, values both led to and was accelerated by the Reformation. I modified this argument by suggesting that Winthrop's Boston, because it was a radical experiment in the wilderness, actually revived old ideas of community, making them somehow more resilient than they had been before 1630. Hence the development of a professional ethic necessarily came only after the inevitable decline of the all-embracing sense of community power and responsibility which was the keystone of Puritan political theory.

This concept of an essentially covert professional ethic organizing the political process is also useful for explaining some of the seeming paradoxes of the American Revolution. In his *Ideological Origins of the American Revolution* (Cambridge, Mass.: Harvard University Press, 1967) Bernard Bailyn argues that the revolutionary crisis revealed a strong, almost paranoid distrust of political power among the colonies' principal leaders. More recently, Gordon S. Wood's "Rhetoric and Reality in the American Revolution," *William and Mary Quarterly,* 3d ser. 23 (1966): 3–23, has suggested that we must look behind the apparent reality of the political situation to understand why this generation of revolutionaries should have distrusted not only England's political institutions and ambitions, but also its own. If, as I have argued, the colonial leader was torn between a public ethic which damned the seeking and exercise of influence and a covert ethic which stressed expediency and the rational seeking of particularistic rewards, the disjunctive nature of these values could have led to the kinds of behavior Bailyn and Wood have described.

John Adams, Upstart (*Chapter 4*)

If, as I suggested, the professional ethic was a covert set of values passed from father to son, finding its historical traces becomes an extraordinarily difficult task. Hence the importance of John Adams, an outsider who gained entrance to the professional community and in the process left a unique record of his journey from one set of values to another. But was he not, perhaps, too unique, too different, too much an exception? There is, in all probability, no answer to this question. As with most statements about the past, we must simply make a guess, assuming that Adams' uniqueness lay in his perception and reporting of things but not in the new values his political education taught him.

Adams is an important source for other reasons as well. Not only did he and his family save everything they wrote, but the publication of the vast collection of documents thus accumulated represents one of this country's major editing achievements. I am, though only impersonally, in great debt to Lyman H. Butterfield, Leonard C. Faber, and Wendell D. Garrett, eds., *Diary and Autobiography of John Adams,* 4 vols. plus supplement (Cambridge, Mass.: Harvard University Press, 1961).

Jonathan Belcher and the Politics of Crisis (*Chapter 5*)

In describing the scope of the governor's power and influence, I probably came closest to explaining the past in its own terms. Indeed no other issue, with the possible exception of the currency, claimed so much space in the Assembly's journal, and for the first three decades of the eighteenth century this debate over the limit of prerogative authority dominated much of the political consciousness. Hence we have traditionally approached the office of royal governor largely in terms of constitutional prerogatives and limits, in terms given their classic form by Leonard Labaree's *Royal Government in America* (New Haven: Yale University Press, 1935).

But there were other categories employed to examine executive authority in the eighteenth century. In his three-volume *History of Massachusetts-Bay,* Thomas Hutchinson was nearly as concerned with the practice of politics as he was in portraying the development and efficacy of royal authority. William Douglass proved a far more radical observer. An Edinburgh-trained physician, Douglass is best known for his quarrel with Cotton Mather over smallpox inoculations and his obsession with a specie currency. But the good doctor was also something of an observer of men and history, and in the 1740s he published his impressions in a series of essays which were later reprinted in his *Summary of British Settlements in North America.* Douglass knew Massachusetts well, and the terms of his analysis are strikingly modern. Governors, he noted, could

> nominate all judges, justices, and sheriffs, which being, with the militia-officers of the several townships, a great majority in the lower House, gives the governor a very great influence there. The power of negativing the members of the upper House makes his influence there so considerable that he has, in a great measure, two negatives in the legislature. . . .
>
> The governor has the opportunity of recommending [his friends and creatures] to the House [to serve as] agents . . . to manage their affairs and his own at the court and boards in Great Britain and to procure for them handsome gratuities. . . . A governor by frequent and long speeches and messages to the House of Representatives . . . seems to act as a member of that House, or rather as the speaker . . . of the House. . . . The governor has a negative not only in all bills of [the] Assembly, but also in all their elections, that of a speaker not excepted. [1:472–73]

Observable patterns rather than theoretical norms caught Douglass' eye.

The data for the sketch of Jonathan Belcher's career came from a variety of sources. Clifford Shipton's capsule biography (*Sibley's Harvard Graduates,* 4:434–50) outlined Belcher's rise and fall from power, though Hutchinson's incisive portrait of Belcher the beleaguered politician is still the most perceptive analysis of the governor's political style (*History of Massachusetts-Bay,* 2:280–82). My own discussion of Belcher's political personality was based on his speeches to the General Court (reprinted in the Assembly's journal), his reports to London (reprinted in *Calendar of State Papers, Colonial Series, American and West Indies* 37 vols. [London: Her Majesty's Stationary Office, 1872–   ], particularly vols. 42 and 43), and his surviving letter-books (largely reprinted in *Collections of the Massachusetts Historical Society,* 6th ser. 6 [1893] and 7 [1894]).

Probably the best account of the Land Bank is still a 1744 pamphlet entitled *An Account of the Rise, Progress and Consequences of the Land Bank* (Boston, 1744). Andrew McFarland Davis' dozen pamphlets and one major work provide the most detailed accounts; see particularly his *Currency and Banking in the Province of the Massachusetts-Bay,* 2 vols. (New York: Macmillan, 1900, 1901). A more recent essay is George Athan Billias' "The Massachusetts Land Bankers," *University of Maine Studies,* 2d ser. 74 (April 1959). Billias, while relying heavily on Davis' earlier work, does demonstrate that the Bank attracted support from some wealthy and prominent citizens. These findings refute previous interpretations of the Land Bank crisis as a classic example of class conflicts disrupting provincial politics; see, for example, John C. Miller, "Religion, Finance, and Democracy," *The New England Quarterly* 6 (1933): 29–54. The pamphlet literature devoted to the currency issue in general and the two Land Banks in particular has been reprinted in Andrew McFarland Davis, ed., *Colonial Currency Reprints, 1682–1751* (New York: the Prince Society, 1910).

William Shirley and the Politics of Persuasion (*Chapter 6*)

My discussion of William Shirley's governorship depended greatly on John A. Schutz, *William Shirley, King's Governor of Massachusetts* (Chapel Hill: University of North Carolina Press 1961). Shirley's correspondence has been reprinted in Charles Henry Lincoln, ed., *Correspondence of William Shirley,* 2 vols. (New York: Macmillan, 1912). Daniel Fowle's short-lived *Independent Advertiser* was a particular useful newspaper for studying Shirley's governorship, in part because Fowle disliked Shirley, in part because of his cleverness as a political commentator. My discussion of the London maneuvering surrounding the parliamentary grant in 1748 was based largely on Malcom Freiberg's "William Bollan, Agent of Massachusetts," *More Books* 23 (1948): 91–98.

Robert Hale and John Choate, Insiders (*Chapter 7*)

Eighteenth-century Massachusetts probably knew no more elusive and yet vital power-brokers than Robert Hale and John Choate. My brief treatment of their careers was possible only because of the detective work of the late Katharine Simonds Thompson, whose manuscript on "John Choate," is to be published by the Ipswich Historical Society. The historical traces that do remain are scattered, among other places, through the town records of Ipswich, the *Essex Institute Historical Collections,* the Massachusetts Historical Society, and the Massachusetts Archives. Choate published two religious pamphlets, the latter with Hale's active assistance: *Reasons of Dissent* (Portsmouth, N.H.,

1760) and *Remarks on the Late Printed Answer* (Boston, 1761). For Hale, at least, the Assembly's journal provided a glimpse of the legislator at work.

Thomas Hancock, Merchant (*Chapter 8*)

In describing the political dimension of Thomas Hancock's merchant enterprises, I adopted Robert Dahl's model for assessing the potential and actual influence of a community's social and economic notables; see his *Who Governs?*, particularly pp. 223–325. The data for my analysis were drawn from Hancock's letter-book, now in the possession of the Massachusetts Historical Society, and his collected papers and additional letter-books in the Baker Library, Harvard University. W. T. Baxter's *The House of Hancock* (Cambridge, Mass.: Harvard University Press, 1945) supplied an outline of Hancock's career and the guide to his accounting practices which allowed my own reconstruction of his business activity. For a brief sketch of Christopher Kilby see Charles Wesley Tuttle, *Captain Francis Chamerowne . . . and other Historical Papers* (Boston, 1886), pp. 225–38. There are three excellent portraits of Thomas Hutchinson's early career: Malcom Freiberg, "Thomas Hutchinson: The First Fifty Years (1711–1761)," *William and Mary Quarterly,* 3 ser. 15 (1958): 35–55; *Sibley's Harvard Graduates,* 7:149–217; and Edmund S. and Helen M. Morgan, *The Stamp Act Crisis* (New York: Collier Books, 1963), pp. 256–79.

A Conservative Balance (*Chapter 9*)

Because it remains a puzzle to historians, the provincial Council has largely been ignored in discussions of colonial politics. Leonard Labaree's *Royal Government in America,* though it offers a narrowly constitutional interpretation of the Council's role and function, still provides the best description of the upper chamber. In part, the gaps in Labaree's analysis have been filled by Jackson Turner Main's *The Upper House in Revolutionary America* (Madison: University of Wisconsin Press, 1967), which focuses on the social and economic backgrounds as well as the political proclivities of those who sat in the Council. What we still lack is an understanding of the thrust and scope of the Council's political activity.

Significantly our failure to come to terms with the Council does not stem from a lack of data. We probably know more about its members than any other group of colonials. And the Council's own records are remarkably well preserved in the Massachusetts Archives. The truth is that we simply do not know what to make of the data. For example, the Council's minutes list the number of votes each successful candidate for the Council received in the May balloting. And yet, try as I might, I could not derive from these tallies a meaningful pattern. Perhaps Council elections did not conform to any pattern, though that seems unlikely given the importance of the office. The alternative is to admit that we lack a conceptual framework which will allow us to make sense of the data and hence of the Council itself. Having exhausted my own imagination, I must leave the development of such a framework to other hands.

A Question of Accountability (*Chapter 10*)

Probably no other issue has been so thoroughly discussed and so completely mangled as the question, "Was eighteenth-century Massachusetts democratic?" I attempted to bring a semblance of order to my own observations, at least, by rather carefully defining democracy in terms of legislative accountability. The actual model I described in this chapter is an amalgam of ideas found in Robert A. Dahl's *A Preface to Democratic Theory* (Chicago: University of Chicago Press, 1956), Warren E. Miller and Donald E. Stoke's "Constituency Influence in Congress," *American Political Science Review* 57 (1963): 45–57, Gabriel A. Almond and Sidney Verba's *The Civic Culture,* and Lewis Anthony Dexter's "The Representative and His District," in Robert L. Peabody and Nelson W. Polsby, eds., *New Perspectives on the House of Representatives,* pp. 3–29.

The logical starting point for reviewing the literature on democracy in Massachusetts is still Robert E. Brown's *Middle-Class Democracy and the Revolution in Massachusetts* (Ithaca: Cornell University Press, 1955). A much shorter and more palatable form of Brown's argument can be found in his "Democracy in Colonial Massachusetts," *New England Quarterly* 25 (1952): 291–313. Also useful is Kenneth Colegrove's "New England Town Mandates," *Publications of the Colonial Society of Massachusetts* 21 (1919): 411–49, which anticipates much of Brown's thesis. For an important correction to our impulse to label Massachusetts a full-fledged, modern democracy, see Michael Zuckerman's "The Social Context of Democracy in Massachusetts," *William and Mary Quarterly,* 3d ser. 25 (1968): 523–44. Probably the best short description of eighteenth-century political thought is Richard Buel, Jr., "Democracy and the American Revolution," *William and Mary Quarterly,* 3d ser. 21 (1964): 165–90. In my discussion of political norms I relied heavily on Buel's sketch of eighteenth-century ideas about representation.

The data on election practices is now largely preserved in the Assembly's journal, the *Acts and Resolves,* and the Massachusetts Archives.

Court and Constituency (*Chapter 11*)

Theoretical models for explaining legislative alignments have little appeal for the historian of colonial America, in part because we simply do not possess enough roll call votes, in part because the models themselves ordinarily assume viable party structures. My own approach in this essay marked a kind of compromise. I was still interested in who voted with whom, but sought not so much working legislative coalitions as clusters of similar attitudes and predilections.

A full list of the roll calls and methods employed in this chapter has already been presented. The data on economic regionalism was drawn from a variety of sources. Probably the best short description of Massachusetts before the Revolution is Francis Bernard's letter to the Board of Trade, September 5, 1763, in J. H. Benton, Jr., *Early Census Making in Massachusetts* (Boston, 1905), pp. 47–64. This same volume also reprints the 1765 census, and all town and regional population figures have been drawn from this source. Three other eighteenth-century descriptions of the province similarly provide a fund of useful information: *American Husbandry: An Account of the Soil, Climate, Production and Agriculture, of the British Colonies* (London, 1774), 1:45–93; Carl Bridenbaugh, ed., *Gentleman's Progress: The Itinerarium of Dr. Alexander Hamilton, 1744* (Chapel Hill: University of North Carolina Press, 1948), pp. 105–50; Douglass, *Summary of British Settlements in North America,* vol. 1. For the development of the province's seaports see Carl Bridenbaugh, *Cities in the Wilderness* (New York: The Ronald Press Co., 1938) and *Cities in Revolt* (New York: Knopf, 1953). For Maine and particularly its lumbering industry see Joseph J. Malone, *Pine Trees and Politics* (Seattle: University of Washington Press, 1964). For the Connecticut Valley see

Robert J. Taylor, *Western Massachusetts in the Revolution* (Providence: Brown University Press, 1954). In the Massachusetts Historical Society (Msc. Bound, vol. 12) there is a 1754 agricultural census of the province's eleven counties indicating the relative productivity of each region. Henry Colman's first three *Reports on the Agriculture of Massachusetts* (Boston, 1837, 1838, 1840) give more extensive but much later agricultural data. Finally Forrest McDonald's *We the People* (Chicago: University of Chicago Press, 1958), pp. 358–99, provides a useful classification of economic interests in America in the 1780s.

The best source of political rhetoric remains the public press, particularly Boston's four papers. The notion that underlying this rhetoric was a debate over the distribution of abundance was first suggested by Perry Miller in *The New England Mind: From Colony to Province* (Cambridge, Mass.: Harvard University Press, 1953), pp. 305–23.

A Method for Our Madness (*Statistical Appendix*)

Discussions of the role of statistics in historical analysis are both endless and, for the most part, useless. Important here only because it spells out some of the lessons learned in the preparation of this study is my "Numbers and History: the Dilemma of Measurement," *Computers and the Humanities* 4 (1969): 31–40. The basic statistical tests described in the appendix can be found in Herbert M. Blalock, *Social Statistics* (New York: McGraw-Hill, 1960), and Hayward R. Alker, *Mathematics and Politics* (New York: Macmillan, 1965), which is a highly readable discussion of the theoretical assumptions underlying some commonly used measures of inequality and association. For a basic description of Guttman scaling applied to legislative roll calls see A. Douglas Price, "Are Southern Democrats Different?," in Nelson W. Polsby et al., eds., *Politics and Social Life* (Boston: Houghton Mifflin, 1963). For cluster analysis see David B. Truman, *Congressional Party* (New York: John Wiley & Son, 1959).

Index